ISRAEL AND THE NATIONS

American Society of Missiology Series, No. 39

ISRAEL AND THE NATIONS

A Mission Theology of the Old Testament

James Chukwuma Okoye

ORBIS BOOKS

Maryknoll, New York 10545

Founded in 1970, Orbis Books endeavors to publish works that enlighten the mind, nourish the spirit, and challenge the conscience. The publishing arm of the Maryknoll Fathers and Brothers, Orbis seeks to explore the global dimensions of the Christian faith and mission, to invite dialogue with diverse cultures and religious traditions, and to serve the cause of reconciliation and peace. The books published reflect the opinions of their authors and are not meant to represent the official position of the Maryknoll Society. To obtain more information about Maryknoll and Orbis Books, please visit our website at www.maryknoll.org.

Library of Congress Cataloging in Publication Data

Okoye, James Chukwuma.
  Israel and the nations : a mission theology of the Old Testament / James Chukwuma Okoye.
      p. cm. — (American Society of Missiology series ; no. 39)
  Includes bibliographical references (p.   ) and index.
  ISBN-13: 978-1-57075-654-2 (pbk.)
1. Missions—Biblical teaching. 2. Bible. O.T.—Theology. 3. Missions—Theory. I. Title. II. Series.
  BS1199.M53O36 2006
  230'.0411—dc22
                                              2005031851

Dedicated to the Memory of
Bishop Godfrey Mary Paul Okoye, C.S.Sp.
1915-1977
Man of God, Man of the Church, Man of the People

and

Robert Belonwu Okoye,
Man of Faith, Beloved Father, Son of Mary
1915-1977

Contents

Foreword

Two contemporary uncertainties are brought together and wrestled with in the pages that follow. First, if God is the source of all our striving for truth and honest living, why try to convert those who are living good lives under the sovereignty of God by another name than that of the Christian God? Second, what is the place of the Old Testament in Christianity? Is it only to prove the superiority of the Christian revelation, or to justify political claims without regard to contemporary suffering?

From the first moments, Christianity has been missionary in essence. Jesus' first efforts, as related in the Gospels, were to reach out with a message of hope to those who needed to hear it. His disciples took up the challenge and continued to proclaim the good news at home and in distant lands. They did so with conscious awareness that they were continuing a tradition, that their words echoed down the centuries past. Their intertextual interpretation of the scriptures provided the base upon which their new gospel was constructed.

In the second century C.E., Marcion proposed a new way of understanding the message of Jesus and Paul, a way in which the Old Testament had no place. The rejection of his teachings by the mainstream church confirmed the conviction that the Hebrew Scriptures have everything to do with the message of Jesus, which is conveyed within its matrix. Marcionism rejected, the question becomes not so much one of Bible *and* Mission as it is Bible *as* Mission. The entire biblical message of both testaments is bound up in the urge to go tell the good news. In this book, James Okoye shows how it is done.

Carolyn Osiek, R.S.C.J.

Preface to the ASM Series

The purpose of the ASM (American Society of Missiology) Series is to publish—without regard for disciplinary, national, or denominational boundaries—scholarly works of high quality and wide interest on missiological themes from the entire spectrum of scholarly pursuits relevant to Christian mission, which is always the focus of books in the Series.

By *mission* is meant the effort to effect passage over the boundary between faith in Jesus Christ and its absence. In this understanding of mission, the basic functions of Christian proclamation, dialogue, witness, service, worship, liberation, and nurture are of special concern. And in that context questions arise, including, How does the transition from one cultural context to another influence the shape and interaction between these dynamic functions, especially in regard to the cultural and religious plurality that comprises the global context of Christian life and mission.

The promotion of scholarly dialogue among missiologists, and among missiologists and scholars in other fields of inquiry, may involve the publication of views that some missiologists cannot accept, and with which members of the Editorial Committee themselves do not agree. Manuscripts published in the Series, accordingly, reflect the opinions of their authors and are not understood to represent the position of the American Society of Missiology or of the Editorial Committee. Selection is guided by such criteria as intrinsic worth, readability, coherence, and accessibility to a range of interested persons and not merely to experts or specialists.

The ASM Series, in collaboration with Orbis Books, seeks to publish scholarly works of high merit and wide interest on numerous aspects of missiology—the scholarly study of mission. Able presentations on new and creative approaches to the practice and understanding of mission will receive close attention.

The ASM Series Committee
Jonathan J. Bonk
Angelyn Dries, O.S.F.
Scott W. Sunquist

Preface

One of the courses I inherited when I began teaching at the Catholic Theological Union, Chicago (CTU) eight years ago was entitled "The Biblical Foundations for Mission." I reoriented it and renamed it "Bible, Mission, and Culture." The course as redesigned paid particular attention to the interplay between text and context. It also paid some attention to issues emerging from this interplay, for example, the dynamics of conversion in context and interreligious dialogue. The course had a New Testament part and an Old Testament part. For the New Testament part, there were excellent textbooks, such as Donald Senior and Carroll Stuhlmueller, *The Biblical Foundations for Mission* (Maryknoll, NY: Orbis, 1983); Lucien Legrand, *Unity and Plurality: Mission in the Bible* (Maryknoll, NY: Orbis, 1990); and David Bosch, *Transforming Mission: Paradigm Shifts in the Theology of Mission* (Maryknoll, NY: Orbis, 1991). Unfortunately, Bosch treated extensively only Matthew, Luke-Acts, and Paul in the biblical section of *Transforming Mission*. For the Old Testament part of the course, however, I found nothing that matched my conception of the theme of mission in that Testament. The treatment by Legrand was close, but unfortunately it was too brief and gave minimal attention to the evolution of the traditions. So I relied mostly on my own exegetical work and on selected articles for class discussion. It was not long before the idea of a book on the theme of mission and its development in the Old Testament began to form in my mind. I worked out a schema and was encouraged by the reception it received from students in the courses I gave at CTU, at the Maryknoll Sisters Mission Institute, New York, and at the Summer Institute on Mission and Spirituality of the Spiritan International School of Theology, Enugu, Nigeria. The opportunity of a sabbatical has allowed me time to flesh out the schema and to write this book. I thank all the students who have stimulated my thoughts with their class participation and questions.

A draft of ten of the fourteen chapters of this book was used as course material at CTU in the spring semester of 2005 in a seminar entitled "Bible, Mission, and Culture," in which students from almost all the five continents were participants. I thank this class in particular for stimulating discussions and for suggestions for adapting the text for class work.

This book has a dual focus, Bible and mission. It is written for students and informed people, be they lay, clergy, or religious, who seek a better

grounding in, and understanding of, the theme of mission and its development in the Old Testament. Some readers will come to it from a mission
perspective, others from a biblical perspective. It is not presumed that readers are adept in both disciplines. It is often the case with treatments of mission in the Bible that the results are given in summary form, glossing over
the exegetical processes that have led to them. This book, on the contrary,
tries to lead the reader, as far as possible, through the processes of interpretation. Where appropriate, I point out the relevance to today's mission
of what is being treated.

I have been particularly sensitive to the integrity of the Old Testament,
which remains fully "word of God." Because Christians regard both the
Old Testament and the New Testament as "word of God," it is important
to respect the organic links of the two without reducing one to the other. It
is also important to show how the believing community has in the course
of time adapted its texts and traditions for its ongoing life of faith. I thus
join the focus on the meaning of the text in context to developments within
the tradition of the Old Testament itself and sometimes into the New Testament. Very often, when a text is read within its total Old Testament tradition the meaning rejoins somewhat, even if not always, the understanding
of that text in the New Testament.

The method used in this book is intertextual and "canon conscious,"
borrowing a phrase from Gerald T. Sheppard.[1] By canon conscious I mean
that the full meaning of a text is not restricted to its immediate context, but
that effort needs be made to trace possible adaptations and reinterpretations of it in the Old Testament itself, and (because I am writing as a Christian) in the New Testament also. By intertextual I mean that the text of the
Bible relates to all other texts, including the literary and religious classics
of humanity at large. I take account of the fact that the biblical text does
not always say the only or last word on issues of religion and human
morality. The literary and religious heritage of humankind sometimes
offers necessary and complementary teaching, and so the text may sometimes be challenged from outside itself. For example, what the Bible says
explicitly on slavery does not compare with the United Nations' *Charter of
Human Rights*, nor with the current positions of Jewish, Islamic, Christian,
and other faiths on the issue.

As practiced in this book, the "canon-conscious" approach is closer to
the method of James Sanders (1984) than to that of Brevard Childs (1979).
Whereas Childs tends to see the final form as "normative," Sanders holds
the view that the canon is "adaptable for life" and that the various layers
of a text should be in dialogue with each other. When such an approach is
applied, it is often seen that Jewish and Christian interpretations are both

---

1. "Canonization: Hearing the Voice of the Same God through Historically Dissimilar Traditions," *Interpretation* 36 (1982): 21-33, here 23.

possible readings of the one tradition, and often share a common ground from which they move in divergent directions. In some parts of the book, it also becomes evident that the "Christian" interpretation is not a mono-lith but a diversity of interpretations often influenced by differing a priori dogmatic or/and hermeneutical stances. Some Christians interpret the Old Testament uniquely from the New, while others speak of a "fuller sense" in the New. I have brought to the task a historical consciousness that allows texts meaning within their historical and cultural contexts, without locking them up within such contexts. My own interpretive tradition belongs to the Roman Catholic tradition.

The chapters of this book are ordered in the following manner. Chapters 1 and 2 give the necessary background to the work by laying out the issues and the approaches used; they should be read first. The chapters following them have been arranged according to the four faces of mission outlined in chapter 1, which faces somehow trace the development of mission in the Old Testament. Chapters 3 to 5 illustrate the first face of mission, namely, the universality of salvation and of righteousness. Chapters 6 to 8 portray the second face of mission in the Old Testament, namely, "community-in-mission." Chapter 9 acts as transition to the remaining faces of mission. The realization of the primacy of the righteousness of God is basic to the further development of mission in the Old Testament and its evolution into the New Testament. The third face of mission in the Old Testament is "cen-tripetal mission," and this is dealt with in chapters 10 to 11. Chapters 12 to 14 finally portray what scholars call "centrifugal mission." A conclud-ing chapter summarizes the foregoing chapters and traces the process of the actual opening up of Israel's covenant with Yahweh to the gentiles. It thus becomes clear how the tension between God's special election of Israel and God's care for the nations is resolved through mission. Israel is chosen to be "a light to the nations so that my salvation may reach to the remotest parts of earth" (Isa 49:6).

One or two quotations head each chapter. These quotations seek to encapsulate the material of the chapter or emphasize some particular aspect of it. Wherever called for, reflections are added that seek to relate the mate-rial discussed to current issues of mission. The bibliography contains works that have been consulted and have been found useful. The standard com-mentaries do not feature in this list, except when the one or other com-mentary has been used in a particular manner.

All biblical quotations are taken from the *New Jerusalem Bible*, unless otherwise stated, and then the version followed is indicated in parentheses.

I thank the Catholic Theological Union, particularly its president, Pro-fessor Don Senior, C.S.P., and its academic dean, Professor Gary Riebe Estrella, S.V.D., for the opportunity of a sabbatical year. My thanks go especially to Dr. William Burrows, managing editor of Orbis Books, Mary-knoll, New York, for his enthusiasm for the work and guidance all through the process of completing and editing the manuscript. I thank also my friend and former colleague Professor Carolyn Osiek, R.S.C.J., and my colleague Professor Dianne Bergant for reading parts of the manuscript and making valuable suggestions. Professor Osiek, the current president of the Society of Biblical Literature, has graciously written the foreword to this book. I accept full responsibility, however, for any shortcomings of the present work. As part of my sabbatical, I spent two months in San Diego with Monsignor John Dickie, the pastor of St. Mary Magdalene, San Diego, to whom thanks are due. Thanks also to the librarians of the Bodleian Library, the Oriental Institute Library, and the Theology Faculty Library, all of Oxford University, for expeditious service during the three months I researched there, my first return visit to Oxford since graduating from there with D. Phil in 1980.

The last chorus of thanks belongs to the heavenly court. The book is dedicated to two persons whose love has left an indelible mark on me and on this world, Bishop Godfrey Mary Paul Okoye, C.S.Sp, and Mr. Robert Belonwu Okoye. Robert Okoye was all a father should be, only that he died before his children could show him their gratitude. May God give him eternal rest. Bishop Godfrey Okoye ordained me to the Catholic priesthood and had me begin ministry as secretary to him and to the Catholic Diocese of Enugu, Nigeria. He also obtained the scholarship from Missio, Aachen, that enabled me study at the Pontifical Biblical Institute, Rome, and at Oxford University, England. Both men passed away the same year, one month after each other. They are still missed after almost thirty years—from heaven may they accompany us still down below.

The final word of thanks goes to the *Little Flower*, who has done little and great things for me and whose presence and spirituality have sustained me in rain and sunshine. Rightly has she been named both Doctor of the Church and Patroness of Mission.

Abbreviations

AACC   All Africa Conference of Churches

ANET   *Ancient Near Eastern Texts relating to the Old Testament,* 3rd edition with supplement (Princeton, N.J.: Princeton University Press, 1969)

LXX   *Septuagint,* the earliest extant Greek translation of the Old Testament from the original Hebrew, presumably made for the Jewish community in Egypt when Greek was the lingua franca of the region, done between the third and second centuries C.E.

MT   *Masoretic Text,* traditional Hebrew text of the Jewish Bible, meticulously assembled and codified, and supplied with diacritical marks to enable correct pronunciation. This monumental work was begun around the sixth century C.E. and completed in the tenth by scholars at Talmudic academies in Babylonia and Palestine.

NAB   New American Bible, Old Testament (1970)

NIV   New International Version

NJB   New Jerusalem Bible (London: Darton, Longman & Todd, 1985)

NJPS   New Jewish Publication Society, *Hebrew-English Tanakh* (1999)

NJSB   New Jewish Study Bible (Oxford University Press, 2004)

NRSV   New Revised Standard Version (1989)

NT   New Testament

OT   Old Testament

REB   Revised English Bible, with Apocrypha (1989)

TEV   Today's English Version (New York: American Bible Society, 1992, 2000)

WCC   World Council of Churches

1

The Hermeneutics of Mission in the Old Testament

What a difference it would make to biblical studies if full justice were done to the Bible as a book about mission from beginning to end, written by missionaries for missionaries! Given its content and intent, how could one study it in any other way?
— Andrew Kirk, *What Is Mission?* 20

A mission theology of the Old Testament? Some people are surprised at the title of this book since they either deny or ignore the theme of mission in the Old Testament. But the title is not meant to be provocative but only to draw attention to a much neglected aspect of Old Testament theology. The book will examine how and when Israel became missionary, or at the least opened up her covenant with Yahweh to the gentiles. It also will investigate the theological foundations for such development.

This chapter will be developed in five movements. It will first outline the tension between election and mission in the Old Testament. It will then examine the works of scholars to see how they address the theme of mission in the Old Testament. An investigation of the theme of mission will then follow in which I shall discern and outline four faces of mission in the Old Testament. Fourth, the question of the hermeneutics of mission in the Old Testament will be addressed. That is, given the diverse nature of the material in the Old Testament, how is the theme of mission in it best approached? This section will also outline the method to be followed in this book. Fifth and finally, the problematic of a Christian reading of the Old Testament will be addressed.

ELECTION AND MISSION

The Old Testament hardly looks like a mission document, for from beginning to end it is focused on Israel. Israel is God's elect, other nations

1

are not. The verb used for the concept of election is בחר (*bāḥar,* "to elect"), a verb that expresses both God's predilection for Israel and God's choice of Israel from among all the nations. In Deut 7:7 Moses says in the name of God:

> Yahweh set his heart on you and chose you, not because you were the most numerous of all peoples—for indeed you were the smallest of all—but because he loved you and meant to keep the oath which he swore to your ancestors.

Only with Israel as a people has Yahweh made a covenant. Only to Israel has Yahweh said, "I shall take you as my people and I shall be your God" (Exod 6:7). The reason for this choice is so that "you, out of all peoples, shall be my personal possession" (Exod 19:5). Yahweh is portrayed as the main protagonist in the early wars of Israel, dispossessing the Canaanites of their homeland in order to make unhindered space for Israel. God commanded Israel to "put them under the curse of destruction; you must not make any treaty with them or show them any pity" (Deut 7:3). In much of the Old Testament, the Canaanites are a symbol of what is hateful to Yahweh, and it is not always clear that they too are enfolded by God's love. A text such as Deut 10:19, however, displays the type of tension that we are drawing attention to, for it recalls that Yahweh loves the stranger and commands Israel to "love the stranger, then, for you were once strangers in Egypt." Though there are quite a few texts of this nature, it is nevertheless true that most texts of the Old Testament evince a one-sided emphasis on the election of Israel and God's partiality towards Israel. They sometimes run the risk of conscripting God into a national agenda. Some of these texts have been lifted out of context and been manipulated by some nations and peoples in the cause of injustice and even genocide against other peoples. All the more important, therefore, that a responsible hermeneutic be brought to bear on such texts.

The classical prophets of Israel created "ethical Yahwism" and fought to liberate the image of God from national agendas. Yet some segments of the prophetic tradition continued to depict Yahweh as partial to Israel in a manner unfair to other nations. In some late prophetic oracles, salvation for Israel was still often intrinsically linked with judgment on its enemies or on the nations. An example is Isaiah 60:12: "for the nation and kingdom that will not serve you will perish, and the nations will be utterly destroyed." Even in liturgy we meet with the war-dance liturgy of Psalm 149:5-7:

> The faithful exult in glory, shout for joy as they worship him, praising God to the heights with their voices, a two-edged sword in their hands, to wreak vengeance on the nations, judgment on the peoples.

The hope that Yahweh will, in the last times, destroy the armies of the nations in the Valley of Jehoshaphat is held out in Joel 3:9-21 and Ezekiel 38-39. In fact, Daniel 7:27 proclaims that finally "the kingship and the rule, and the splendors of all the kingdoms under heaven will be given to the people of the holy ones of the Most High . . . whom every empire will serve and obey." "The people of the holy ones of the Most High" are Israel, whose heavenly patrons are the "holy ones of the Most High," that is, the divine beings who formed the council of Yahweh. There is an undeniable "Israel-focus" in segments of the Old Testament story. But one of the contentions of this book is that such a focus is to be read not in isolation but in relation to internal transformations of the tradition that indicate that Israel's election had a missionary intention.

Israelite tradition in the Old Testament has indeed also many texts that show that Yahweh cares for all humanity and the entire creation. Some texts even seem to place the election of Israel in function of the salvation and welfare of the world. Developing this thesis is the burden of this book. We here give a few examples. The account of creation in Genesis 1 shows the unity of humanity under the one God and creator who cares for all. The narrative of the election of Abraham, the ancestor of Israel, has God's care for all humanity written all over it. Abraham is destined to be both father of Israel and father of many nations (Gen 17:5). God promised him, "I will make of you a great nation, and I will bless you." But God also established him as an instrument of blessing for all families when God said, "in you all the families of the earth shall be blessed" (Gen 12:2-3 NRSV). The choice of Abraham could therefore be seen in function of "blessing" for all humanity. When Israel left Egypt an ʿēreb rab ("mixed multitude," Exod 12:38) went up with them. The reference is most probably to other enslaved ethnic groups in Egypt.[1] These were equally beneficiaries of Yahweh's redemption and stood with Israel at Sinai. They were all bound both to Yahweh and to each other by covenant. The power of the covenant at Sinai (Exod 19-24) was to make them all the one people of God. Already the point was being made that Israel was more a covenant community than heredity linked by blood. Some scholars (for example, Norman Gottwald) even posit that Israel as a nation was formed in Canaan when the revolution of oppressed peasants came under the influence of the Moses group coming from Egypt and thus under the banner of Yahweh as the liberating deity. Although this hypothesis leaves many questions unanswered, it radically reinterprets the notion of election. In this scenario, Israel would be the

---

1. Reading this text in light of Lev 24:10 (the case of the man whose mother was an Israelite woman but whose father was an Egyptian), some have interpreted the "mixed multitude" as products of miscegenation between Israelites and Egyptians.

covenant community that is meant to manifest the nature of Yahweh and
the benefits of life under Yahweh. Election would in this case be intimately
connected with mission.

Many psalms sing of the universal and just rule of Yahweh and thus
evince Yahweh's concern for all creation. Psalm 82 depicts how God
demoted to mortals the erstwhile heavenly rulers (*ʾelōhîm*)[2] and removed
them from rule over the nations, because they would not "let the weak and
the orphan have justice, be fair to the wretched and the destitute" (Ps 82:3).
The psalmist ends with the plea: "arise, God, judge the world, for all
nations belong to you" (v. 8). The universal and just rule of God is both
anticipated and celebrated in the liturgy of the Psalms of Yahweh's
Enthronement (Pss 47; 93; 96-99; 100).

The anonymous prophet of the exile presents Yahweh as commissioning
Yahweh's servant to become "a light to the nations, so that my salvation
may reach to the ends of the earth" (Isa 49:6). This commissioning is contrasted with an earlier commission "to restore the tribes of Jacob and bring
back the survivors of Israel." The "servant" in Deutero-Isaiah is often
explicitly called "Israel" (Isa 41:8, 9; 44:1, "Jacob, my servant"), though in
the so-called Servant Songs (Isa 42:1-4; 49:1-6; 50:4-9, and 52:13-53:12)
the reference seems to be to an individual who somehow represents Israel.
The servant, that is, Israel or an individual who assumes the vocation of
Israel, has a commission and an effectiveness that go beyond Israel and
unto the nations.

Israel's wisdom literature is international and universal: "the God who
is revealed in wisdom is the 'teacher of the nations'" (Gunkel and Begrich
1998, 294). The themes of election, covenant, and *torah* do not appear.
The religion of wisdom is based on human life and experience, not on
revealed religion. The "fear of the Lord," which is the beginning of wisdom
(Prov 1:7), is primarily not response to God's covenant with the one nation
Israel, but the universal human response to the experience of the Holy.
Though wisdom will later be identified with *torah* (Sirach 24), the path of
wisdom universalizes human daily experience as the arena for living faith.
In so doing, wisdom places Israel and the nations on the same footing with
respect to the experience of God and the practice of true religion.

Our brief survey thus shows that the Old Testament focuses not only on
Israel but also on the world outside of Israel. God's purposes relate to all of
humankind, and it is within the working out of this universal purpose that
the apparent focus on Israel must be understood. Hence, the theme of mission shows itself to be the necessary accompaniment of that of election.

---

2. The obvious sense of *ʾelōhîm* is "gods," or "heavenly beings." In ancient mythology,
these were members of the divine council who were given rule over nations and constellations.
Some avoid the obvious sense by translating *ʾelōhîm* as "the mighty" (Rashi) or "judges."

SCHOLARS AND MISSION IN THE OLD TESTAMENT

Book-length treatments of mission in the Old Testament are few. H. H. Rowley was one of the first in recent memory to offer such a treatment in English. He dealt with the question in *Israel's Mission to the World* and five years later in *The Missionary Message of the Old Testament*. In the latter book, he asserted that "the Old Testament is a missionary book" (p. 76), although it is undeniable that Judaism is not essentially and notably a missionary religion. The thesis of the earlier work was that Israel had a "wider vision that passed beyond the borders of Israel, and embraced aliens as well as Jews in the Kingdom of God" (pp. 2, 18). Israel came slowly to the conviction of a universal purpose of God. It appeared clearly and definitely only in the exilic and postexilic periods. The great vision of Isaiah 2:2-4 (parallel in Mic 4:1-4) is probably exilic or postexilic. It portrays the nations streaming on pilgrimage to Zion in the final days. Several texts of this period portray the nations as open to the faith of Israel or called to share in Israel's religious inheritance. For example, Isaiah 11:9 says that "the earth[3] will be full of the knowledge of Yahweh as the waters cover the sea."

Rowley sees the monotheistic faith of Deutero-Isaiah as having corollaries, one of which is that "he who created all must be God of all, and must desire the worship not alone of Israel, but of all [humankind]" (1939, 8). The election of Israel is not given up; rather, Israel is seen to be elect in order to be light to the nations (Isa 49:6). Rowley interprets this as meaning "that Israel in active worship shall share the faith which is her glory with all people" (1944, 51).

Robert Martin-Achard warns that the idea of mission must be distinguished from that of universalism, for universalism, as in Amos, may still not envisage the conversion of the peoples nor reflect the responsibility of Israel toward them.[4] In addition, texts where captives, slaves, and strangers (*gērim*) are integrated into Israel present us not with mission but with the normal process of assimilation. Mission implies a community's conviction of responsibility toward the rest of humankind. Martin-Achard begins with Deutero-Isaiah, whom P. Volz called the "founder of mission," but concludes that the message of Deutero-Isaiah is not missionary in the ordinary sense of the word. He finds that in this prophet Israel is "light to the nations" in the sense that its very existence is a testimony to the grandeur

---

3. Some, however, translate הארץ (*hā-ʾāreṣ*) here as "the country" or "the land" (NJB, NJPS).

4. I had access to Martin-Achard only in the French edition listed in the bibliography, but an English edition exists: *A Light to the Nations: A Study of the Old Testament Conception of Israel's Mission to the World* (London: Oliver & Boyd, 1962).

of Yahweh. For "it is in giving life to his people that Yahweh makes of them light to the nations" (1959, 29; my translation). In other words, the focus is on the deeds of Yahweh in favor of Yahweh's people, seeing in which deeds the nations will render Yahweh the glory due to Yahweh. The blessing of Abraham (Gen 12:1-3) has a universalistic attraction, in the sense that the peoples would want to participate in it, but this text is not missionary, for no initiatives for the conversion of others are commanded by Abraham. Martin-Achard stresses that Israel plays no active part in all texts which scholars cite in relation to mission in the Old Testament. It is rather the action of Yahweh in and for Israel that is stressed. As the history of the Old Testament reaches its term, what is depicted is centripetal movement (Isa 2:2-4 // Mic 4:1-4), not Israel going to the nations but the nations streaming to Israel's sanctuary in Zion. He concludes that the mission of Israel to the nations consisted not in evangelizing but in being the chosen people, that is, the nation where Yahweh acts and whose existence has no sense but by reason of divine intervention. This role of Israel has been shared by the church, which also evangelizes only to the extent that its Lord lives in it. There is thus a unity of perspective on mission in the entire Bible. Mission is first and foremost an affair not of words and activities but of presence—the presence of God in the midst of God's people and the presence of this people in the midst of humanity (1959, 69-72). Although it is questionable that what Martin-Achard describes comprises mission in its entirety, he underlines an important aspect of mission that needs to be taken into account. His insight will be incorporated below as part of the second face of mission in the Old Testament.

A. Rétif and P. Lamarche (1966) study mission in the Old Testament under the aspect of universalism. They point out the tension running through this Testament between universalism and narrow nationalism, with universalism being more of an aspiration until the cross of Christ. There is universalism of origin in the Table of the Nations (Gen 10), and universalism of the promise of salvation in Genesis 3:15 ("he shall crush your head"). The blessing of Abram perhaps originally read, "by you the nations will bless themselves," though with the growth of universalism after the exile it came to be read as "in you the nations will be blessed" (1966, 21). The P creation account in Genesis 1 is universalistic, for all humankind is created in the image and likeness of God. Amos presents a universalism of judgment, not yet of salvation—God's universal law governs all peoples and before it all are accountable. The universal peace of Isaiah 11:6-8 includes all humanity. The insistence on individual responsibility (Ezek 18; Jer 31:29-30) breaks the bond to communal destiny and thus relativizes the Jew/gentile dichotomy (1966, 60). Jeremiah 18 presents Yahweh as a potter molding the destiny of all nations—any nation that repents of evil attracts Yahweh's mercy. Deutero-Isaiah presents Yahweh as calling the nations to conversion: "turn to me and be saved, all you ends of the earth, for I am God and there is no other" (Isa 45:22). The Songs of the Servant trace a mission of "light to the nations." The sufferings and death of the servant become a source of blessing for many. Isaiah 66:18-21 sees strangers admitted even to the priesthood following an outreach to, and ingathering of, the nations. The author of Jonah wanted the hearers to embrace the mission of preaching conversion to the multitudes of Nineveh, whose fate God shows to be God's concern. Joel 3:1-5 promises an out-pouring of God's spirit on all humankind when "all who call on the name of Yahweh will be saved" (Joel 3:5). The insights of Rétif and Lamarche are welcome and will be integrated somewhat into the fourfold schema of mission in the Old Testament to be sketched out below.

For many evangelicals all scripture has one key and it is christological. All scripture speaks with one voice to give a unified testimony to Jesus as the Christ. The book by Walter Kaiser is in this tradition and expresses the belief that "the goal of the Old Testament was to see both Jews and Gentiles come to a saving knowledge of the Messiah who was to come" (Kaiser 2000, 10). The object of faith is the same in the Old Testament as in the New, namely, Christ. Kaiser writes that "the plan of God had from the very beginning the central figure of the 'Seed' who was to come in the person of the Man of Promise, the Messiah" (p. 27). The Bible begins with the theme of mission in the Book of Genesis and maintains that drive throughout the Old Testament and into the New Testament. "If an Old Testament Great Commission must be identified, then it will be Gen 12:3 (all the peoples of the earth will be blessed through you [Abraham])" (Kaiser 2000, 7). The nations and gentiles were envisaged right from the beginning as equal recipients of the same good news (cf. Gen 12:3), for

> the "people of God" in all ages have been one. Together they have been called to the same privilege of service and ministry on behalf of the coming Man of Promise. All were to be agents of God's blessing to all on earth. Nothing could be clearer from the missionary and ministry call issued in Exodus 19:4-6. (Kaiser 2000, 24)

The Servant of Yahweh (Israel) received the commission to establish the manner of serving Yahweh among the nations; his task is spiritual, not political or judicial. Mission in the Old Testament can thus be dubbed "centrifugal witnessing" (Kaiser 2000, 9). Kaiser is particularly insistent that it was God's intention to bless the whole earth through David. So he translates *tōrat ha-ʾadam* in 2 Sam 7:19b not as "human destiny" (NJB) or "instruction for the people" (NRSV) but as "charter for humanity" (ibid., 26). The Davidic dynasty was to symbolize God's rule on earth in the hands of the messiah to come. Seen from the unity of scripture and the eternal intentions of God, the Old Testament is fundamentally and pervasively missionary. Kaiser has done scholarship a service in focusing on the unity

of the divine missionary purpose in both Testaments and in showing the
organic links between them. His interpretation is grounded squarely in
evangelical principles and is to that extent valid. Denominations, like individuals, bring differing interpretive perspectives to bear on scripture. With
this perspective, however, there is a chance that the reader could miss a
sense of the historical development of ideas of mission in the Old Testament and the tension manifest in its pages between divine mission and
national agenda.

Some authors treat the theme of mission in the Old Testament as part of
a treatise on mission in the Bible. Carroll Stuhlmueller's treatment is quite
extensive (138 pages of 348). It is a thematic approach that emphasizes the
aspect of acculturation. Israel lived in osmosis with the surrounding culture. There was a continuous cycle of indigenization, prophetic challenge,
and purification. The ancestors of Israel shared the same origin as the other
nations (Gen 10). When Israel left Egypt it was a "mixed group" (Exod
12:38), and in Canaan the nation was formed out of uprooted and
oppressed *apiru* (outlaws and people with no citizen rights). Other nations
continued to have great impact on Israel's religious and secular traditions.
For example, the ideology of kingship, the priesthood, and the sacrificial
system were all borrowed from Canaan. Hosea transformed and incorporated Canaanite fertility language into Israelite worship and theology, and
so "the earlier covenantal language of Lord and vassal is now modulated
to read husband and wife" (Stuhlmueller and Senior 1983, 68). Possible
universal elements in Israelite tradition are the pattern of God's care for the
oppressed and God's love for Israel, which, being gratuitous, can also in
principle be offered to other nations. Deutero-Isaiah saw Israel as given the
task of being a "light to the nations" (Isa 49:6). Israel's liturgical prayer
served to "kindle and preserve intuitions of God's universal sovereignty—
and therefore of the universal scope of his salvation" (Stuhlmueller and
Senior 1983, 318). Later tradition would see renewed Zion as symbol of
cosmic salvation. There is mission in the Old Testament, but it is centripetal
mission. For contemporary mission, the Old Testament has much to teach
us about the assimilation of cultural patterns into the expression of the
faith. It also affords us a textbook case of the dialectic between outreach
and identity.

Lucien Legrand (1990), in an incisive but brief treatment (37 of 161
pages), concentrates on the motif of election and the nations. He uses the
categories of "universalism centered on Zion" and "de-centralized universalism" (1990, 15-27). The eschatological pilgrimage of the nations to
Zion represents universalism centered on Zion, but some texts go beyond
this to imply that God's covenant with Israel will be extended to other
nations, who would then stand on the same footing with God as Israel. Isaiah 19:19-25 says that "Israel will be third with Egypt and Assyria, a blessing in the midst of the earth" and calls Egypt "my people." Blessing is a

prerogative of Abraham and his progeny in Genesis 12:3, and "my people" is the term usually used for Israel as covenant partner of Yahweh. Thus, here covenantal terms are being used of nations other than Israel. Isaiah 56:6-7 has Yahweh promise to lead "to my holy mountain" eunuchs and foreigners who join themselves to Yahweh, "for my house will be called a house of prayer for all nations." Isaiah 66:18-21 contemplates sending messengers to Tarshish, Put and Lud, Meshech, Tubal and Javan, and "they will proclaim my glory to the nations" (v. 19). Job is the story of a non-Israelite with a universal human problem and a divine response that has universal validity. Jonah illustrates universal divine compassion in the face of universal human misery. Legrand concludes that in the Old Testament universalism and election are incomprehensible in disjunction, for "God's call is addressed to the world, but it begins with Israel and invites the nations to join with the people of the election" (1990, 27).

David J. Bosch unfortunately devotes only four pages to the Old Testament, under the heading of "Reflections on the New Testament as a Missionary Document" (1991, 15-55). He emphasizes the aspect of God's compassion, a compassion that embraces the nations also. He states that "if there is a missionary in the Old Testament it is God [Godself] who will, as [God's] eschatological deed *par excellence*, bring the nations to Jerusalem to worship [God] there together with [God's] covenant people" (Bosch 1991, 19).

Andreas J. Köstenberger and Peter T. O'Brien give a concise but insightful treatment of mission in the Old Testament (2001, 19-71).

The authors of the book by Arthur F. Glasser et al. (2003) are in the evangelical tradition. Using the theme of the kingdom of God as key for the study of mission in both Testaments, the authors posit a covenantal rule of God over Israel and a universal rule of God over the world, the former being in the service of the latter. They write that "the salvation of the nations was God's ultimate motivation in making Abraham's name great and in being the God of Abraham's innumerable progeny" (2003, 59). They cite approvingly (p. 17) the dictum of George A. F. Knight (1959, 8) that "God was in Israel, seeking to reconcile the world unto himself (cf. 2 Cor 5:19)."

WHAT IS MISSION IN THE OLD TESTAMENT?

It is clear that the various scholars operate with divergent ideas of mission. For example, Martin-Achard distinguishes mission from universalism, while Rétif and Lamarche seem to equate both. For Rowley the text, "a light to the nations" (Isa 49:6), makes of Deutero-Isaiah *the* missionary of the Old Testament, while for Martin-Achard this text is not missionary in the ordinary sense of the word. Because scholars differ on what constitutes mission in the Old Testament, it is necessary to clarify the sense or senses in which "mission" is being used in this work.

The word "mission" derives from the Latin word *missio*, which means "a sending." Until the sixteenth century C.E., "mission" referred to the outward activity of the Trinity, the Father's sending of the Son and the sending of the Holy Spirit by Father and Son. It was the Jesuits, the Carmelites, and the Congregation for the Propagation of the Faith who in the sixteenth century gave it new content and began to use it for the missions of the church. Because mission refers to a sending, some seek to relate mission in the Old Testament uniquely to the root שלח ("to send"), or to the concept of a mandate for preaching to outsiders for the purpose of converting them to faith in Yahweh. Not finding much of this in the Old Testament, they deny that there is mission in it. But, as will become clearer in the course of this work, the Bible contains different models of mission operative in different faith communities at different times. Legrand is right in insisting that "like the Christian life itself, mission is *koinonia*, the communion of a plurality and variety of gifts in the Spirit" (1990, 7). He outlines a number of models of mission. The exodus model of mission as the pilgrimage of a liberated people, the Abraham model of mission as a blessing to all, a pilgrimage of faith and dialogue. There is also the creation model of responsibility for God's world. The Johannine model consists in the sharing of life and spiritual experience. The Pauline model of an itinerant mission of proclamation, conversion, and the founding of believing communities is thus only one model of mission among many. A similar divergence of models of mission obtains in the Old Testament as well.

FOUR FACES OF MISSION IN THE OLD TESTAMENT

Mission being part of the identity of any faith community, it cannot be defined without reference to the life and traditions of that particular community. For the faith community of Israel, mission is intimately related to election. A problem for our subject is that Israel did not always maintain a unique idea of what constituted the "goal" of her election. As she evolved into different forms of being—tribal community, nation, remnant scattered among the nations—her views of her place and function in God's universe and of her relation to other peoples varied. It is nevertheless a fact that sometime in the later Persian period Israel began to welcome people of other nations to partnership in her covenant with God. Jewish apologetic and missionary propaganda directed toward gentiles began to appear in the Diaspora, especially in Egypt. Scot McKnight is right on target when he writes that

> the old view that Judaism had no mission because it did not evangelize is mistaken. If Judaism did use propaganda, that would constitute a mission because mission is a broader term about one's orientation.

In other words, such a view of propaganda reflects mission consciousness. Moreover, the use of "good works" to affect non-Jews is another reflection of a mission to the world, although such is not "evangelism." (1991, 50)

What McKnight says here about mission in the later Persian period applies also to the Old Testament period. Direct evangelism is not the only form of mission. Mission in the Old Testament has had many faces, and I shall outline four of them. These faces serve as both a heuristic tool and an instrument for the organization of the chapters to follow.

The first face of mission in the Old Testament I identify as the aspect of universality, universality of salvation and universality of righteousness before Yahweh. It is the consciousness that all people can be righteous or evil before Yahweh. Some texts in this category may go one step further and indicate some consciousness of the responsibility of Israel vis-à-vis the nations, a consciousness of mission that is not yet missionary activity proper.[5] Wisdom 18:4 is one such text. It reads: "but well those others deserved to be deprived of light and imprisoned in darkness, for they had kept in captivity your children, by whom the incorruptible light of the Law was to be given to the world." This text interprets "light of nations" in Isaiah 49:6 in relation to the *torah* and implicitly understands the *torah* of Israel as having some missionary function vis-à-vis the nations, without specifying what this function is. It nevertheless affirms that *torah* as light is to illuminate not only Israel but other nations also. Yahweh is not limited to or constrained by any racial or cultural boundaries. Chapters 3-5 explore this face of mission in the Old Testament.

The second face of mission in the Old Testament I designate as "community-in-mission." It is the awareness that Israel's very existence is bound up with the knowledge and glory of Yahweh among the peoples and that Israel's election serves the glory of God. Martin-Achard expressed this idea when he affirmed that Yahweh was present in Israel and acted in Israel so that the nations might recognize Yahweh and give Yahweh due honor and glory. Israel was meant to be a divine pattern for individual and social life that will draw all humanity to Yahweh. The classical prophets, beginning with Amos, sought to bring Israel to this awareness in practice. Scholars need to recover the important lesson that a primary aspect of Israel's mission is to be fully the Israel that God has desired it to be, a revelation of God to the nations. In modern times the same idea is expressed of the church when it is said that "the pilgrim church is missionary by her very nature."[6] Jeremiah expressed this idea when he said,

---

5. The distinction between "mission consciousness" and "evangelism" is borrowed from Scot McKnight (1991, 50).

6. Vatican II, *Ad Gentes*, Decree on the Missionary Activity of the Church, no. 2.

if you come back to me Israel . . . if you take your horrors out of my sight, if you go roving no more, if you swear, "as Yahweh lives!" truthfully, justly, uprightly, then the nations will bless themselves by him and glory in him. (Jer 4: 1-2)

This aspect of mission in the Old Testament may correspond to what Kaiser called "centrifugal witnessing" (2000, 9). Chapters 6 to 8 will develop this face of mission in the Old Testament.

Chapter 9, "The Primacy of the Righteousness of God," is a transitional chapter that investigates the theological foundations that made possible Israel's inclusion of gentiles in the covenant with God.

The third face of mission in the Old Testament is what scholars generally call "centripetal mission." It is explicit in texts such as Isaiah 2:2-5, where all the nations stream on pilgrimage to Zion, there to be instructed in God's *torah* and in God's ways. Some of the texts that come under this heading qualify as what has been called the "mission of moral monotheism." In several texts, the Old Testament calls upon the nations or the ends of the earth to acknowledge Yahweh. When such texts are examined, it is seen that what is at stake is the acknowledgment of Yahweh as the only God and the avoidance of immorality associated with idolatry. Such calls are not always invitations to the nations to participate in the Yahweh covenant. In the Diaspora, Jewish apologetic and missionary literature directed to gentiles led some of the gentiles to profess Yahweh, the God of Heaven, as the only true God and to adhere to Judaism in some form. A few converted fully to Judaism as proselytes, but most became "god-fearers" and generally accepted monotheism, observed the Sabbath, and attended synagogue worship, but were not fully aggregated to Judaism. Texts that portray centripetal mission or the mission of moral monotheism are dealt with in chapters 10-11.

The fourth and final face of mission will be dealt with in chapters 12-14. Scholars speak here of "centrifugal mission," in which active effort is made to reach outsiders and through conversion include them in the covenant as "proselytes." The first text in this category was apparently Isaiah 56:1-8, which for the first time opened the possibility of the religious conversion of gentiles and evolved an instrument for it (see chapter 12).

SURVEY OF CONTEXTS OF MISSION
IN THE OLD TESTAMENT

Many contexts and movements affected the development of mission consciousness in the Old Testament. Of these I single out three.

Until the eighth century B.C.E., Israel was sheltered from the vortex of international politics and its focus was mainly inward. The rise of Assyria and its imperial ambitions initiated an era of love-hate relationships with other peoples that were reflected in some texts. Moments of severe national or group crisis were likely to elicit particularistic texts, while eras of peace and good relations with the surrounding nations would generate more universalistic and inclusive texts.

The second period is that of the exile. In exile Israel was no longer a political or national entity, but rather became a confessional community into which people entered or remained by free choice. Israel's religious difference from other peoples came to be highlighted. This was the case especially for the contrast between worship of the one God and idolatry. Deutero-Isaiah interpreted the presence of Israel among the nations as that of a witness in Yahweh's lawsuit against the nations and their gods (Isa 43:10). Yahweh was about to use Yahweh's might to restore Israel to its land so that "the glory of Yahweh will be revealed and all flesh will see it together" (Isa 40:5). Yahweh was commissioning Yahweh's servant Israel to be "a light to the nations, so that my salvation may reach the ends of the earth" (Isa 49:6). The ministry of this prophet is important for significant developments in mission consciousness in Israel, but it is not clear that Deutero-Isaiah envisaged the equal participation of gentiles with Jews in the covenant. The distinction of making the leap to envisage the full and equal religious integration of gentiles into the covenant belongs to "Trito-Isaiah."

Apocalyptic was a third force in the development of mission consciousness in Israel, for it located Israel within a universal current. Unlike prophecy, apocalyptic does not stress Israel's salvation history; rather, apocalyptic writers viewed history in universal terms as cosmic drama. This drama moves from the absolute beginning of time (creation) to the absolute end, when history will be completely transfigured and transformed in the new creation (Anderson 1967, 136-37). Many of the more inclusive texts of the Old Testament, for example, Isaiah 65:17-25, belong to that "apocalyptic rendering of the Isaiah tradition" which universalizes Israelite tradition, moving it from the national plane to the cosmic. The centrality of Zion is, however, not dismissed, for "if the peoples would know and worship the God whose sovereignty is universal, they must come to the symbolic 'center'" (Anderson 1988, 21).

INTERPRETING THE TEXT

The Old Testament collapses into a unity over a thousand years of the transmission of a people's growing knowledge of God and of God's demands on them. The first several centuries of this tradition were purely oral in form. When the material came to be written down, the editors did not systematically eliminate what no longer seemed to apply, as modern editors would, but sometimes preserved the traditions beside the new beliefs. If they found two or three traditions of a certain event or saying, they preserved these as best they could, with editorial updating where necessary. For example, Deuteronomy 5:4-5 now reads:

on the mountain, from the heart of the fire, Yahweh spoke to you face to face, while I stood between you and Yahweh to let you know what Yahweh was saying, since you were afraid of the fire, and had not gone up the mountain.

Verse 4 seems to have the people on the mountain, while v. 5 denies this explicitly. This tension reflects the unresolved debate in the Sinai/Horeb narrative as to whether Yahweh spoke the Ten Commandments directly to the people or only to Moses, who then communicated them to the people. The final editor has here juxtaposed two divergent traditions and left them in tension with each other! Humanity's knowledge of God has been a hit-and-miss affair. There is no guarantee that either the original or the most recent tradition portrays God and God's relationship with people more truly. Thus, the Old Testament, indeed the Bible as a whole, speaks with many voices, and we need to hear all these voices together.

Texts have meaning in themselves and meaning in relation to one another. Therefore, the final literary shaping of the material may suggest meanings that are not to be found in the disparate pieces considered apart from one another. The Primeval History (Gen 1-11) is a case in point. Israel prefaced its history with eleven chapters of universal history. Some Midrashim (collections of Jewish interpretations of the Bible using very broad and elastic principles of interpretation) seize on this fact to declare that the world was created for the sake of Israel. But the chapters are more probably to be read in the inverse sense, namely, that God, who created the universe, chose Israel in function of God's purposes for the universe. The distinction between the disparate materials in themselves and the meaning that accrues to them in relation to texts in context is important. So is the literary shaping or reshaping of texts by editors or redactors.

The final literary shaping often juxtaposes later insertions with universalistic import beside texts whose atmosphere is that of restrictive nationalism. Isaiah 18:1-7 may serve as an example. The first six verses denounced "*a nation tall and bronzed . . . a people feared far and near*" (v. 2) on whom the birds of prey will feast in summer (v. 6). However, v. 7 says that "in that time, an offering will be brought to Yahweh Sabaoth on behalf of *a people tall and bronzed, on behalf of a people feared far and near . . .* to the place where the name of Yahweh Sabaoth resides, Mount Zion." The editor has employed the strategy of "repetition with commentary" in order to qualify (and correct) an earlier oracle along a universalistic trajectory. Similarly, the proclamation against Egypt in Isa 19:1-16 suddenly turns into an oracle of the deliverance of Egypt in Isa 19:18-25, even of the conversion of Egypt along with Assyria to the worship of Yahweh. Such tensions of universalistic and particularistic readings in proximate juxtaposition call for attentiveness in the exercise of interpretation.

Taking all the above into consideration, here is an outline of the interpretive method followed in this book. Four different approaches will be applied to the text, though they need not always follow each other in the order given here. Moreover, some of the approaches may not apply to some texts.

First, then, the text will be considered in its literary context and in its function within the larger complex and the whole. Attention will be given to possible layers in the text, particularly in prophetic literature, where the later strata often comment upon and adapt the earlier ones. Second, historical analysis will be applied to the text insofar as this is possible or called for. Third, the reception of the particular text within the Old Testament, and sometimes into the New Testament, will be investigated with the aim of elucidating the text's total field of meaning. Finally, texts in diverse contexts but with similar content will be compared. Such comparison often manifests the variety of points of view on particular subjects and issues within the Old Testament tradition itself. The method is thus attentive both to context and to rereadings and intertextual linkages.

A CHRISTIAN READING OF THE OLD TESTAMENT

Christians are uncomfortable with the term "Old Testament," for it seems to imply that God's covenant with Israel has either been revoked or been bypassed by the Christian dispensation. Paul firmly rejected such an idea in Romans 11:1. The Christian church fought Marcion in the second century on the same question. The resort to the term "First Testament" is not really appropriate, for Jews do not accept a second testament or any addition to the words of Moses (see Deut 4:2; 34:10). Nor is the term "Hebrew Scriptures" adequate, for the Catholic and Orthodox canons contain some books written originally in Greek and regarded as sacred by Jews in Alexandria, but perhaps not by the Hebrew-speaking scribes in Palestine. With the above qualifiers in mind, we shall continue to use the term "Old Testament."

Gerhard von Rad (1965, 321) draws our attention to the "confusion of views on the relationship of the Old Testament to the New and the way in which theological definitions of this contradict one another." Some Christians interpret the Old Testament christologically and almost silence its independent voice. But the Old Testament is as much "word of God" as the New Testament. The literal sense of the text of the Old Testament may receive a "fuller sense" through the Christ-event, but is not thereby negated or laid aside. Because the canon is a synchronic statement, every book in it, every chapter and every verse, is contemporaneous with every other (Levenson 1985, 1), and so intertextual allusions within the canon may advance, qualify, or take something away from the sense of an earlier text.

Christians and Jews differ in the "hermeneutical perspective" they bring to the text. For Jews, the Torah (Pentateuch) contains "the essential institutions revealed by God . . . governing the religious, moral, juridical and political life of the Jewish nation after the Exile," while for Christians "the general tendency is to give more importance to the prophetic texts, understood as foretelling the mystery of Christ" (Pontifical Biblical Commission 2002, no. 11). Jews read the Old Testament from the perspective of "*torah*/law," Christians from the perspective of "promise." Jews consider many eschatological promises to be objects of future hope, while Christians see these as already fulfilled in Christ. Thus, for Christians the Old Testament is not a self-contained revelation, for "the very structure of the Christian Bible makes the theological claim that the Old Testament can be read in a broader literary and theological context" (Schramm 2000, 347). The Catholic and Orthodox Old Testament contains more books than the Jewish Old Testament. Besides, the canon establishes a context of its own that must be considered in understanding each of its parts, for "by placing scripture alongside scripture a whole new range of interpretations became possible" (Clements 1978, 153).

The Bible itself does not assume that texts can have only one original and "correct" meaning. Prophetic sayings, for example, were constantly reinterpreted and reapplied within the Old Testament itself. Some texts of the Old Testament receive further reinterpretations in the New Testament. Even in a Christian reading, however, these texts are not thereby divested of their original Old Testament meaning. The New Testament often builds on the Old by further developing an allusion or an implicit aspect of that text (see, e.g., the treatment of Exod 19:3-8 in chapter 6). As von Rad said long ago, "the way in which the Old Testament is absorbed in the New is the logical end of the process initiated by the Old Testament itself" (1965, 321). Jewish interpretive tradition has also applied its own techniques, sometimes with a view to "clarifying" the meaning of texts that Christians use to argue their own point of view. It is in this manner that the Testaments (and their interpretive traditions) comment on each other, and mutually correct each other (Schramm 2000, 347). Divergent faith perspectives may thus be a factor in the divergence of interpretations, not only between Christians and Jews but also between Christian denominations. This author's faith and interpretive perspectives align with those of the Roman Catholic tradition. The Catholic tradition insists on the continuity of the Old in the New, but is also attentive to context, allowing each Testament its own integrity—"Novum Testamentum in Vetere latet, et in Novo Vetus patet," "the New Testament lies hidden in the Old, and the Old becomes clear in the New" (St. Augustine).

DISCUSSION

1. Universalism is not yet mission (Martin-Achard).
2. Mission is primarily the presence of God in the midst of God's people and the presence of this people in the midst of humanity (Martin-Achard).

3. "God was in Israel reconciling the world to Godself" (Knight).
4. What are the four faces of mission in the Old Testament and what do you think about such a schema?
5. Comment on the method of interpretation outlined in this chapter.
6. How should Christians interpret the Old Testament?

2

A Brief Survey of Trends in Mission

Until the sixteenth century the word "mission" was used of the Trinity to designate the Father's sending of the Son and the sending of the Holy Spirit by Father and Son. From the sixteenth century onward, the Jesuits, the Carmelites, and the Roman Congregation for the Propagation of the Faith began using it for spreading the Christian faith. So until the 1950s "mission" meant the spreading of the faith, the conversion of nonbelievers, and the planting of new churches (Bosch 1991, 1). Events in the world would lead to attempts at a redefinition.

Karl Barth in a paper in 1932 presented mission as the activity of God. He was followed in 1933 by Karl Hartenstein, who was the first to coin the phrase *missio Dei*. Both men were concerned to confine mission to God, thus preventing it from being secularized and horizontalized (Bosch 1991, 390). The 1952 "Fifth International Missionary Conference" in Willingen, Germany (just after World War II and the mission debacle in China), both gave the term *missio Dei* currency and explicated it. Mission refers primarily to the purposes and activities of the triune God for the whole universe. Mission, as an activity of the church, is only "a participation in the sending of the Son, in the *missio Dei*, with the inclusive aim of establishing the lordship of Christ over the whole redeemed creation" (cited from Vicedom 1965, 5).

If the church's mission merely participates in and serves God's mission, which enfolds all people and all dimensions of existence, then it cannot be limited to church-centered goals like planting churches and saving souls. It must equally be as directed toward the full well-being of humanity and the cosmos as the *missio Dei* itself. The election of Israel and of the church is to be understood in terms of the universal goals of God's mission.

Discussion now centered on the place of evangelism in mission. Does the *missio Dei* work itself out in ordinary human history or exclusively in and through the church? The 1960s and 1970s were an era of "new mission" in the World Council of Churches (WCC). This new mission focused on "salvation today" through humanization and working for the transformation of the unjust structures of society. It provoked a lively discussion to which different denominations brought diverging perspectives.

The Orthodox have always insisted that pneumatology is inseparable from christology—the Holy Spirit is the Spirit of Christ and leads to Christ. They had the substance of the concept of *missio Dei* without using that term. For them the primary goal of mission is the glory of God reflected in humans through praise. God's glory is the communion of life within the Trinity, which overflows to enfold and transfigure everyone and everything; it is *theōsis,* a process of divinization (Stamoolis 1986, 49). Liturgy is both the motivation for and the goal of mission: if mission establishes the church, the church is established to worship the triune God (ibid., 87).

On the Protestant side, evangelicals emphasized the role of the church and insisted that Christ be at the center; mission should be seen as the line that separates belief from unbelief.[1] In March 2000, a statement by the Commission on World Mission and Evangelism, *Mission and Evangelism in Unity Today,* proposed to lay out God's mission without neglecting the role of the church and to delineate a trinitarian approach to the concept of *missio Dei* that does not separate the presence of God or the Spirit from that of the Son (Matthey 2001, 431). It also proposed to distinguish mission and evangelism, using *mission* for the holistic mandate of the church within God's mission, and *evangelism* for an essential part of it, namely, "naming the Name," voicing the gospel and inviting to conversion and discipleship in Christ (statement, no. 12; see Matthey 2001, 430).

On the Catholic side, the 1965 Vatican II document *Ad Gentes,* the Decree on the Missionary Activity of the Church, took up the ideas of *missio Dei* and the trinitarian dimension of mission that were found in the Orthodox tradition and in the Willingen Conference. Mission flows from the "fountain of love" within God the Father:

> the pilgrim church is missionary by her very nature. For it is from the mission of the Son and the mission of the Holy Spirit that she takes her origin, in accordance with the decree of God the Father. (2)

In the definition of mission, the intimate link of the church's mission with the *missio Dei* appears: "missionary activity is nothing else and nothing less than a manifestation and epiphany of God's will and the fulfillment of that will in the world and in world history" (9).

In no. 4, it is stated that "doubtless the Holy Spirit was already at work in the world before Christ was glorified"—a text that would generate varied concepts of the relation of the Spirit to mission. When it came to the

---

1. WCC Commission on World Mission and Evangelism, Mexico, 1963; cited from Kirk 2000, 23.

mission of the church, the document unfortunately retained the plural, *missions*, and located these geographically as "commonly exercised in certain territories recognized by the Holy See." It explained the missionary task as that of "preaching the gospel and planting the church among peoples or groups who do not yet believe in Christ" (6).

The Catholic Church is necessary for salvation to the extent that no one would be saved who, knowing that the church was made so by God, yet refused to join the church; yet God, in ways known to God alone, can lead those inculpably ignorant of the gospel to that faith without which it is impossible to please God (Heb 11:6) (*Ad Gentes* 7).[2]

The Synod of 1971 on "Justice in the World" underlined the link between mission and justice when it said in the introduction to its document:

> action on behalf of justice and participation in the transformation of the world fully appear to us as a constitutive dimension of the preaching of the Gospel, or, in other words, of the Church's mission for the redemption of the human race and its liberation from every oppressive situation.

In 1974, the Synod on Evangelization was held. In the many nations freed from colonialism in the 1960s and 1970s, "missionary" had become an ugly word. Yet the new idea that non-Christians did not require explicit faith in Christ in order to be saved unnerved many missionaries who felt that this undermined all their efforts. Burgess Carr (1974) added to the turmoil when he proposed a "moratorium" on mission in the Two-Thirds World. Eboussi-Boulaga (1974, 287) sharpened the turmoil when he declared: "Let Europe and America give priority to their own evangelization; let us plan the orderly departure of missionaries from Africa." In the face of all this, Paul VI in the encyclical *Evangelii Nuntiandi* (Evangelization in the Modern World, 1975) proposed a shift from mission to evangelization, and from focus on the church to focus on the kingdom—integral salvation. This double shift allowed the inclusion in the evangelizing mission of the church of many activities considered necessary in the current historical situation.

In the meantime, every activity of the church seemed to come under the term "evangelization." Mission was being drawn so far into ecclesiology as to seem to lose specificity, to be no longer a specific task of the church. As early as 1958, Lesslie Newbigin (1958, 21) had proposed distinguishing the missionary *dimension* of the church from her missionary *intention*, but this

---

2. See also the Pastoral Constitution on the Church in the Modern World (*Gaudium et Spes*), 22.

did not seem to catch on. In 1984, the Pontifical Council for Interreligious Dialogue weighed in with *Reflections and Orientations on Dialogue and Mission.* This document insisted that the evangelizing mission of the church was "a single but complex and articulated reality." It is comprised of elements that include presence and witness, commitment to social development and human liberation, liturgical life, prayer and contemplation, interreligious dialogue, proclamation and catechesis (13).

In 1991, the Pontifical Council for Interreligious Dialogue and the Congregation for the Evangelization of Peoples issued an important document, *Dialogue and Proclamation: Reflections on Interreligious Dialogue and the Proclamation of the Gospel of Jesus Christ.* There is one plan of salvation for humankind with its center in Jesus Christ (28). The firm faith in the religions is an effect of the Spirit of truth operating outside the confines of the Mystical Body (26); "concretely, it will be in the sincere practice of what is good in their religious traditions and by following the dictates of their conscience" (29) that these share in the mystery of Christ. However, insofar as they respond to God's call they are related (*ordinantur*) to the church as the sacrament in which the kingdom of God is present in mystery (35; cf. *Lumen Gentium*, 16).

On December 7, 1991, Pope John Paul II issued the encyclical *Redemptoris Missio* (On the Permanent Validity of the Church's Missionary Mandate). In §41, he referred to the 1984 document of the Pontifical Council for Interreligious Dialogue, "The Attitude of the Church towards the Followers of Other Religions: Reflections and Orientations on Dialogue and Mission," which stated that the evangelizing mission of the church was "a single but complex and articulated reality,"[3] with principal elements as presence and witness, commitment to social development and human liberation, liturgical life, prayer and contemplation, interreligious dialogue, and proclamation and catechesis. The pope summarized the elements in a slightly different way as witness, proclamation, dialogue, inculturation, and promoting development by forming consciences. Of these the specific missionary activity is mission *ad gentes* (initial proclamation, missionary evangelization or missionary work among non-Christians). He writes that "proclamation is the permanent priority of mission. The church cannot elude Christ's explicit mandate, nor deprive men and women of the 'Good News' about their being loved and saved by God" (44). Mission *ad gentes* is to be distinguished from the new evangelization of formerly Christian lands. Although "every authentic prayer is prompted by the Holy Spirit, who is mysteriously present in every human heart" (29), the Spirit is not an alternative to Christ, nor is his universal activity to be separated from his

---

3. *Dialogue and Mission* 13, which was taken up in *Evangelii Nuntiandi* 24: "evangelization is a complex process."

particular activity in the church. The Word is not to be separated from Jesus Christ, nor Jesus from the Christ (6). Christ is the fullest and definitive self-revelation of God and is therefore the only Savior; all participated forms of mediation acquire meaning and value only from Christ's own mediation (5).

The 1990s saw the theology of religions as the "epitome of mission theology" (Bosch 1991, 477). In response to some of the currents in this field, the Congregation for the Doctrine of the Faith in August 2000 issued the Declaration "*Dominus Jesus*: On the Unicity and Salvific Universality of Jesus Christ and the Church." This document insisted that theological *faith* is to be distinguished from *belief* in other religions (7). Faith is the personal adherence of a person to God who reveals and the truth God reveals and is a supernatural virtue infused in persons. Belief is human and consists of that treasury of wisdom and religious aspiration which persons conceive in their search for absolute truth, but which still lacks assent to the God who reveals himself (7). "The action of the Spirit is not outside or parallel to the action of Christ" (12). The Scriptures of other religions suffer from gaps, insufficiencies, and errors. They may reflect a ray of that truth that enlightens every person (*Nostra Aetate* 2),[4] but they receive this from the mystery of Christ (*Dominus Jesus* 8). It is contrary to the faith to introduce a separation between the salvific action of the Word as such and that of the Word made human, for the one single person operates in the two natures (10). It must be firmly believed that the pilgrim church is necessary for salvation, being the universal sacrament of salvation (*Lumen Gentium*, Dogmatic Constitution on the Church, 48). This does not contradict, but must be held together with 1 Timothy 2:4, which says that God wishes all humans to be saved and to come to a knowledge of the truth.

Until recently mission was mainly a one-way street, from Europe and North America to Africa, Asia, and Latin America. Today mission is from everywhere to everywhere. Particularly dynamic is the current of missionaries from the former recipients of mission to the former centers of mission, and much of this new current belongs to charismatic and Pentecostal Christianity.

REFLECTION

It is clear that consensus is lacking on the theory and practice of mission, and that there are also confessional differences and divergent accents in the matter among Christians. The following are some of the outstanding issues.

---

4. The Vatican II Declaration on the Relationship of the Church to Non-Christian Religions.

How is the statement that "the pilgrim church is missionary by her very nature" (*Ad Gentes* 2) to be understood? What is said about the universal church applies equally to the local church. If the church exists for mission, is there room for distinction in its activity? Is there room for a distinct missionary vocation? Do "missionary congregations" still have a role to play in the local church? Is the distinction between "missionary intention" and "missionary dimension" helpful?

There is need to clarify the mission dimension of witness, proclamation, dialogue, inculturation, and promoting development (*Redemptoris Missio* 41). Asian theologians tend to reduce proclamation to dialogue, while African theologians tend to see mission as mainly inculturation.

The Orthodox have always considered liturgy to be the radiating center for mission. The Eucharist as a vortex draws humanity and creation into itself in order to transfigure and divinize them. The divine living communicated to the assembly in the liturgy is a potent witness to the living and triune God for all outside. Perhaps this is a dimension of the liturgy that needs be recovered among the "Western" churches.

The affirmation that "doubtless the Holy Spirit was already at work in the world before Christ was glorified" (*Ad Gentes* 4) has raised a number of issues. What is the place of Jesus Christ in mission, and what is the relation to Christ of the Spirit already at work in the cultures and religions? If the Spirit is at work in other religious traditions, are they then means of salvation for their adherents? Can these traditions convey saving faith to their members? What is the role of the church vis-à-vis other religious traditions and their members? And regarding the members of the Jewish faith, whose covenant with God is still valid, how is Paul's saying in Romans 11:26 that "all Israel will be saved" to be achieved? Will Israel be saved through its covenant with God or by obedience to the gospel of Jesus Christ?

There is an increasing divergence between church-based mission and kingdom-based mission. The latter is seen by some as embracing activities that are not necessarily based on the explicit confession of faith in Jesus Christ, nor do the activities even tend toward conversion to and aggregation to the church.

The mission of the Two-Thirds World to Europe and North America is bringing to the fore many new perspectives on faith and on styles of worship. It has also raised many questions, not the least of which concerns the proper object of mission. If the earlier mission to the Two-Thirds World appeared to be based on need—those who have coming to the aid of those who have not—how would one begin to understand reverse mission? Should one then not speak rather of mission as a sharing of varied gifts of the churches?

3

Genesis 1 as Blueprint for Mission

The earthly Temple is the world *in nuce*, the world is the Temple *in extenso*.

—Jon D. Levenson, *Sinai and Zion*, 141

As I indicated in chapter 1, chapters 3 to 5 will consider texts that portray the universality of salvation and of righteousness before God. Genesis 1 is considered to unfold the blueprint for mission, in that it depicts both the purpose of creation and the responsibility of humanity in it and for it.

Genesis 1:1–2:4a is P material. P (the Priestly writer) is one of the four "sources"[1] that scholars posit as underlying the present text of the Pentateuch. The "implied reader," that is, the addressees as far as one can make out from the text itself, is in exile away from the native land and is submerged under forces that resemble primeval chaos. The text seeks to give reassurance about the power of God over all hostile forces and about God's gracious purposes for God's people. In this sense, the account of the creation of the universe is a theological reflection, not a straightforward historical description.

Myths of origin seek to justify and to ground what is most essential to society and human life by recourse to the divine intent embedded in the primeval structure of things. The scientific explanation of the physical universe reckons with long periods of evolution from one level of existence to another. Creation myths do not focus on the evolution of humanity, but generally depict humanity as an already organized society at creation, as here in Genesis 1.

Myths of creation abounded in the ancient Near East, and so creation faith may have been part of the environment that Israel breathed. It is pos-

---

1. The four are usually designated by the siglum JEDP, namely, the Yahwist, the Elohist, the Deuteronomist, and the Priestly writer.

sible that the Jerusalem temple ideology during the monarchy already proclaimed Yahweh as creator of the universe, even if not yet perhaps in an
exclusive sense. In Genesis 14:19, 22 the god of Salem, El Elyon, is given
the epithet *qōnēh*[2] *šāmayîm wā'āreṣ* ("creator of heaven and earth"). Salem
is Jerusalem and the Jerusalem priesthood may have taken up such a belief.
It was Deutero-Isaiah, however, who demythologized the ancient myths of
creation and brought them into intrinsic relationship with God's acts of salvation in history. He stressed thereby the soteriological meaning of creation
and the creative significance of redemption (Anderson 1994, 27). That is,
the act of creation was a salvific act, while redemption itself was an act of
new creation.

FAITH AND CULTURE

P's text is implicitly polemical; it reapplies ancient myth in conformity
with the faith of Israel. A fundamental transformation is that P's creator god
stands over against creation, while in the ancient Near Eastern myths of creation the gods themselves emanated from the primeval elements of chaos.
The will and personal activity of the creator are paramount; the creator controls creation throughout all its history until the creator's purposes are
accomplished (see Robinson 1946, 18, 21). In many of the creation myths,
creation is associated with conflict against primeval forces of chaos. For
example, in the Babylonian myth *Enuma elish*, Marduk slew Tiamat (standing for the salt waters) and split her body into two to form the waters above
and the waters beneath. P rejects every concept of conflict at creation and
subordinates everything to the word of God. Tiamat, however, has left
traces in *tĕhôm*, the watery deep of Genesis 1:2. This word never takes the
article and is always feminine, like Tiamat, though its grammatical form is
masculine. In ancient myth, light emanated from the gods, and both the sun
and the moon were forces that controlled the destinies of nations and of
individuals. For P, primeval light appeared by the word of God, and both
sun and moon are merely "two great lights" that serve humans by dividing
day from night and marking the times for festivals. At the command of God,
the earth produced vegetation "bearing fruit with their seed inside" (Gen
1:11). This means that propagation is a power given by God at creation and
does not depend on fertility rites (Bird 1981, 129-59). There is no primor-
dial principle of evil, for God looked on all God had made and found it
"very good" (Gen 1:31). The great sea monsters (*tannînim*, Gen 1:21), elsewhere called Leviathan, Rahab, and Yam (sea), are no longer primeval

---

2. A Ugaritic fragment uses the same root, *qanah*, as epithet of El as, *qn 'rṣ* ("creator of
earth").

adversaries of God but creatures obedient to Yahweh. Poetry will, however, retain the old motif of the "cosmic battle," but now in a manner to enhance the power of the creator (cf. Ps 74:13-17). The myths saw human beings as created to relieve the lesser gods of toil and to provide food for the gods. P's creation account is human-centered: all things are created for humanity, and it is God who provides food for them (Gen 1:29). P's story of creation rejects the aristocratic split between a leisure-class divinity and a humanity that serves this divinity through slave labor. Rather, God works and rests and thus sets the pattern for humans to follow in their relation to the land and to the animals in the covenant of creation (Ruether 1999, 115).

STRUCTURAL AND LITERARY ANALYSIS

I read v. 1 as an interpretive summary statement: "in the beginning, God created heaven and earth."[3] The number seven is used to organize the material into six days of creation and a seventh day of rest. The reader is thus prepared to discover resonances of the theology of the Sabbath. Creation descends from heaven in two parallel movements of heaven–waters–earth, with correspondence between both sides of the diptych, and two works each on the third and sixth days (see Anderson 1977, 148-62). The first day corresponds to the fourth, the second to the fifth, and the third to the sixth.

Day 1	light	Day 4	luminaries
Day 2	waters separated sea and sky appear	Day 5	sea and air creatures
Day 3	earth/vegetation	Day 6	animals/humankind
	Day 7 rest	of God	

This pattern means that God first prepares a sphere, then creates the user of that sphere, delineates its nature and function, then installs it. For example, God first separates the upper and lower waters, thus preparing the

---

3. The NRSV interprets differently: "in the beginning, when God created the heavens and the earth, the earth was a formless void and darkness covered the face of the deep, while a wind from God swept over the face of the waters. Then God said…". Likewise, *Enuma elish* begins, "when on high the heaven had not been named."

habitat of sea and air creatures; then God creates and installs fish and birds, the creatures that use this habitat.

For P, order in the world hangs on obedience to the word of God. The world would be a perfect place were human beings to obey God's word as the elements do. Hence, P presents creation in a command–execution pattern:[4]

Introduction:	and God said
Command:	let there be . . .
Execution:	and it was so
Judgment:	and God saw that it was good (except for the firmament and humankind)
Time sequence:	and it was evening and morning . . .

It is clear that creation by word has been superimposed on material that perhaps conceived the creation differently, for creation by word is not carried through consistently. The text speaks also of the actions of dividing (*wayabdēl*) and making (*'āśāh*): God divided light from darkness (Gen 1:4) and made the two great lights (1:16). Further, God directly created human beings (Gen 1:27) without employing the command "let there be." For all new beginnings, P carefully uses the verb *bārā'* ("to create," Gen 1:1, 21, 27; 2:3). This verb did not yet mean "to create out of nothing," for uncreated chaos, in the form of darkness and the watery deep, formed the background to God's act. Yet this verb has God always as subject; hence it designates an action conceived as proper to God alone.[5] No creation is mentioned for the beings with God in Genesis 1:26. Creation out of nothing is not found in the Old Testament. As late as 50 B.C.E., Wisdom 11:17 still held the doctrine of creation "from formless matter." Creation out of nothing begins to appear in biblical literature in Romans 4:17 and Hebrews 11:3.

Blessing, the divine force for fruitfulness and success, is given only to the living creatures (*nepheš ḥayyāh*), that is, animals and humans (Gen 1:22, 28). The seventh day is also blessed (Gen 2:3) as being life-giving for these two species (we shall see later that animals are included in the command of rest on the Sabbath). In Hebrew thinking, plants do not have life as such; they are not *nepheš ḥayyāh* (living creatures) and so do not receive blessing.

---

4. P has Exodus 25-31 detail commands for the tabernacle and Exodus 35-40 correspondingly the execution.

5. The use of *bārā'* is concentrated in Deutero-Isaiah (eleven times), where the standard epithet for Yahweh is Creator of Israel (*bôrē' Yiśra'ēl*) and Creator of the Earth. It is also very common in P (eleven times), again for God's action in creation and God's deeds in history (see, e.g., Exod 34:10; Num 16:30). Three other uses of this verb, Amos 4:13, Jer 31:22 and Deut 4:32, are probably also exilic or postexilic.

P considers this blessing important, for it is repeated after the flood in 9:1, "and God blessed Noah and his sons, 'breed, multiply and fill the earth.'" It should be noted that the blessing of all humankind parallels the blessing of Abraham, the ancestor of Israel, in Genesis 12:2-3, but more about this later. The evaluation of the creator (it was good, very good in Gen 1:31) denotes the joy of a maker who sees that his product conforms to his purposes. This divine evaluation functions to focus the reader on conscious design in this creation story. Conscious design appears in the manner in which the unit reaches a twofold climax, namely, the creation and commissioning of human beings (Gen 1:26-28) and the resting of God (2:3).

THE RESTING OF GOD

Umberto Cassuto (1961, 61, 63)[6] insists that *wayyišbōt* of Genesis 2:2b means neither "and he rested," nor "and he ceased work," but rather "and he refrained from work." The NRSV, however (similarly the NAB and NJB), rightly translates the phrase as "and he rested on the seventh day." Exodus 20:11 cites our passage rendering it, "and he rested on the seventh day" (וינח ביום השביעי), using the root, *nwḥ* ("to rest"). In Exodus 31:17, P makes his mind clearer by saying that on the seventh day Yahweh "rested and drew breath" (שבת וינפש), that is, refreshed Godself. As already mentioned, this "rest" of God is one of the goals toward which the creation account moves. But, because the dominant motif has been one of creation by word, the evocation of "rest" here presents the reader with a "gap," something unexpected. The reader cannot take it to mean repose from the tiredness of labor, for the creator God has been presented as speaking only eight words. The reader notices that the concept of rest is rendered through the use of the denominative of Sabbath:

Gen 2:2b: *wayyišbōt bayyôm haššĕbî'î*
                and he rested on the seventh day
Gen 2:3b: *kî bô šābat mikkol mĕla'ktô*
                for on that day he rested from all his work.

The reader is thus led to seek further enlightenment in the theology of the Sabbath. The Sabbath proclaims that "to Yahweh belong the earth and all it contains, the world and all who live there" (Ps 24:1). It also draws the attention of humankind to the fact that there is more to life than all its striving. The Decalogue in Exodus 20:10-11 cites our text to support the command of Sabbath rest:

---

6. It becomes clear in Cassuto's discussion that he is concerned to avoid all anthropomorphism.

you shall do no work that day, neither you, nor your son nor your daughter nor your servants, men or women, nor your animals, nor the alien living with you. For in six days Yahweh made the heavens, earth and sea and all that these contain, but on the seventh day he rested; that is why Yahweh has blessed the Sabbath day and made it sacred.

The legislation is careful to specify that rest from work is not only for the master of the house, but applies also to the slaves and even the animals. The significance of this becomes evident in a text about the festival of the New Year in Lagash (third millennium), which says, "During seven days no grain was ground, the maidservant made herself equal to her mistress, the manservant walked side by side with his master."[7]

In other words, the feast of the New Year in that milieu reminded everyone of the basic equality and dignity of every person. Thus, it was potentially subversive of the ordering of society into master and slave. So it is with Sabbath rest in Israel. "The rest of God is a promised rest for humankind" (Brueggemann 1982, 36). It proclaims the lordship of God over all humanity as something that guarantees the welfare of everyone and everything. By God's act of setting the Sabbath apart, all human beings are gifted with a cycle of work and rest, not only masters but also slaves and animals. Israel professes its hope in the coming time when the master/slave dichotomy will disappear in the universal reign of God. When that day comes, "Yahweh will become king of the whole world . . . Yahweh will be the one and only and his name the one name" (Zech 14:9-10).

It may be asked, if the Sabbath is a particular Israelite observance, why does P insert it into the very foundations of creation? The answer must be that in observing the Sabbath, Israel is holding brief for all of humanity. At the conclusion of the temple service, the priests give the blessing (Num 6:22-27) so that worshipers may carry God's force for life home with them. At the conclusion of God's act of creation, God equally blessed the seventh day, that is, endowed it with force and vitality for all creatures. In the words of Claus Westermann (1978, 59), "the blessing bestowed on the community gathered for worship is now applied to the whole human race, indeed to all living beings, just as blessing in its original sense meant the power of life."

Rest is also the reason for creation in some myths of the ancient Near East. In these myths, the rest of the higher gods was being disturbed by rebelling lower gods. Human beings were created to quiet the "noise"

---

7. Cited from Niels-Erik Andreasen, "Festival and Freedom: A Study of an Old Testament Theme," *Interpretation* 28 (1974): 281-97, here 282 no. 3. He translated the text from B. Meissner, *Babylonien und Assyrien* II (Heidelberg, 1925), 94.

(rebellion) of the lower gods, by taking over from them the drudgery of maintaining the irrigation canals and providing food for the gods.[8] In some of these myths, however, the motif of rest is an element that follows the victory of the god over the forces of chaos. The creation of the world (including human beings) happens in a chain that links victory over the forces of chaos with the building of a temple/palace for the victorious god and his enthronement/rest on the temple throne. The forces of chaos in the Babylonian creation myth, *Enuma elish,* are represented by Tiamat. Marduk split her body into two to form the waters above and the waters beneath. From earth mixed with the blood of Tiamat's second husband, Qingu, Marduk fashioned human beings. The gods then decided to build him the palace/temple of Esagila as place of rest:

> Now, O lord, thou who hast caused our deliverance, what shall be our homage to thee? Let us build a shrine whose name shall be called "Lo, a chamber for our nightly rest"; let us repose in it! Let us build a throne, a recess for his abode![9]

"Rest" means that everything is under control; Marduk's sovereignty is now unchallenged and will remain so. So he hung his no-longer-needed bow in the sky. The order established by him will continue. In the light of this background, the rest of God in Gen 2:2 is the declaration of sovereignty over the world that Yahweh has created. Admittedly some (poetic) texts posit chaos as confined, not eliminated. Such texts see primeval chaos as now and then seeking to surge forth in historical events and figures, only to be pushed back by the rebuke of Yahweh (Isa 51:9-10; Ps 74:12-17). But this does nothing to diminish the universal sway of Yahweh.

THE EARTHLY TEMPLE

The P writers relate the creation of the world and the establishment of the wilderness tabernacle. Just as creation ended in God's solemn day of

---

8. In the Atrahasis myth, the lower gods (*igigi*), who had to plow the fields and dig the irrigation canals, rebelled, and their "cries" disturbed the rest of Enlil and the higher gods (*anunnaki*). Enlil decided to fashion human beings out of earth mixed with the blood of the slain rebel god We-ila, so they could relieve the lesser gods of their drudgery. But no sooner were these created than they too began to disturb the rest of the gods with cries of rebellion, for they had inherited the spirit of rebellion. When devestation wrought by plagues, drought, and famine failed to reduce human "noise," the gods readjusted the pattern for creation to include death and sent a flood to annihilate all human beings. Enki saved his devotee Atrahasis in a ship, and he became the progenitor of postdiluvian humankind.

9. ANET, 68; *Enuma elish* in the translation of E. A. Speiser.

rest, so the erection of the tabernacle ended in a solemn day of rest (Exod 31:12-17 and 35:1-3). Further, P relates three things to one another, namely, the creation of the world, the construction of the tabernacle (Exod 39-40), and the distribution of the land in the book of Joshua (Blenkinsopp 1976; Weinfeld 1981, 501-12; Levenson 1988, 78-120). In each case, there is a "conclusion formula" using a form of the verb, *kālāh* (to finish, to complete):

Thus the heavens and earth were *finished* . . . God *finished* his work. (Gen 2:1-2)

So all the work was *finished* . . . so Moses *finished* the work. (Exod 39:22; 40:33)

So they *finished* dividing the land. (Josh 19:51)

A comparison of Genesis 2:1-4a and Exodus 39-40 is enlightening:

Genesis 2:1-3	Exodus 39-40
And God saw all that he had made and found it (והנה, and behold) very good (Gen 1:31)	Moses saw that they had performed all the tasks, as the Lord had commanded, (והנה, and behold) so they had done (39:43)
The heavens and the earth were completed (ויכלו) and all their array (2:1)	Thus was completed (ותכל) all the work of the tabernacle of the tent of meeting (39:22)
God finished (ויכל) the work which he had been doing (2:2)	When Moses had finished (ויכל) the work (40:33)
And God blessed (ויברך) (2:3)	Moses blessed (ויברך) them (39:43)
And sanctified it (ויקדש) (2:3)	to sanctify it (וקדשת) and all its furnishings (40:9)

Thus, in the theology of P, creation, tabernacle, and the land of Israel have one thing in common: they are all meant to represent a world in perfect conformity with the designs of the Creator. When the Creator looked at all the Creator had made, the Creator saw that it was very good (Gen 1:31)—it contained nothing against the Creator's wishes. The tabernacle was erected exactly according to a heavenly pattern shown to Moses. The craftsman, Bezalel, was endowed with God's spirit, which assured perfect conformity to the heavenly pattern that was shown to Moses on the mountain. The promised land, symbolized by Zion, is God's chosen home, "for Yahweh has chosen Zion, Yahweh has desired it as a home. 'Here shall I rest for evermore, here shall I make my home as I have wished'" (Ps 132:13-14). This whole world, with the sign of the Sabbath over it, is meant to be a sanctuary, a place of "rest" for God, a place where God's sovereignty is acclaimed and where God may dwell with God's creation. Tabernacle and temple are truly the world in microcosm. Israel bears within itself the vocation of the whole earth to be the home of God. God's rest in Zion is a concrete symbol of the promised rest of God in creation.

Jon D. Levenson draws a very interesting parallel between covenant and combat myth. In the myth, the gods gladly accept the kingship of their heroic savior and grant him the right to determine their destinies, for establishing his kingship ensures their survival: "Covenant and combat myth are two variant idioms for one ideal—the exclusive enthronement of YHWH and the radical and uncompromising commitment of the House of Israel to carrying out his commands" (1988, 135). The "rest" of God at creation is promise and demand: promise that God will finally come to rest in God's creation, demand that Israel function to bring all things to that rest. As a pledge of this, the Sabbath of Israel hangs over all creation.

IN THE LIKENESS OF GOD HE CREATED THEM

In Genesis 1, rather than human beings being created for the relief of the gods, God created everything for the sake of human beings. God created the world as a place for human beings and as where God can dwell with them as in a sanctuary. In the Yahwistic account of creation (Gen 2:4b-3:24), the human attempt to be like God is *hybris* and is punished by the setting up of boundaries between the divine and the human realms and finally by expulsion from the garden (Gen 3:22). For P, God made human beings, male and female, in God's own image and likeness. In the light of the prohibition of all images of Yahweh, this saying is very significant, for it means that human beings disclose something of the nature of God. That disclosure is tied to two Hebrew words, צלם (*ṣelem*, "image/statue") and דמות (*dĕmût*, "likeness"). Scholars are agreed that both mean roughly the same thing, though it is possible that "in our likeness" is meant to soften the plasticity of "in our own image." At any rate, both terms appear in Genesis 5:3. At the age of 130, Adam fathered a son in his likeness, after his image. The meaning here is certainly physical resemblance—Seth was physically like Adam. So also in our text: human beings are as physically related to God as Seth was to Adam, though this resemblance is not through physical generation. In the Hebrew thinking of the period, the human person is not body and soul, but a "body" with "diffused consciousness" (Robinson 1946, 20, 279). In Egyptian court style, the pharaoh is often called "image of Re," and the god calls him "my living image." These terms designate him as viceroy or representative of the god on earth, with something of divinity present in him. The image is like an icon—it represents the figure it depicts. Some scholars see in Genesis 1 a democratization of this royal attribute, which is now transferred to all human beings—every person is royalty. Because human beings are theomorphic (von Rad 1962, 145), to see a human person is to be presented with something of God.

Westermann (1994, 153) thinks that such a view is foreign to P, whose theology is dominated by God's holiness; God reveals Godself only at the holy place. He states that God appears in God's *kābôd* (glory) as a manifestation before human beings, not in human beings. With Karl Barth, Westermann would rather see the "image of God" as qualifying human beings in their ability to enter into relationship with God. He thus writes that "human [beings] are created in such a way that their very existence is intended to be their relationship to God" (1994, 158). But this reasoning about P and *kābôd* can be countered by the fact that in Ps 8:5 God crowned human beings with glory and majesty (*kābôd wĕhādār*), attributes of God and derivatively of the king. By doing so, God aligned them with the divine realm, making them only "little lower than the heavenly beings," or in the translation of the NRSV "a little lower than God."[10] The faith of Israel speaks here of humanity as such. The nations share with Israel this likeness to God, which is more fundamental than Israel's election. God will call Israel "my firstborn son" (Exod 4:23), but Israel will not be alone in the fundamental likeness to God and the inherent demand to live according to the pattern of God, to imitate God.

As "image," human beings are to fill the earth and subdue it (וכבשׁה, Gen 1:28) and tread down (ורדו) the fish of the sea, the birds of heaven, the cattle and wild animals (Gen 1:26). The verbs *rdh* ("trample down") and *kbš* ("subdue") are usual for royal subjection of enemies. In Genesis 9:2, God's blessing of human beings makes terror and dread of them fall upon the animals, who are all given into human hands. The creator of the heavens, who shaped the earth and made it, did not create it to be chaos, but formed it to be lived in (cf. Isa 45:18). The earth was created in a "frontier" state, and human beings under God are to "green" the earth, subdue and beautify it. As "image of God" they are viceroys of the Creator on earth. Their stewardship is meant to reflect the intentions of the Creator and to bring God's creation to the purposes intended by God. God had already created everything according to its kind, each according to its species, with inher-

---

10. *Elōhîm* is a plural form that is used as one of the names of God, but it is also used as a true plural for the heavenly beings, who were the gods that formed the pantheons of the peoples in the ancient Near East.

ent laws proper to each. These laws will serve human beings as a blueprint for their stewardship over creation. It is to be noted that nothing is said here about ruling or subduing fellow human beings—every human being is royalty. We are thus left with a double divine commission—to humanity and to Israel, the one serving the other: "Gen 1-11 concerns the affirmation that God calls the world into being to be his faithful world. . . . Gen 12-50 concerns the affirmation that God calls a special people to be faithfully his people" (Brueggemann 1982, 1).

CONCLUSION

Israel enshrined in her religious tradition the awareness that the purposes of God enfold the entire creation and that somehow Israel holds brief for humanity. Creation, as portrayed in the myths, is God's first act of redemption. The choice of Abraham and the election of Israel in him will come later and will depict the redemption of a particular people. But God's redemption has already touched the whole of creation. God confers blessing on all living creatures and rests on the seventh day. In Genesis 12:2-3 Abraham, and Israel in him, will be enabled and commissioned to further this blessing to all families of the earth. Human beings are made in the image and likeness of God. They are God's regents on earth and receive tasks parallel to those later to be entrusted to Israel. In pursuance of God's redemptive purposes, God commissions human beings to green the earth and to be stewards over God's creation. Israel cannot carry out this commission alone; creation itself is meant to be a space where God can dwell with people: "the earthly temple is the world *in nuce*, the world is the temple *in extenso*" (Levenson 1985, 141). Just as the particular temple of Zion symbolizes creation, so Israel will be called as representing the world as sacred space for God. The cycle of rest, in imitation of God's rest on the seventh day, is a perpetual reminder of the lordship of God over all creation. It is also a pledge that a time will come for God's own just order, in which there will be no masters and slaves, no citizens and foreigners with unequal rights. In this new order, Israel and the nations will finally rest together in the rest of God.

DISCUSSION

1. Discuss the conflict of faith and culture in the first account of creation.
2. Give a structural analysis of Genesis 1:1-2:4a.
3. Discuss the "rest" of God in Genesis 2:2.
4. What are the implications of human beings being in the "image and likeness" of God?
5. What is the mission task in Genesis 1?

4

"You have put all things under his feet"

Psalm 8

Because the psalmist has learned to recognize the remembrance and visitation of God in the history of Israel, he perceives its hidden working in the life of all humankind. The special history of Adonai with Israel is a disclosure of the ways of God with all people.
—James L. Mays, "What Is a Human Being?" 519

We saw in the preceding chapter that the rest of God on the seventh day is, as it were, a signal of God's sovereignty over creation. It is both promise and demand—promise that God's sovereignty over creation will become fully manifested in the new order God is bringing about, demand that humankind enter into this sovereignty and bring everything into it. Psalm 8 celebrates in the one breath the sovereignty of God and the trusteeship of humanity over creation.

A HYMN

Psalm 8 is a hymn, the first hymn in the Psalter. The fundamental attitude in a hymn is that of awe, joy, and thanksgiving. A hymn usually opens with an introductory summons to praise God, then moves through a transitional phrase (usually indicated by the word, *kî* ("for," "because")) to the content of praise itself. This structure can be seen in the first verse of Psalm 136, which is a hymn in miniature: "give thanks to the Lord *for* he is good, *for* his faithful love endures for ever." The topic of praise is either what Yahweh has done or what Yahweh is or shows Godself to be.

Psalm 8 stands out from all other hymns in the Psalter in having no introductory summons and in being entirely an address to God. The theme

35

of the hymn is the "name" of Yahweh, as manifested in heaven and on earth. The psalmist is moved with awe at the majesty of this name; wherever he turns in the vast universe he sees imprints of the power and the presence of this name. Paradoxically, this name is magnified, not diminished, by the commanding position allotted to human beings on earth. So insignificant compared with the vast expanses of space and the constellations, human beings nevertheless have everything under their feet, put there by God. The psalmist thus sings in one breath of the glory of God and the glory of humankind—*gloria Dei vivens homo* ("the glory of God, human beings fully alive"), says Irenaeus. Psalm 8 was appropriately the first biblical text to reach the moon, brought there in the first manned landing by Apollo II, on July 20, 1969 (Clifford 2002).

This psalm moves along two trajectories, a refrain in the first person plural and a narration in the first person singular. The refrain, the "our" exclamation in vv. 1 and 9, is the voice of the choir or of the people and constructs a frame around the "I" narration. In another movement, the heavens (vv. 1-3) are contrasted with the earth (vv. 4-9).

TRANSLATION

The superscription is "for the choirmaster, according to the Gittith; a psalm of David." Many think that "Gittith" refers to an instrument or tune from Gath, a Philistine stronghold. "*Gath*" (גַּת) in Hebrew means "winepress," so the LXX renders "for the winepress," which some understand to refer to a hymn for the vintage.

As shown below, vv. 1b-2a (vv. 2b-3a in the Hebrew and the NJPS) have received differing translations. In this text, which may be corrupt, there are two problems for translation.

The first problem is v. 1b. תנה is the imperative singular masculine of נתן ("to give"), but a rendering "give" is inappropriate in the context. The Brown-Driver-Briggs *Hebrew and English Lexicon of the Old Testament* proposes to emend the text to נתתה ("you have given"), and thus to translate the verse as follows, "thou hast set your majesty upon (over) the heavens." The phrase, נתן הוד על, usually means to endow a person or thing with majesty. Thus, Moses is to endow the priest Eleazar with some of his authority (Num 27:20; and see 1 Chr 29:25; Dan 11:21). The NJPS follows this trend when it translates as follows, "You who have covered the heavens with Your splendor." In this rendering, earth and heaven sing with one voice of God's majesty, the earth lifting up the Name, the heavens manifesting God's splendor.

The second problem is the syntactical connection of the phrase "from the mouths of infants and sucklings." Should it be read with what follows or

NJPS	NRSV	NIV	NJB
2[1] O Lord, our Lord, How majestic is Your name throughout the earth, You who have covered the heavens with Your splendor!	1 O Lord, our Sovereign, how majestic is your name in all the earth! You have set your glory above the heavens.	1 O Lord, our Lord, how majestic is your name in all the earth! You have set your glory above the heavens.	1 Yahweh, our Lord, how majestic is your name throughout the world! Whoever keeps singing of your majesty higher than the heavens
3 From the mouths of infants and sucklings You have founded strength on account of Your foes, to put an end to enemy and avenger	2 Out of the mouths of babes and infants you have founded a bulwark because of your foes, to silence the enemy and the avenger.	2 From the lips of children and infants you have ordained praise because of your enemies, to silence the the foe and the avenger	2 even through the mouths of children, or of babes in arms, you make him a fortress, firm against your foes, to subdue the enemy and the rebel.

with what precedes? Robert Alter (1985, 118) reads it with what precedes and renders as follows, "you whose splendor was told over the heavens, from the mouths of babes and sucklings." In this rendering, 'ōz is splendor, which is aligned with glory: the whole gamut of creation, from the beauty of the heavens to the prattle of infants, bears witness to the splendor and glory of Yahweh. The NJPS, on the contrary, reads the phrase "from the mouths of infants and sucklings" with what follows and thus renders, "from the mouths of infants and sucklings, you have founded strength on account of your foes." But the meaning of "you have founded strength" remains obscure in this translation.

The LXX, followed by the NIV, thinks that 'ōz here refers to praise and renders, "from the lips of children and infants you have ordained praise because of your enemies."

The NRSV and NJB take a different tack; they interpret 'ōz ("strength") as a bulwark or fortress which Yahweh erects against Yahweh's foes. But for the NJB, the fortress is the one who praises Yahweh. The continuous praise of God makes the singer impregnable against attacks (doubts?) brought on by the enemies of God.

---

1. The Hebrew Bible, followed by the NJPS (New Jewish Publication Society Bible) starts numbering psalms from the superscription.

THE FRAME

"How majestic is your name in all the earth" could simply be a state-ment that all on earth are singing the praise of God's name. Some, how-ever, see the symbolizing force of the name in ancient cultures at play here. The name is bound up with the individual; it represents the person and connotes the attributes of his or her character. Thus, it can stand for one's fame, honor, or might. The name of Yahweh would thus refer to the nature of Yahweh's being as made manifest in the divine self-disclosure. Yahweh's name is the sum of Yahweh's majesty, glory, and might as revealed in creation and in history (Woude 1997, 1363). If this meaning is accepted, then the psalmist sees the entire universe as pointing to God, its maker.

The Code of the Covenant in Exodus 20:24 still leaves open the possi-bility that God may cause God's name to dwell in any place, thus legitimizing that place as a place of worship of Yahweh. But the Deuteron-omistic tradition (see Deut 12:11, 14) restricts the name of Yahweh to the one place that Yahweh would choose on earth; this was eventually shown to be the temple in Jerusalem (1 Kgs 8:29). The name of Yahweh takes the place that is occupied by the cultic image in other religions (von Rad 1962, 183). But for our psalmist, not just the holy place but all creation, not just Israel but the entire humanity, bears the imprint of God and speaks of God and of God's mighty presence.

God is addressed as ʾAdōnênû (our sovereign). ʾĀdôn (lord) was a title of deity in the ancient Near East and also a common address for the king. It refers to a master who can dispose of the subject entirely as he wills. "Our" points to the community of Israel. This means that the universe is seen from the point of view of Israel's faith. At the same time, "our" includes all humanity—in her praise of Yahweh, Israel holds brief for humanity.

Yahweh is the particular name of Israel's God. The meaning of the name "Yahweh" is disputed. Some writers derive the name from the causative of the verb "to be," hence translating the name as "he who causes to be/exist," that is, the creator. But it should probably be rendered "he will be who he will be" (Exod 3:14). Yahweh tells Moses that Yahweh will be known from what Yahweh will prove to be in relation to Israel. According to the Yahwist, the name Yahweh was known already in primeval times (Gen 4:1, 26) and thus was not a preserve of Israel; but E and P regard this name as first revealed to Moses (Exod 3:14-15; 6:2). The psalmist pro-claims the God of Israel as lord of the universe, who has instituted human beings, not just the children of Israel, as lords on earth.

THE NARRATION: THE HEAVENS

God put God's name in all the earth and fills the heavens with God's *hôd* ("glory," "splendor"). *Hôd* is the effulgence and radiance that emanate from the person of the king. In heaven above, God is sovereign, clothed in majesty and splendor (*hôd wĕhādār*), wearing the light as a robe (Ps 104:2). Other peoples view the sun, the moon, and the stars as gods; the stars in particular were believed to control human destinies on earth. For Israel and the psalmist, these elements are the work of Yahweh. It was Yahweh who made them, fixed them in their places, and determined their courses.

"From the mouths of infants and sucklings You have founded strength on account of Your foes, to put an end to enemy and avenger" (v. 3). This verse continues to perplex scholars. Some think of the cosmic battle at creation in which Yahweh dispatched adversaries, sometimes called Rahab, Leviathan, and Yamm (Ps 74:13-17). But these adversaries in the creation myths are not usually called "infants and sucklings." Helmer Ringgren (1953, 267-68) proposes reading, "from the mouths of the *yônᵉqîm* [sucklings] thou hast founded a bulwark."[2] The "sucklings" would refer to the mythological *ynqm* at Ugarit, children of El who devoured the birds of the air and the fish of the sea and had to be remanded to the desert for seven or eight years. Mark S. Smith (1997) suggests that the threat against which God laid the foundations of the earth securely as a bulwark was the mouths of these devouring children of El. Others interpret the bulwark as the firmament of heaven, which was so strongly made as to hold in check the forces of chaos (cf. Bratcher and Reyburn 1991, 79). Job 38:6-7 incorporates an enigmatic fragment of myth that refers to the sons of God shouting for joy when God founded the earth:[3]

> into what were its [earth's] pedestals sunk, and who laid the cornerstone, while the morning stars sang in chorus and all the sons of God shouted for joy? (NAB)

Early Jewish exegesis understood the babes and infants to refer to Israel as a weak and helpless nation. The enemy and avenger referred to those who sought to snuff out Israel's chorus of praise. In the thought of the

---

2. See also H. Ringgren, "קִין," *Theological Dictionary of the Old Testament*, edited by G. Johannes Botterweck and Helmer Ringgren (Grand Rapids: Eerdmans, 1974–), 6:108.

3. The verb, יסד ("to lay a foundation"), however, does not occur there; rather the verbs טבע ("to sink") and ירה ("to cast, throw").

evangelist Matthew (Matt 21:16), the chief priests and scribes were playing exactly this role when they tried to stop the little children from singing
"hosanna to the son of David."

In many texts, 'ōz retains its literal meaning of "strength." For example,
Psalm 29:1 (//Ps 96:7) issues the summons to "ascribe to Yahweh glory
(kābôd) and strength ('ōz)," where 'ōz means might and power. As referring to might and power, 'ōz is used in close connection with kābôd
("glory"), ge'ut ("exaltation, majesty") and hādār ("splendor"). What is
intriguing is when this word is used in close connection with beauty
(tiph'eret), as when the psalmist says that in God's sanctuary are 'ōz and
beauty (Ps 96:6). A passage that indicates the possible meaning of this
word when so used is Isaiah 52:1, where the summons to Jerusalem to
awake runs as follows, "clothe yourself in splendor / put on your strength
(libšî 'uzzēk). The synonymous parallelism indicates that "put on your
strength" refers to decking oneself out in clothes of splendor and majesty.
When this sense is transferred to the use of 'ōz in Psalm 8, it points to God
as decking Godself out in the praise of the babes and infants. The praise of
infants and of the humble lays the foundation for the majesty of God as if
this were a building. It is true that the praise of creatures adds nothing to
God's glory, yet doxology is theological, for "praise as confession says who
God is" (Mays 1994a, 65).

THE NARRATION: THE EARTH

Human beings are not compared with the creatures of earth, but with
those of heaven—they are just a little lower than the 'elōhîm, the heavenly
beings (NIV). There is division of labor in the ruling of the universe: "the
heavenly world is ruled by God through heavenly servants. The earthly
world, subordinate yet parallel to the heavenly world, is ruled by human
servants" (Clifford 2002, 69). Human beings, as God's stand-ins on earth,
are crowned by God with God's own glory. We already saw that glory
(kābôd) and splendor (hādār) are attributes of God as king. Isaiah 35:2
sings of a time when "they will see the glory (kābôd) of Yahweh, the splendor (hādār) of our God." In crowning human beings with glory and splendor, God establishes them as kings and queens over creation and visible
manifestations of the Godhead.

Tribute is put at the feet of a conquering king as a symbol of possession.
The great suzerain lays certain territories at the feet of a vassal as a symbol
of dominion and oversight on his behalf. God made human beings lords of
the earth, which is the work of God's hands, and put all things under their
feet. Sheep and cattle, the wild beasts, and even the birds of the air and the
fish of the sea—all are given over to humanity. As the vassal rules the territories in the name of and for the honor of the suzerain, human beings are
meant to rule the world as stewards of the divine Sovereign.

There is no proportion between humankind and what God entrusts to it. One look at the heavens and the stars and human beings are overwhelmed with feelings of insignificance and ephemerality. These feelings are induced not only by the vastness of the universe but also by the magnificence and power of the One who firmly established it and upholds it in being. The verb כוננתה in v. 3 derives from the root *kwn*, which means "to set firmly in place, not to be moved." This word evokes images of the myth of creation, in which God overcame primeval waters and caused the earth to stand firmly on the underground waters. That the earth does not totter is due to the continuing activity of God, who holds it firmly in check: "it is he who laid [the earth's] foundations on the seas, on the flowing waters he fixed it firm" (Ps 24:2). Yet this majestic and powerful God remembers and cares for the puny and insignificant creatures that human beings are. What the Deuteronomist said of God's love for Israel can equally well be said of God's love of humanity: "Yahweh set [Yahweh's] heart on you" not because of your greatness but "because [Yahweh] loved you" (Deut 7:7). It is all unmerited love.

The verbs *zākar* ("remember") and *pāqad* ("visit, pay heed to") are embedded in Israel's memory of their deliverer God. Though both verbs can be used in the sense of God's remembering and visiting to punish, more often God remembers the covenant, the promises to the patriarchs, or God's merciful love, in order to preserve them for Israel. God promises not to remember Israel's sins (Jer 31:34), meaning that God will forgive them. What the psalmist has learned of Israel's God, he now applies to God's relation to all God's creatures. Mays (1994b, 519) expresses it this way:

> Because the psalmist has learned to recognize the remembrance and visitation of God in the history of Israel, he perceives its hidden working in the life of all humankind. The special history of Adonai with Israel is a disclosure of the ways of God with all people.

Psalm 8 is important for the theme of mission in the Old Testament. God remembers and visits every man and woman in the same manner that God remembers and visits Israel. Mission is founded on this basic universal and nonexclusive address of God to all humankind.

In much of the Old Testament, dominion over the nations is given to Israel or to God's anointed on Mount Zion (Ps 2). But what this psalm says of the dignity of every human person is unrivaled even by what the Old Testament says of the election of Israel and the dominion conferred on it. This psalm makes the human person as such God's regent on earth. Ecojustice and the stewardship of creation here entrusted to humankind are fundamental aspects of mission.

The New Testament read this psalm not as a statement about humanity but as prophecy concerning the Christ, the representative of the New

Humanity. There is perceived conflict between the promised dominion of humankind over all creation and the present condition of humankind in thrall to the forces of creation. In the present order, not everything is under humanity's feet, and death is still a force to be reckoned with. The conflict is resolved by pointing to a representative of humankind, Jesus, whom God made "for a little while" lower than the angels (Heb 2:5-9).[4] Being crowned with glory and honor belongs not to humanity in its present condition, but to the risen condition of the New Man who has tasted death on behalf of all (Heb 2:9) and who will surely in the future destroy the last enemy of humanity, which is death (1 Cor 15:26-27).

DISCUSSION

1. How does Psalm 8 differ from the hymn pattern?
2. Compare the election of human beings in this psalm with the election of Israel in various parts of the Old Testament.
3. How is the stewardship of creation, which is entrusted to humanity, mission?
4. Explain how the Letter to the Hebrews reapplies Psalm 8.

---

4. The LXX translated *'elōhîm* (heavenly beings) as "angels" and Hebrew *mĕ'at* (a little lower) as *brachy*, meaning "a little" (time or space). The author of Hebrews chose the sense "a little time" and understood the "son of man" of Psalm 8:5 as Jesus.

5

The Blessing of Abraham

Genesis 12:1-3

In calling Abraham, God had begun a task which [God] had not completed.

—Ronald E. Clements, *Old Testament Theology*, 147

THE DIVINE INITIATIVE IN MISSION

The Bible began with the creation of the cosmos and of the first human being, Adam. After the sin in the garden, the generations of humankind gradually degenerated until "Yahweh saw that human wickedness was great on earth and that their hearts contrived nothing but wicked schemes all day long" (Gen 6:5). Only Noah found favor with God. Yahweh brought on them the flood, an agent of un-creation. It wiped off the face of the earth all living creatures except the one family of Noah. After the flood, Yahweh began again with Noah as the first man. Yahweh blessed Noah and his sons, saying to them, "Breed and multiply and fill the earth" (Gen 9:1). Yahweh restored to them dominion over the beasts of the earth and the birds of the air. For the first time Yahweh allowed human beings to kill animals and birds for food, only that "you must not eat flesh with the life, that is to say, the blood, in it" (Gen 9:4). In Genesis 1:29 the food foreseen for human beings and animals was to be the seed-bearing plants.

This new beginning soon came to grief. The whole world then spoke one language. Moving eastward they found a valley in the land of Shinar and settled there. They projected to build themselves a city and tower with its top reaching heaven and thus to make a name for themselves, so as not to scatter all over the world (Gen 11:4). Yahweh came down and confused their language and scattered them all over the world and they stopped building the city (Gen 11:9). Terah was part of this migration. He took his son Abram and his grandson Lot and their wives and left Ur of the Chaldees to go to Canaan, but when they arrived at Haran they settled there (Gen 11:31). But God did not let the matter rest there. God inaugurated anew God's purpose in the world through the calling of Abraham (Gen 12:1). Thus began a history initiated by God and uniquely related to God, a history that is meant to be both model and agent of God's relationship with humankind.

A plot of new beginnings links the *first* man of creation to the *first* man after the flood to the *single* man upon whom the story will concentrate (Muilenburg 1965, 389). Adam and Noah bore in themselves the destiny of humankind. Abraham is to serve God's project of blessing to all families of the earth. The Primeval History explains why all the peoples of the earth need blessing. Ever since the sin of Genesis 3, the story has been dominated by curse (Wolff 1966, 145). God cursed the serpent (Gen 3:14) and cursed the soil because of humankind, with the result that the soil would yield only brambles and thistles (Gen 3:18). God cursed Cain and banned him from the ground that received his brother's blood (Gen 4:11). Noah cursed Canaan so that he would become his brothers' meanest slave (Gen 9:25-27). That the story could continue thus far has been owing to divine grace and forbearance. Muilenburg (1965, 389) traces four paradigmatic episodes in the Primeval History: the story of paradise (Gen 2:4b-3:24), the two brothers (Gen 4:1-16), the cohabitation of divine beings with human women (Gen 6:1-4), and the Tower of Babel (Gen 11:1-9). In each case, the same theological movement is in play—the sin of human beings is followed by divine judgment/punishment and then by divine grace beyond the judgment. The disobedience of the first couple is punished by expulsion from the Garden, but Yahweh not only relents from the decree of death but also makes clothes for the ashamed couple. Cain's fratricide is followed by expulsion from fertile land, yet Yahweh puts a sign of divine protection on him. The mixing of divine beings and the daughters of human beings calls down the flood, but not only is Noah spared but Yahweh also commits Godself never again to curse the earth despite the inveterate evil of the human heart. The fourth episode seems at first to lack the element of divine grace: the hubris of the tower builders is punished with dispersion and the story seems to end there. On closer examination, however, it seems that

> the merciful grace of Yahweh which persists through all the narratives of the prologue save the last now overcomes the final treason of the nations in their zealous efforts to build civilization without God . . . Abram becomes the embodiment of divine grace. (Muilenburg 1965, 393)

THE STORY LINE

Yahweh said to Abram, "Leave your country, your kindred and your father's house for a country which I shall show you; and I shall make you a great nation, I shall bless you and make your name famous; you are to be a blessing! I shall bless those who bless you, and shall curse those who curse you, [and in you all the families of the earth shall be blessed." (Gen 12:1-3 NRSV)

The narrator identifies Yahweh as Abram's God. Abraham actually knew his god as El Shaddai (Exod 6:3). The god of Isaac in Genesis 31:42 was called *Paḥad Yiṣḥāq*, that is, "Fear of Isaac" (NJPS) or "Kinsman of Isaac" (NJB). The god of Jacob was "*'Ăbîr Yaʿăqōb*," that is, the "Mighty One of Jacob" or the "Bull of Jacob" (Gen 49:24). The patriarchs each worshiped a "god of the father," a personal protector, but the narrator has assimilated their experience with their protector god to Israel's experience with Yahweh.

To leave one's land and kin, then, as in Africa of a couple of centuries ago, was to face an uncertain future and to subject oneself to grave danger. The stranger was liable to be mistreated or abused. Yahweh assured Abraham of guidance and protection on the way. The promise "I shall bless those who bless you, and curse those who curse you" can thus be understood as a "protection formula" (Westermann 1985, 151).

Yahweh spoke simply of "a land which I shall show you." When Abram left on his journey he did not know the goal to which Yahweh would lead him. Divested of country and kin and not yet identified with a new land, Abram undertook a journey that was a pilgrimage of faith in full confidence in the Lord who called him. Whereas the men of the tower sought to make a name for themselves (Gen 11:4), Yahweh promised to make the name of Abraham great and to make of him a "great nation." Great nation alludes to the future nation of Israel, which is here foreseen as the effect of the blessing of Abraham. *Gôy* ("nation"), as distinct from *'am* ("people, ethnic unit"), refers to a people constituted politically. The promise of becoming a great nation was made to one whose wife was barren (Gen 11:30) and who was seventy-five years old (Gen 12:4)! That the matriarchs of Israel were almost all initially barren shows that Israel was a creative act of God.

"You are to be a blessing." Blessing originates in God, but as a power of the soul; the seat of blessing is the soul of the person, and it is there that God works (Pedersen 1926, 194). The action of God does not fall outside of the human recipient but affects the very center of one's being. What blessing gives is not just something external, but the inward energy to create results. This power of the soul creates all progress; it contains the strength to produce and the full power to find and use the necessary means for achieving full life and happiness. Blessing is shown in the power of fertility. The first blessing of God for humans was "be fruitful, multiply, fill the earth and subdue it" (Gen 1:28). Blessing is also the power to create wealth and prosperity. It appears in the gift of rain and abundant harvests that go with it. It manifests itself in protection from enemies and/or power over them (Pedersen 1926, 211-12). Blessing is, of course, not automatic; the one blessed must continue to maintain good relationships with God and people. So the state of being blessed is sometimes expressed by saying that God is with the one who is blessed. Blessing in the Old Testament is primarily this-worldly and refers to the actual conditions in which people pass their worldly existence, even if it implies continuing good relationship with God. Israel never gave up its rooting in this world. Christians must learn from Israel not to overspiritualize the blessings of their mission.

MISSION AS BLESSING FOR ALL FAMILIES
OF THE EARTH

The word for family here is *mišpāḥāh*. The exact denotation of *mišpāḥāh* is unclear, but it is a category somewhere between *šēbeṭ* ("tribe") and *bayît* ("house"). It is sometimes rendered as "clan" (NJB). It is significant that the recipient of blessing is the family, not tribes or nations: the family is the true ecumenical experience of all humankind (Mann 1991, 352). The focus in Genesis is on families, and the patriarchs were heads of families. In the exilic period from which this unit probably derives, Israel was no longer a nation but equally a series of *mišpāḥôt* (extended families).

The versions diverge into two traditions concerning Abraham's blessing for all the families of the earth. One interpretation understands the blessing in a reflexive sense; the other takes it as passive. The Hebrew verb is the *niphal*, ונברכו בך. The Hebrew *niphal* usually has a passive sense, although it can also bear a reflexive meaning. The true reflexive is the *hitpael*. The versions that take the *niphal* as a reflexive render the phrase as follows:

> and all clans on earth will bless themselves by you (NJB)
> And all the families of the earth shall bless themselves by you (NJPS)

In these versions, Abraham is to be a paradigm of blessing. The families of earth may use his name for blessing and may wish to be blessed as he is, but it is not said explicitly that blessing comes to them through Abraham. The sense would be close to that expressed in Genesis 48:20, where Jacob blessed Ephraim and Manasseh, saying "by you shall Israel bless itself, saying 'God make you like Ephraim and Manasseh.'"[1] There is a similar sense

---

1. The MT lacks the word "itself" and has only the *piel* verb, יברך, "shall bless."

in Genesis 22:18 when the blessing is joined to a promise that Abraham's descendants will overpower other nations and gain possession of their cities: "your descendants will gain possession of the gates of their enemies. And all nations on earth will bless themselves by your descendants. . . ." Here the true reflexive, the *hitpael* (התברכו), is used.

The other tradition of interpretation takes the *niphal* as a true passive, as follows:

and in you all the families of the earth shall be blessed (NRSV)
and all peoples on earth will be blessed through you (NIV)

In these versions, Abraham is to be a source or agent of blessing to all families of earth.

The promise is repeated to Abraham in Genesis 18:18 and to Jacob in Genesis 28:14, both in the *niphal*. But it also occurs in the *hitpael* when repeated to Abraham in Genesis 22:18 (as above) and to Isaac in Genesis 26:4. Westermann (1985, 152) argues that, as far as the promise is concerned, the *niphal* and the *hitpael* have the same meaning and that both have a universal import. For God's promise to Abraham is not limited to him and his posterity, but reaches its goal only when it includes all the families of the earth. However, the example above in which conquest and blessing are conjoined and which uses the *hitpael* seems to indicate some awareness of difference between the two. The suggestion of Rétif and Lamarche (1966, 21) seems to me to be deserving of merit. They argue that the promise originally read, "by you all the families of earth will bless themselves." With the growth of universalism after the exile, however, it came to be read as "in you all families of earth will be blessed." One indication in support of this proposal is that the LXX translated the verb in the passive, *eneulogēthēsontai* ("in [you] will *be* blessed"). The particular context also makes this meaning likely. "I shall bless those who bless you" means that in some way blessing comes to others through Abraham. In Genesis 18:18 Yahweh invokes the fact that "in you all nations on earth shall be blessed" (using the *niphal* as in Gen 12:3) to reveal to Abraham the divine project of the punishment of Sodom and Gomorrah. Thereupon Abraham exercised the office of intercession and succeeded in getting a reprieve for Sodom if only ten people were found righteous in that city. A further indication that the universalistic perspective in the promise of blessing derives from later tradition can be found in the work of Rolf Rendtorff. Rendtorff (1977, 7) has shown that the speeches of divine promise that now link the patriarchs to one another were not original to the patriarchal stories themselves, but indicate a unifying and comprehensive theological editing of all three patriarchal stories (Abraham, Isaac, Jacob). The editors would have imported into the texts the more universalizing tendencies that are evident in some exilic traditions.

The promise of blessing to Abraham contains an internal and creative tension. Abraham is the physical progenitor of Israel, and in blessing Abraham God is conferring the blessing on his descendants, on Israel. Yet God surprisingly links this blessing to blessing for all families of the earth (Khoury 2003, 189). It means that the blessing of Israel consists precisely in being a blessing for all families of earth. The special favors of God to Abraham and his descendants are to make them agents of blessing for all of humankind. The temptation is that Israel may seek to grasp the blessing for itself alone. The promise is that Israel will eventually discover that God means it to serve God as servant so that God's salvation may reach the ends of the earth. Israel will then knowingly invite the nations to share in the blessing.

Wolff (1966) sees this happening already with the Yahwist when he interprets this passage as belonging to the "kerygma" of the Yahwist. By "kerygma" he meant a message from God that has the character of a claim and is addressed to a specific hour in history. The Yahwist is said to posit blessing as the key for Israel's relationship to other peoples and their relationship to Israel (1966, 137). The Yahwist writing during the empire of Solomon wanted it to be known that it was God's desire that the nations being incorporated into the Solomonic empire should find blessing in Israel (1966, 147), that is, abundant and fruitful life. It must be mentioned, though, that some scholars (for example, John van Seters) see the Yahwist as relating to the sixth century B.C.E. and not to the tenth century, which was the era of Solomon.

There is further indication that earliest Israel did not yet understand the blessing of Abraham in a missionary and universalistic sense. George W. Coats (1981, 40) speaks of a curse in the blessing. If the blessing is to come to all families, they must support the family of Abraham. Those who relate negatively to Abraham and his family must live apart from this source of blessing and thus must miss the fruits of God's blessing. Ishmael was the firstborn of Abraham. He and Abraham were circumcised on the same day (Gen 17:24). Genesis 17:10-11 makes circumcision the sign of the covenant between Yahweh and Abraham's descendants. But one day Sarah saw the son that Hagar the Egyptian had borne to Abraham playing (*měṣaḥēq*, Gen 21:9). The LXX and other versions add, "with her son Isaac." *Měṣaḥēq* is a pun on *yiṣḥāq* (Isaac). Coats (1981, 37-38) underlines the pun by saying that Sarah saw Ishmael "Isaacing" (pretending to be Isaac, taking the place of Isaac). She insisted that Abraham cast out mother and child, and God supported her against the hesitations of Abraham. Ishmael was thus excluded from the inheritance of Abraham, from possession of the promised land, and from the special covenant with God, despite his having been circumcised! Where then is the blessing for Ishmael? He receives the "blessing" of being a "great nation," but as "a wild donkey of a man," in the desert, and with the hand of all against him and his hand against all his brothers (Gen 16:12). In the early tradition, Ishmael had to be excluded because the blessing was being construed in too ethnic and political a manner. Later rereadings of the blessing, however, would be more inclusive and universalistic in perspective.

REAPPLICATIONS OF THE BLESSING OF ABRAHAM

When the blessing of Abraham is reapplied in various parts of the Old Testament, it clearly tends toward a universalistic sense.

Psalm 47 is one the Songs of Yahweh's Enthronement (Pss 47; 93; 96-99).[2] These psalms sing of a universal kingship of Yahweh and of the advent of an entirely new world order with Zion as the center. Psalm 47 envisions God as ascending the throne to the fanfare of the ram's horn (v. 5) and, seated on God's holy throne, reigning over the nations (v. 8). The nations are summoned to clap their hands and shout to God with shouts of joy (v. 1), just as the crowds would do at the accession of a king. There follows the procession to do homage to this enthroned God. What is important is who forms the procession and how they are described. The information is contained in v. 9, which says literally: "the leaders of the peoples (*'ammîm*) are gathered // the people (*'am*) of the God of Abraham." The peoples of the world are represented by their leaders; these peoples are further specified in the parallelism as "the people of the God of Abraham." Their acknowledgment of the one God makes them the fruit of Abraham's blessing for all families of the earth. It also makes them deserving of the title "people of God," usually reserved for Israel. Such universalistic views appear in the prophets, especially Deutero-Isaiah; but whereas the prophets spoke of the future, these psalms speak of the present (Gunkel and Begrich 1998, 25). It may be that this psalm is describing an actual event in the temple in Jerusalem, when many leaders of the nations were so gathered. Even though these leaders may not have been able to enter the holy place, the psalm can still be read as part of that leap of faith that is possible in prayer and cult. Accepting these leaders as "people of the God of Abraham" must somehow act quietly to transform the attitudes of the worshipers toward closer inclusion of these.

---

2. Sigmund Mowinckel posited an annual Israelite festival of the enthronement of Yahweh corresponding to the New Year festival in Babylon, where each New Year Marduk entered his sanctuary-throne anew and renewed his kingship. The *mythos* for this event was the creation myth. The Old Testament nowhere speaks explicitly of such a festival, but scholars have found intimations especially in the psalms. Hermann Gunkel, who is skeptical, nevertheless sees in Psalm 47 the two necessary elements that would suggest its use in a similar ritual: it posits both the entry of Yahweh into the sanctuary and the renewal of his kingship. See Gunkel and Begrich 1998, 66-81.

Psalm 72 is a royal psalm. Royal psalms are so called because they are about the king or are pronounced by him. By the time the Psalter received its final shape, the Davidic monarchy was obsolescent; hence, the royal psalms sang of hopes for future deliverance and conditions of salvation to be ushered in by an anointed one of God, the messiah (*māšîaḥ* means "anointed one"). Psalm 72 hopes and prays that this coming "anointed one" will rule from sea to sea, and from the river to the ends of the earth (v. 8). Then v. 17 says: ויתברכו בו כל־גוים יאשרוהו, which the NJPS translates as follows: "let men invoke his blessedness upon themselves; let all nations count him happy." The reading "let all nations count him happy" respects the disjunctive accent (*ʾatnaḥ*) placed under *bô* ("him"). The LXX, however, rendered the phrase as, "and all families of the earth will bless themselves in him" (a literal translation of the Hebrew, which used the *hitpael,* that is, the reflexive tense). Clearly the name of this coming king is to be used in blessings, and in this sense he will be a paradigm of blessing. But the entire context seems to say more than this. Verse 1 begins with a prayer to God to endow this king with God's own justice and righteousness. As a result, "in his days, uprightness shall flourish, and peace in plenty till the moon is no more" (v. 7). Like rain on mown grass and showers moistening the land (v. 6), he will be the source of life and vitality for his people. All kings will do him homage, all nations become his servants (v. 11). But this is because (*kî,* "for," v. 12) "he rescues any needy person who calls upon him, and the poor who have no one to help them. . . . From oppression and violence he redeems their lives; their blood is precious in his sight" (v. 14). The context thus justifies the translation, "all nations will be blessed through him" (NIV and similarly the NJB). God's anointed king in Zion will be the source of blessings of peace, justice, and fullness of life for all nations and in this way will be an agent of the blessing of Abraham.

Jeremiah 4:1-2 is part of God's response to the incipient pleas of repentance on the part of the people of Judah. It lays out what the people need to do in order truly to return to God and gives the motivation for this. The motivation is founded on the blessing of Abraham evoked in the *hitpael* (reflexive sense):

> If you come back, Israel, Yahweh declares, if you come back to me, if you take your Horrors out of my sight, if you go roving no more, if you swear, "as Yahweh lives!" truthfully, justly, uprightly, then the nations will bless themselves by him and glory in him.

The NJPS translates, "the nations shall bless themselves by you and praise themselves by you," but the Hebrew text has "him," which can refer to Abraham or more especially to God. The reason is that the expression "to glory in" usually has God as the object. In chapter 1 we designated this aspect of mission as "community-in-mission." It is the realization that Israel's moral and religious existence is meant to glorify God and eventually to lead the nations to turn to God: "the turning of Israel to her true self is inextricably bound up with the confessions and praises of the nations" (Muilenburg 1965, 396).

Isaiah 19:18-25 will receive more extended treatment in chapter 12. Here it is sufficient to remark upon v. 25, "that day Israel will make a third with Egypt and Assyria, a blessing at the center of the world, and Yahweh Sabaoth will bless them in the words, 'Blessed be my people Egypt, Assyria my creation and Israel my heritage.'" In the actual history of Israel, Egypt and Assyria have been the powers to fear. Now these three become partners who are united through the worship of the one Yahweh (Isa 19:23). The ancient world powers of the Fertile Crescent were Egypt in the west and Assyria and Babylon, the kingdoms of the east. Most of the wars and upheavals originated from the imperial designs of the world powers on either side of the crescent. Now the two warring factions are at peace and work together, and the agent of their peace has been Israel. Israel and its God have proven to be "blessing at the center of the world." Like Israel, Egypt now becomes "my people." Also like Israel, Assyria becomes "the work of my hands," an epithet of Israel especially in Deutero-Isaiah. A highway from Egypt to Assyria in the world of that time would be like a highway from Alaska to Australia through the length of Africa. The image is that of world peace founded on the common worship of Yahweh. In the very center of the world stand the temple and throne of Yahweh, from which emanate blessings not only for Israel but for the entire world. The promise "in you shall all the families of the earth be blessed" is coming true.

Sirach 44:19-21 is part of the "Eulogy of the Ancestors." Though Hebrew fragments of this book were discovered at Qumran, the entire text has been handed down only in the LXX. In the LXX tradition, the text understands Abraham and his progeny to be a source of blessing for the nations. It also understands the "land" that Abraham was promised as to extend throughout the entire earth:

> The Lord therefore promised him on oath to bless the nations through his descendants, to multiply him like the dust on the ground, to exalt his descendants like the stars, and to give them the land as their heritage, from one sea to the other, from the River to the ends of the earth. (Sir 44:21)

So, while some texts of the Old Testament tended to restrict the blessing of Abraham to Israel, others extended the boundaries.

THE BLESSING OF ABRAHAM
IN ACTS 3:25 AND GALATIANS 3-4

The New Testament will focus on the blessing of Abraham as an important argument for the inclusion of the gentiles. Paul read Genesis 12:3 in
the LXX version, hence in the passive sense. He realized that "in calling
Abraham, God had begun a task which [God] had not completed"
(Clements 1978, 147), but whose completion could only be in Christ. The
transition from the text of Ben Sira above to the reapplications of Genesis
12:3 in the New Testament is quite smooth.

After the cure of the lame man at the Beautiful Gate of the temple, Peter
proclaimed the resurrection of Jesus to the crowd that gathered around him
and the cured person. The resurrection of Jesus is a blessing in the first
place to Israel: "it was for you in the first place that God raised up his servant and sent him to bless you as every one of you turns from his wicked
ways" (Acts 3:26). But it is also the fulfillment of God's promise to Abraham that "all the nations of the earth will be blessed in your descendants"
(Acts 3:25).

In Galatians 3-4, Paul argued on three convergent lines. First, the
promise was made unconditionally to Abraham. God's covenant with him
(Gen 15) preceded any precept of circumcision (Gen 17). This covenant
was pure grace on the part of God and was not prefaced on any "works."
In a similar way, God was now calling all peoples, Jew and gentile, a call
based on God's grace and not prefaced on "works."

Second, the promise of God was made to Abraham and to his seed, in
the singular, not the plural: "now the promises were addressed to Abraham
and to his progeny. The words were not, and to his progenies in the plural,
but in the singular, and to your progeny, which means Christ" (Gal 3:16).
This emphasis indicates that Paul had before him a text that bore the words
"and to his seed" (*sperma*) in the singular (Williams 1988, 717). The
promise refers to the words of God to Abraham in Genesis 12:3, namely,
"in you shall all families of the earth be blessed." A repetition of this
promise—with the exact addition "and to your seed" in the singular—
occurs in the LXX of Genesis 13:15 and 17:8, and in both cases the reference is to possession of the land. Sam K. Williams points out that Paul must
have read land (*gē*) as the "inhabited earth." Both Greek *gē* and Hebrew
'ereṣ are ambivalent: they can refer to the promised land of Canaan or to
the whole inhabited earth. There is a Jewish tradition that the inheritance
of God's people is the whole earth.[3] See also Sirach 44:21 cited above.

---

3. See Matthew 5:5: "Blessed are the gentle; they shall have the earth as inheritance"; see
also *Jub.* 22:14-15; *1 Enoch* 5:6-7 and *4 Ezra* 6:55-59; Williams 1988, 718.

Romans 4:13 clearly says that what was promised to Abraham was that he would inherit the world (*klēronomos kosmou*). If the "seed" of Abraham is singular (Christ), and Abraham is promised the inheritance of the world, then Christ was promised inheritance of the world. Paul did not explicitly draw this conclusion in Galatians, but in Philippians 2:6-11 everything on earth and in heaven is subjected to Christ and all must confess that Jesus Christ is Lord to the glory of the Father. Paul's argument then runs as follows:

> Abraham is given the world as his descendants become the "lords of all," free from the enslaving power of the *stoicheia* [the elemental principles of this world]. And Christ is given the world in so far as the peoples of the earth acknowledge him as Lord. (Williams 1988, 719)

The question then is, How will God fulfill this promise to Abraham and to Christ that they will possess the world?

That brings us to the third point. Galatians 3:14 relates the blessing of Abraham closely to "the promise of the Spirit" (*tēn epangelian tou pneumatos*) when it says "that the blessing of Abraham might come to the gentiles in Christ Jesus, and so that we might receive the promised Spirit [literally, the promise of the Spirit] through him." The genitive "the promise of the Spirit" indicates identity (epexegetical genitive), and thus the content of the promise is the Spirit (Williams 1988, 712). But where is the Spirit promised to Abraham? Genesis 15:6 says that Abraham believed God and this was reckoned to him as righteousness. What he believed was God's promise that his seed (*sperma*) would be like the stars of heaven, even though at the moment he was childless and his wife was barren. But for Paul the promise of numerous descendants is the promise of the Spirit (Williams 1988, 714), for Abraham begot Isaac miraculously through the power of the Spirit. Romans 4:18-21 describes the begetting of Isaac as "according to the Spirit." Like Isaac, only those begotten "according to the Spirit" are children of the promise." In other words, both for Abraham and for his seed/Christ, the true children who will inherit the world are those begotten not by flesh but by the Spirit. The Galatians themselves can testify to their reception of the Spirit through faith in Christ and not through works. The Spirit has made them to be "in Christ," "and simply by being Christ's, you are that progeny of Abraham, the heirs named in the promise" (Gal 3:29). And because scripture foresaw that God would give saving justice to the gentiles through faith, it announced the future gospel to Abraham saying, "all nations will be blessed in you" (Gal 3:8). In other words, Genesis 15:6 and Habakkuk 2:4 ("the upright will live through faith," cited in Gal 3:11) make it clear that all along God envisaged only one demarcating line—not the ethnic line of Jew and gentile, but that of faith. Faith is produced by the Spirit and gives participation in the blessing of

Abraham (Dumbrell 2000, 21) independently of circumcision and the Law, as was the case with Abraham. Christ, the true seed of Abraham, communicates Abraham's blessing to the gentiles, that is, brings the light to the nations (Wright 1991, 154)—something that Abraham's physical descendants had failed to do.

CONCLUSION

God is *the* missionary, who "makes a way where there is no way." God's initiative and grace keep open the options for life for humans. Mission is rooted in divine *com*-passion.

The call of Abraham is never predicated on merit, but was entirely by the grace of Yahweh. The covenants that Yahweh made with him (Gen 15 and 17) were also entirely unconditioned. The unconditional call of Abraham is the founding experience of the religion of Israel. The embers of mission would not glow in Israel until Israel rediscovered the primacy of the righteousness of God, who freely calls all humanity to Godself.

God called Abraham to be a blessing for all the families of the earth. Blessing to all the families of the earth is God's response to the problems of Genesis 1-11 (von Rad 1972, 160). Mission must be experienced by the peoples as blessing, as new force and energy for integral human existence.

The promise to make Abraham a great nation shows God's need of a servant people, who may bear God's redemptive purposes for the nations and be God's means of achieving it (Glasser et al. 2003, 56). In calling Abraham, God had begun a task that God had not completed (Clements 1978, 147). Israel is summoned to the fulfillment of that task. The task was assumed by Christ, the seed of Abraham, and will be completed only when, having banished all forces of death and brought full blessing to all families of earth, Christ hands over the reign to the Father (cf. 1 Cor 15:28). Meanwhile, mission is the process through which all receive blessing.

Abraham's was a pilgrimage of faith trusting in the God who called him. He engaged in a dialogue of faith with the Canaanites he met on the land. God gave him the whole land in trust, but he negotiated with the inhabitants for every piece of land he actually acquired. He was shown worshiping his God at various Canaanite sacred sites. In the Abraham narratives,

> there is no denunciation of Canaanite worship, no condemnation of Canaanite inhabitants, no rejection of Canaanite rulers as oppressors, and no concern about acknowledging a Canaanite deity. The militant ideology of the book of Deuteronomy, which demanded a cleansing of the land of Canaanite religious culture, does not surface in this ideology. (Habel 1995, 127)

The Abraham narrative is thus a model of how religions and peoples may live in peace together and in mutual respect for one another. The religions of the world have a duty to promote the peace and prosperity of all peoples in the name of God. The document *Dialogue and Proclamation* (Pontifical Council 1991, no. 26) recognizes that the firm faith in the religions is an effect of the Spirit of truth operating outside the confines of the mystical body. Mission calls for a genuine dialogue of spiritual experience, for such experience is always of God and from God. Mission is at heart a dialogue of faith, not imposition of beliefs or of alienating institutions.

DISCUSSION

1. What patterns do you discover in the primeval cycle?
2. What is blessing in the Old Testament?
3. What do you think of Hans Walter Wolff's interpretation of blessing with reference to the Yahwist?
4. Discuss the meaning of blessing as used in Psalm 72.
5. How is Christ the blessing of Abraham in Paul?

6

"For the whole world is mine"
Exodus 19:3-8

Sinai is the expression of a particular intimacy that does not negate
the possibility of other intimacies . . . while God deals personally and
with particular communities, the way of the Creator is open to all
[humankind].
—David Hartman, "Sinai and Exodus," 386

The angel of Yahweh who appeared to Moses at the burning bush by
Horeb, the mountain of God (Exod 3:1), gave him a sign saying, "after you
have led the people out of Egypt, you will worship God on this mountain"
(Exod 3:12). This mountain is thus presented as the goal of the exodus
right from the start. Horeb is the name of the mountain of revelation in the
Elohist strand and in the Book of Deuteronomy and works dependent on
that book; in Exodus, it occurs only here and in Exodus 17:6 as a gloss.
Otherwise the "mountain of God" is identified in the Book of Exodus as
Mount Sinai.

Sinai traditions form the dominant center of the Pentateuch, stretching
from Exodus 19 to Numbers 10:10. Within this block are placed most of
the laws, and these are presented as revealed by God to Moses on Mount
Sinai. All law in Israel has thus been embedded within the context of
covenant, making all the laws covenant stipulations (Levenson 1985, 50).
It is surprising, however, that not all biblical traditions mention Sinai. For
example, the so-called credo of Deuteronomy 26:5-9 mentions the oppression in Egypt and the deliverance by God and immediately thereafter the
settlement in the land of Canaan, ignoring any stationing of the people at
Sinai or divine revelation to them there. Besides, Kadesh traditions both
precede and follow the Sinai pericope, suggesting that the Sinai pericope
was a massive and secondary insertion (von Rad 1962, 187). It may be that
behind the exodus-Kadesh narratives and the Sinai narratives lie events
involving two separate groups whose traditions were combined after the

settlement. "According to the one [account] they proceeded straight to Kadesh, and there offered sacrifice to Yahweh and received his statutes. They remained there for thirty-eight years and then advanced northwards into the territory occupied by Judah. According to the other, they proceeded to the sacred mount of Sinai or Horeb, where they received the divine ordinances, and had a two years' period of wandering in the wilderness" (Rowley 1950, 106). At any rate, this would mean that historically not all of what became "Israel" had the Sinai experience.

Scholars see Exodus 19-24 as a closely interwoven unit. Chapter 19 begins with the divine promise of a covenant, which is enacted only in chapter 24. The people's pledge, "whatever Yahweh has said, we will do," occurs as an *inclusio* at 19:8 and 24:7. In between are placed the theophany on Sinai, the giving of the Ten Commandments, and the Book of the Covenant; then comes the ratification of the covenant in Exodus 24:1-8. In this larger complex, Moses climbs up and descends from the mountain in a manner that defies all perspective; the reader also loses any sense of the sequence of events or development in the narrative. Scholars speak in this connection of "spatial form devices" (Dozeman 1989a, 87-101), which by subverting chronological development force the reader to focus on the characters. The characters here are Yahweh on the mountain, the people below, and Moses mediating between the two.

Exodus 19:3-8 forms a clear unit. The people arrived from Rephidim to the desert of Sinai and pitched camp facing the mountain (Exod 19:2). Moses then went up to God to receive words from the Lord. He descended, summoned the elders, and told them all that Yahweh had bidden him. All the people with one accord replied, "whatever Yahweh has said, we will do." Moses then went up and reported to Yahweh what the people had said. Verse 9 begins a new unit by relating further instructions of Yahweh about the need for the people to sanctify themselves before entering into the presence of Yahweh.

The reader notices that the people were pledging themselves to keep Yahweh's covenant before it was enacted and to obey all that Yahweh commanded before the very commands were given. The commands and stipulations would come only later, in Exodus 20-23 (the Decalogue and the Book of the Covenant). Hence, the unit is chronologically displaced and should be read as a summary of the Horeb event, which has been placed at the beginning to alert the reader to the way in which it is to be understood (Blenkinsopp 1997a, 117; Noth 1962, 154). To say that it is a proleptic summary suggests that it belongs to the editorial process and could be quite late. Earlier scholars tended to attribute the unit to the Elohist, regarding it as quite early. Muilenburg (1959, 352) even considered Exodus 19:3-6 to be a "special covenantal Gattung" *in nuce* the *fons et origo* (source and origin) of covenantal pericopes in the Old Testament. Consensus is emerging, however, that the unit has received Deuteronomic, and perhaps also Priestly, editing. The word *sĕgullāh* ("treasured possession"), applied to the people of Israel, appears only in Deuteronomy (Deut 7:6; 13:2; 26:18). In Malachi 3:17 God speaks of the righteous (not Israel as a whole) as "my treasured possession." "A kingdom of priests, a holy nation" may derive from the Priestly tradition.

The word *běrît* ("covenant") appears in v. 5. *Běrît* is used in the Old Testament in three senses. The first sense is that of a solemn promise, sometimes confirmed by oath; as promise, it is not based on any conditions or on what the recipient has done or will do. We find this sense in God's covenant with Noah (Gen 9:9-11), the promise to Abraham in Genesis 15 and 17, and Nathan's words to David in 2 Samuel 7. The second sense is that of a bilateral commitment between two parties. It may be between a suzerain and his vassal (vassal treaty) or between equals (parity treaty). The third sense is found, for example, in Hosea 2:20, where Yahweh promises to make a covenant on behalf of Israel with the wild animals, with the birds of heaven, and with the creeping things of earth.

Because the unit is a proleptic summary, covenant here refers to the process that is concluded in Exodus 24. There the people's pledge of obedience in 24:7 relates to "all Yahweh's words and all the laws" (Exod 24:3), the "words" being the Ten Commandments and "the laws" being the Book of the Covenant. It was therefore a bilateral covenant with stipulations. There is fierce debate as to when the idea of covenant entered the religious vocabulary of Israel, whether the description of Yahweh's relation to Israel as covenant predated the seventh century B.C.E. (it appeared in Hos 8:1) or first became current in Deuteronomy. We need not go into that dispute here; our analysis assumes that Exodus 19:3-8 was a proleptic summary and hence belonged to the editorial process. We already posited Deuteronomic editorial influence, and perhaps also some influence from the Priestly tradition.

Some scholars speak of Exodus 19-24 as patterned on the suzerain treaty form, which usually had six elements. The *self-presentation* of the suzerain is followed by a *historical prologue* that outlines the course of events leading to the treaty. Then follow *stipulations* that form the central pivot, which in turn are followed by the provision for *deposition of the treaty in a public place and for periodic public readings*. The covenant is brought to a close with a list of *witnesses* (heaven and earth, and the gods of the parties) and *blessings and curses* for keeping or breaking the covenant. The full pattern of the suzerain treaty, however, is not fully verified in our unit. For example, the curses and blessings appear elsewhere, in Deuteronomy 27-28, and the provision for deposition and periodic public reading in Deuteronomy 17:19 and 31:10.

"*You have seen for yourselves what I did to the Egyptians, and how I carried you away on eagle's wings and brought you to me.*" Yahweh did not need any self-presentation, but the above imitates the historical prologue. The action of deliverance was a demonstration of Yahweh's good will toward these former slaves in Egypt and of Yahweh's desire to have

> **Suzerain Covenant**
>
> Preamble—Self-introduction
>
> Historical Prologue
>
> Stipulations
>
> Preservations + periodic public
>
> reading
>
> Witnesses—the gods of the parties
>
> Blessings and curses

them for Yahweh alone. The eagle is supposed to soar higher than other birds of prey, so no other bird can snatch its prey from it. "I have carried you away on eagle's wings," therefore, means that I have brought you away quickly and securely. Rashi[1] cites Midrash Mechilta and says that all birds place their young between their feet, because they are afraid of birds above them, while the eagle flies higher than any bird and fears only humankind, who may cast an arrow at it. So it says, "better that the arrow pierce me than my young."

"And brought you to me." The Targum interprets this as Yahweh bringing Israel near to Yahweh's service. But it is clear that the earliest strand of the tradition, which spoke of the "mountain of God," identified God and the mountain (see Dozeman 1989b, 16). This explains the strict orders to mark out the limits of the mountain, and the prohibition, on the pain of death, against going up the mountain or even touching it (Exod 19:12-13). In this ancient strand, "and brought you to me" would mean literally bringing them to the place of Yahweh's dwelling. The Book of Exodus attributes a triple motive to the exodus event. The first is deliverance from slavery to Pharaoh for covenant with Yahweh at Sinai, hence "and brought you to me." The covenant people are then to form and model a just society in the promised land. The second is the worship of Yahweh. This was already indicated in Exod 7:16, 26, where Moses made the plea to Pharaoh on behalf of Yahweh saying, "let my people go that they may serve/worship me in the desert." The verb, וַעֲבָדֻנִי (*wĕ'abdûnî*), is a play on *'ebed* ("slave") and *'ābad* ("serve, worship"). The Hebrews who "served" Pharaoh (in slave labor) are to come away in order to "serve" (worship and obey) Yahweh. According to this strand, represented by the P tradition, the goal of the exodus is the establishment of a sacral and worshiping commu-

---

1. *Pentateuch with Targum Onkelos, Haphtaroth and Rashi's Commentary* (New York: Hebrew Publishing Company, 1935), 98.

nity. So in P what Moses receives from God on the mountain are not laws but the *tabnît* (blueprint) of the wilderness sanctuary (Exod 25:9, 40), the locus of God's presence in the community. God leaves the mountain of remoteness and moves into a "mobile home" to be always with a people on the move: "God here begins a 'descent' that will climax in the incarnational move God makes in Jesus (see John 1:14)" (Fretheim 1996, 232). The third motive was so that Israel might be the embodiment of the universal kingship of Yahweh. The Song of the Sea in Exodus 15 ends (v. 18) with the triumphant cry that "Yahweh will be king for ever and ever" on Yahweh's holy mount. The community serves the universal kingship of Yahweh.

Themes of the Book of Exodus

Liberation for covenant with Yahweh at Sinai

Liberation for worship: "let my people go and worship me in the desert" (7:16)

Sacral community, with Yahweh tabernacling in its midst (7:25-31, 35-40)

Universal and eternal kingship of Yahweh

"*So now if*" (אם ועתה). In a covenant formula, this strong conjunction introduces the stipulations. We have here a conditional proposal on the part of Yahweh. Yahweh proposes to make the Israelites Yahweh's special possession and a holy nation, *if* they would obey Yahweh's voice and keep Yahweh's covenant. In Deuteronomy 7:6, no condition is attached—Israel is a nation holy to Yahweh. The meaning of "special possession" is further explained as their becoming a "kingdom of priests" and a "holy nation."

Səgullāh is a prized personal possession; for a king it may signify an estate or territory that belongs to him in person, not to the state. David captured the Jebusite citadel of Zion, which then became the "city of David" (2 Sam 5:7). The temple mount is the peculiar possession of Yahweh. The sense of *səgullāh* is clear in Deuteronomy 7:6: "for you are a people consecrated to Yahweh, your God; of all the peoples on earth, you have been chosen by Yahweh, your God, to be his own people." A similar categorization of Israel occurs in Deuteronomy 10:14-15; 14:2. Psalm 147:20 celebrates this divine choice of Israel: "for no other nation has he done this, no other has known his judgments." Because Israel is God's "special possession," God addresses Israel as "*my* people" and promises in various places that "I will be their God and they shall be my people." This last phrase is often called the "covenant formula."

Gôy qādôš ("holy nation") occurs only here in the Hebrew Bible, though *'am qādôš* ("holy people") is frequent in Deuteronomy (Deut 7:6; 14:2, 21; 26:19). *Gôy* ("nation") looks beyond the bonds of blood and kinship toward sociological and political organization. God had promised Abraham that he would be a *gôy gādôl* ("great nation"). In the postexilic period when the Torah was finalized, the restored community lived under Persian rule and was a minority among other peoples on the land. It was a "citizen-temple community," that is, it was no longer a nation in which citizenship was by birth. Rather, it was a community into which people entered by free choice and which was defined by affiliation to the temple of Yahweh—in essence, a sacral community. *Gôy qādôš* ("holy nation") can be read as a reapplication of the promise to Abraham of his becoming a "great nation." When so read, it means that the greatness of Israel can be found neither in numbers nor in political might, but in its distinctiveness, its standing for, and manifesting, Yahweh within the surrounding culture. God is holy; to be taken into the presence and sphere of God is to be holy. Israel is distinct because of being a people marked by the name and character of Yahweh. Israel exists for the glory of Yahweh and the worship of Yahweh. God's holiness becomes evident to all especially through the holiness of Israel (Wells 2000, 242). But some texts understand this holiness of Israel as having to do with the separation of pure and impure, and this is the predominant sense of holiness in the Holiness Code (Lev 19-26). It includes not only not living "according to the customs of the nations I am going to drive out before you" (Lev 20:23 NIV), but also distinguishing clean and unclean animals (והבדלתם, "and you will separate," just as "I have separated you [ואבדל] from the other peoples to be mine [להיות לי]). The technical language of *hibdil* (to separate) includes the sense of not mixing things that do not go together. In such texts, holiness is defined by separation from other nations, whereas in the text under consideration it is defined by aggregation to Yahweh.

Mamleket kōhănîm, usually translated as "a kingdom of priests," has received diverse interpretations. Moran (1962, 7-20) takes holy nation (*gôy qādôš*) and *mamleket kōhănîm* together as making up a whole. Holy nation refers to the people and *mamleket kōhănîm* refers to priest kings. The "holy nation" (the people) is to be ruled by a class of priest kings. But the parallelism of *mamleket kōhănîm* and *gôy qādôš* suggests that it is the whole people who are referred to in the two designations. Rashi remarks that all Israel cannot be priests because priesthood is reserved for the tribe of Levi; hence with the Midrash he interpreted *kōhănîm*, not as priests but as princes. Following in his steps, Jon D. Levenson invokes the analogy of the treaty of the suzerain Mursilis with Duppi-Tessub, in which the Hittite suzerain placed all Amurru land under his vassal. So,

as reward of loyalty in covenant, YHWH confers upon Israel the status of royalty. Their special position in a world entirely God's is the position of priestly kings. . . . "The whole world" is to Israel as the Amurru land . . . is to Duppi-Tessub. In each case, the suzerain establishes the vassal as the royal figure in a larger community which is itself under the great king's suzerainty. (Levenson 1985, 31)

The idea that it is the destiny of Israel to rule over the nations is fairly widespread in the tradition of the Old Testament. The king in Jerusalem is given worldwide rule (Ps 2:7; 72:8). The people are also recipients of this rule, as in Jacob's blessing of Isaac, "let peoples serve you and nations bow low before you" (Gen 27:29). In Deuteronomy 15:6, the blessing for obedience to the covenant is that "you will be creditors to many nations but debtors to none; you will rule over many nations, and be ruled by none" (Hamlin 1976, 518). Isaiah 61:5-6 added its voice when it understood Exodus 19:5-6 in the sense of Israelites being royal priests. It says that "foreigners will be your ploughmen and vinedressers; but you will be called 'priests of Yahweh' (*kōhănê YHWH*) and be addressed as 'ministers of our God' (*mĕšārtê 'ĕlōhênû*)." Foreigners will serve Israel as servants serve kings. The religious concept of exclusive service to Yahweh is here combined with mundane political expectations. All the agricultural work is to be done by incorporated foreigners, allowing all Israel leisure to serve Yahweh's altar. Daniel 7:27 carried this idea to its term when it predicted that "kingship and rule and the splendors of all the kingdoms under heaven will be given to the people of the holy ones of the Most High, whose royal power is an eternal power, whom every empire will serve and obey." The "people of the holy ones of the Most High" are Israel.

Understood in this way, it would seem that Exodus 19:5-6 focuses uniquely on the relationships of Yahweh and Israel and the benefits accruing to Israel from these. But this meaning seems subverted in two ways. First is the choice of the word *kōhănîm* (priests). Priests serve a community by bringing them closer to God and serve God by mediating God's revelation and decrees to the community. The surprising thing here is that God promises to make priests of the entire community of Israel. Martin Noth thus suggested that "Israel has the role of the priestly member in the number of earthly states; it has the priestly privilege of 'drawing near' to God to do service for all the world" (1962, 157).

Danie C. van Zyl put the same idea a bit differently:

Priest and holy suggest separation and devotion to Yahweh, but in a functional way, oriented to service: they were to represent and mediate God, his glory and his goodness to others. (1992, 267)

At first sight, it looks as if the religious terms (priestly, holy) and political images (kingdom, nation) are incompatible. But precisely the jarring effect of such a combination is meant to signify that all aspects of Israel's life are pertinent to the fulfillment of God's purposes, not just the religious sphere (Fretheim 1996, 235).

A second pointer to the subversion of the text is the gloss, *"for (kî) the whole world is mine."* The Hebrew particle *kî* usually gives the motive or grounding for what preceded. The sentence reads smoothly without this gloss; if it were removed, it would not be missed. But its presence introduces possible fields of meaning that would not be there otherwise. It was added out of concern for the universal sovereignty of Yahweh over all the earth and over all nations, lest it might appear that Yahweh's ownership and rule extended over Israel alone. In fact, this latter view is found in the text of Deuteronomy 32:8:

> when the Most High gave the nations each their heritage, when he partitioned out the human race, he assigned the boundaries of the nations according to the number of the children of God, but Yahweh's portion was his people, Jacob was to be the measure of his inheritance.

It is also striking that the construction of this gloss is parallel with the phrase about Israel belonging to Yahweh, both being constructed with the pronominal suffix *lî* ("to me, mine"):

> and you will be *to me* a treasure out of all peoples,
> for *to me* is all the earth.

The versions struggle with the nuances introduced by the gloss. Here are some of the versions.

> you shall be My treasured possession among all the peoples. *Indeed*, all the earth is Mine, *but* you shall be to Me a kingdom of priests and a holy nation. (NJPS; italics mine)

> *Although* the whole earth is mine, you will be for me a kingdom of priests and a holy nation. (NIV; italics mine)

> You, out of all peoples, shall be my personal possession, *for* the whole world is mine. For me you shall be a kingdom of priests, a holy nation. (NJB; italics mine)

The NJPS renders *kî* as "indeed." It can be so rendered, but this is not usual. The NJPS focuses on the prerogatives of Israel. It agrees with various statements in Deuteronomy that underline the identity of Israel by focusing on her prerogatives vis-à-vis the nations. An example is Deuteronomy 10:14:

> Look, to Yahweh your God belong heaven and the heaven of heav-
> ens, the earth and everything on it; yet it was on your ancestors, for
> love of them, that Yahweh set his heart to love them, and he chose
> their descendants after them, you yourselves, out of all nations, up to
> the present day.

Ezra 9:1-2 (see also Neh 13:23-27) would rely on such traditions, in combination with Deut 23:4-7 (which excludes certain nations and categories
of Israelites from the "assembly of Yahweh") to exclude the "people of the
land" from the postexilic covenant community (Fishbane 1985, 124-29). A
separatist understanding of holiness mandated the expulsion of foreign
women so that the community might remain "holy seed."

Our passage, however, is susceptible of a different rendering. When rendered in the manner of the NJB, the question arises as to how Israel as "my
personal possession" is related to the phrase, "the whole earth is mine."
Terence Fretheim answers the question in this way: "because all the earth
is mine, so you, you shall be to me a kingdom of priests and a holy nation.
. . . Israel is commissioned to be God's people on behalf of the earth which
is God's" (1991, 212). It is clear from the Primeval History and from many
parts of the Old Testament that God's purposes are wider than the overall
biblical focus on Israel may lead one to believe. Fretheim (1996, 230)
insists that Exodus must be read in relation to Genesis. Thus, the themes of
creation, promise, and universal divine purpose set in place by the Genesis
narrative become the lens through which Exodus is read. When Exodus is
read in this manner, it becomes clear that God's actions in Exodus on
Israel's behalf are for the sake of the world, "that my name may be declared
through all the earth" (Exod 9:6). If Sinai expresses God's particular intimacy with Israel, it is not to negate the possibility of other intimacies
(Hartman 1978, 386). Rather God's dealings with Israel manifest the universal divine self-offer to all peoples and all nations, an offer that Israel is
called to mediate as priests. It does not suffice to dismiss election as the
"confessional language of the insiders" (Boring 1999, 99), as if in fact all
are elect. The immediate goal of election is not salvation but mission. The
privilege of Israel is not erased by our reading, only that other peoples are
meant to enter into her unique relationship with her God.

REAPPLICATION IN REVELATION
AND 1 PETER 2:4-10

Exodus 19:5-6 receives a reapplication in Revelation and 1 Peter 2:4-10.
For this to happen, a number of shifts must be made. The Christians
addressed are neither a nation nor a people. They cannot claim direct
descent from Abraham nor former religious association with the original
recipients of the promises. The shift consists in showing that through
Christ, the heir of Abraham, Christians accede to the promises to Abra-

ham. Also in him they form a spiritual household, hence become people of the same God of Abraham, Father of Jesus Christ. On election, a shift from the communal plane to the individual plane is needed: Israel may be elect as a community that accepts God's grace and call, but Christians are elect as persons who do the same, and whom God gathers together into his household in Christ.

The Book of Revelation does not shift the keys but is quite literal in its interpretation. It understands a "kingdom of priests" (Exod 19:6) as referring to "a kingdom and priests" (*basileian kai hiereis*, Rev 5:10; see 1:6) and proceeds to make priests and kings of Christian martyrs (Rev 20). As priests, martyred Christians serve at the heavenly altar, where their blood makes supplication for divine retribution (Rev 6:10-11). As kings, they come to life after the binding of the Dragon to reign with Christ for a thousand years (Rev 20:4-5). By virtue of their being constituted a kingdom and priests, they are set over the world to rule over it (Rev 5:10). They accede to this rule, however, by "conquering" with Christ, that is, by giving their blood for the confession of Christ.

First Peter is written to "the elect living as resident aliens in the Diaspora" (ἐκλεκτοῖς παρεπιδήμοις διασπορᾶς) of Pontus, Galatia, Cappadocia, Asia and Bythinia (1:1). One notes already the transfer to the Christian community of the titles of Israel. "Elect" or chosen ones is a consistent title of Israel, especially in Deuteronomy. "Diaspora" referred originally to the Jewish dispersion in the exile of the northern kingdom in the late eighth century B.C.E. and of the southern kingdom in 597 and 587 B.C.E. The term is here transferred to the Christian addressees as similarly lacking citizens' rights where they dwell and as living on the margins of the surrounding culture, which in some ways was alien to the Christian faith and lifestyle. These communities suffered great pressure to conform and assimilate to the dominant culture. They could not attain citizenship status in their various cities, for their new faith prevented them from participating in the religious rites of city and family that were constitutive of citizenship (Boring 1999, 103). This left them open to the charge of atheism and disrespect for the gods of the city. It is in this context that the author in 2:4-5, 9-10 sought to re-franchise the community by crafting for them a new identity founded on Christ. He does this by a massive transfer of the prerogatives of Israel. They are a chosen race, a holy nation, once not a people but now the people of God (*laos theou*, the term for Israel as people of God), a people who are God's personal possession, a people once outside God's pity but who have received pity (recalling Hos 2:3). Their new identity is to form a people in Christ and to be built on Christ, the living stone, into living stones forming a spiritual house or household. Then occurs the reapplication of Exodus 19:5-6. The LXX had rendered *mamleket kōhănîm* ("kingdom of priests") with βασίλειον ἱεράτευμα ("a royal priesthood"). This reading is retained in 1 Peter 2:9, but now the focus is on "priesthood." The author assigns to Christians three functions of this priesthood, namely, to offer spiritual sacrifices (2:5), to give testimony, and to "sing the praises of God who called you out of darkness into his wonderful light" (2:9). Doxology is missiological, for it tells of the deeds of God and the character of God. In a complex metaphor (1 Pet 2:4-5), the author speaks of Christ as the living stone and of the community as "like living stones, [who] are being built into a spiritual house to be a *holy* priesthood (εἰς ἱεράτευμα ἅγιον)" (NIV). The author could do little with the epithet "royal," since it obviously did not conform to the condition of his addressees, so he shifted keys to the epithet "holy," which in the text of Exodus was used with "nation" (holy nation). The metaphor, however, is complex, because the idea of a "spiritual house" evokes the image of a temple—the Spirit makes the Christian community a fit dwelling place for God. The idea of a holy priesthood, on the other hand, evokes the image of liturgy, in which priests carry out the worship of God through offerings. The composite image refers to the life and bearing of the Christian community as the place both of the dwelling/manifestation of God and where God is given due and proper worship. Christians glorify God in worship and behavior: "the Christian mission is the outworking of Christians living out their difference" (Wells 2000, 229). Non-Christians are to be drawn to God by observing the Christian way and lifestyle in the world. They are especially to be drawn to seek the reason for the hope that sustains Christians, a hope that enables them to be patient under unjust treatment (1 Pet 3:15). Thus in 1 Peter a "missionary intention" informs the very worship and the daily life of holiness of the Christian community: the Christian community incarnates God's holiness and glory in the world and thus draws others to God's holy presence (Wells 2000, 243).

CONCLUSION

As Lucien Legrand (1990, 35) well pointed out, Exodus 19:5-6 helps us perceive that the life of a people is a vehicle for mission. The effort to be true to the character of God as the Holy One of Israel also manifests God to the world. Such an effort to conform to God must be integral and not merely limited to what is "spiritual"; hence it must be apparent in all levels of the life of the elect people.

DISCUSSION

1. Argue the point of view that Exodus 19:5-6 speaks only of Yahweh's preferential love for Israel and that Israel's election is particular to it alone.
2. Analyze and evaluate the method used in this chapter.
3. As the author of 1 Peter 2:4-10, explain and justify your interpretation of Exodus 19:5-6.

7

God of Righteousness

The Prophetic Protest of Amos

Do not you and the Cushites all belong to me, children of Israel? – declares Yahweh. Did I not bring Israel up from Egypt and the Philistines from Caphtor, and the Arameans from Kir?

—Amos 9:7

The purpose of election is not that the world might serve Israel, but that Israel might serve the world.

—C. Howie, "Expressly for Our Time," 282

We saw in the previous chapter that Israel existed for the glory of Yahweh and not primarily for its own self-exaltation. The credit for burning this idea into the conscience of Israel goes to the prophets of the eighth century B.C.E., among them particularly Amos. Elijah also had a similar message in the preceding century, but mainly in deeds and not in written and preserved oracles. For these prophets, Yahweh was

> the God of righteousness in the first place, and the God of Israel in the second place, and even that only in so far as Israel came up to the righteous demands which in [God's] grace [God] had revealed to him. (Wellhausen 1957, 417)

Amos from Tekoa in Judah was called to prophesy sometime during the long reigns of Uzziah (783-742 B.C.E.) in Judah and Jeroboam II (786-746 B.C.E.) in Israel. Although from Judah, he was sent by God to the northern kingdom of Israel to preach at the central sanctuary of Bethel. His ministry there was short-lived, as the high priest of Bethel, Amaziah, both denounced him to the king as a conspirator and urged him to return to Judah and earn his living there. For, said he, "there you can prophesy, but never again will you prophesy at Bethel, for this is a royal sanctuary, a national temple" (Amos 7:12-13).

The Book of Amos has been subjected to diverse scholarly analyses, with some defending its basic unity (e.g., Paul 1991, 6) and others finding as many as six layers (e.g., Wolff 1977, 106-13). Most scholars accept chapters 3-6 as substantially the words of Amos of Tekoa. What is in dispute is the extent of the Deuteronomistic and other redactions in these chapters and in the rest of the book. For our purposes, some adaptation of the theory of Robert Coote (1981, 1-8) will suffice. According to Coote, Amos, the eighth-century prophet, preached to the ruling elite of Samaria a message of divine judgment because of social injustice. A seventh-century editor made adaptations and additions concerned with cult. Coote calls this editor the "Bethel editor," but others prefer to speak of a Deuteronomistic redaction, but the extent of this is disputed. In the exilic period a Judean editor, who also published the book in its final form, is credited with the references to Judah and Zion and the promises of salvation in Amos 9:11-15. It was he who reapplied what was prophesied of Israel, the northern kingdom, to the "Israel" of the exile and thereafter to Judah and the Jewish Diaspora.

> **Coote's Analysis of Amos**
>
> Eighth century: addressees, the ruling elite of Samaria
>
> Seventh century: "Bethel editor"—concerned with cult
>
> Sixth century: Judean editor—refers to Judah and Zion and inserts the promises in 9:11-15

In what follows, we adopt a literary approach that seeks to understand the message of the book as a whole, but with attention to possible diverse layers. For reasons of space, we will focus on only three texts of Amos, namely, 1:2; 1:3–2:16; 9:7.

AMOS 1:2: YAHWEH'S PRESENCE IN ZION IS FRAUGHT WITH DIRE RESPONSIBILITY

After the superscription (Amos 1:1), the Judean editor of the book set the tone in Amos 1:2, a summary of the prophet's message given in poetic parallelism.[1] What the verse describes is "a completely contrary experience of God" (Jeremias 1998, 14). A consistent thread that runs through the

---

1. Some scholars, however, believe that this verse summarizes only chapters 1-2 and that 3:1-2 is another summary for the collection in chapters 3-8.

entire message of the book is that of the overturning of expectations founded upon the popular view of a "favored-nation" relationship with Yahweh. In most of Amos, the prerogatives and particular institutions of Israel are mentioned only as grounds for punishment or rejection. "Go to Bethel and sin, to Gilgal, and sin even harder!" (Amos 4:4). Bethel and Gilgal were central shrines of the northern kingdom. The indictment is not that these sanctuaries were unlawful—the eighth-century prophet shows no knowledge of the Deuteronomic injunction of the unique sanctuary (Deut 12). The indictment is rather that the unjust lives of the worshipers rendered their very acts of worship acts of transgression against God. "Prepare to meet your God" (Amos 4:12) is the traditional summons to prepare for encounter with God in theophany, but in Amos the hoped-for encounter with God becomes a threat, something that is death-dealing and not life-giving.[2] So in Amos 1:2, the presence of Yahweh on Zion, Yahweh's holy mountain, traditionally the source of Israel's security and blessing, becomes a threat. Psalm 46, a Psalm of Zion, intones the belief (vv. 1-2) that, "God is both refuge and strength for us, a help always ready in trouble; so we shall not be afraid though the earth be in turmoil, though the mountains tumble into the depths of the sea, and its waters roar and seethe, and the mountains totter as it heaves." The refrain to this recitation is, "Yahweh Sabaoth is with us, our citadel, the God of Jacob" (vv. 3, 7, 11). Yahweh Sabaoth (the Lord of hosts) is the title of Yahweh as divine warrior who is enthroned over the Ark; the "hosts" are the armies of heaven. Yahweh is deemed to command these armies to Israel's advantage. Amos 1:2 presents a contrary experience of theophany—Yahweh in Zion is to be the source of national catastrophe and mourning.

"The Lord roars from Zion and thunders from Jerusalem" (NIV). Zion is the temple mount and symbolizes the sanctuary and abode of Yahweh. The imagery is that of terrifying sounds that portend imminent danger and/or death. The root *š'g* ("roar") evokes the roar of the lion in front of prey (Amos 3:3-4). In Amos 3:8 the prophet refers again to this roar of Yahweh: "the lion roars, who is not afraid? Lord Yahweh has spoken: who will not prophesy?" In other words, the word of doom entrusted to the prophet is the roar of the "lion," and it presages imminent death for Israel. The verb translated "thunders" is literally "lets out his voice" (*yittēn qôlô*). *Qôl* is voice; the plural, *qôlôt*, is used for peals of thunder. The intended effect of this line is that of shuddering before terrifying peals of thunder and the potentially deadly roar of the lion.

"The shepherds' pastures mourn, and the crown of Carmel dries up." The summit of Carmel stands for the highland, the meadows for the lowlands. In Amos 9:3 the "top of Carmel" is contrasted with the "sea bed"

---

2. Walter Brueggemann gives a different interpretation of Amos 4:6-12, understanding "prepare to meet your God" as summons to covenant renewal (1965).

as places where the fleeing survivors might try to hide from Yahweh. Hence what is described in our verse is a merism, meaning that every person and every place is affected. That the pastures "mourn" is personification; their "mourning" anticipates the human mourning and wailing that will be the response to the devastating action of Yahweh. Everywhere God's voice produces mourning, and that voice is articulated in the words spoken by God's prophet. In normal experience, thunder presages rain and rain holds out the promise of life. The very opposite is the case here, where thunder brings drought and death. Carmel is famous for evergreen and lush vegetation, so much so that it became a symbol for full and luxuriant growth. Isaiah 35:2 paints the glory of the restored Jerusalem as its having "the glory of Lebanon . . . bestowed on it, the splendor of Carmel and Sharon." Yet even this Carmel dries up at the thundering voice of Yahweh. To say that even Carmel, the most luxuriant vegetation in the land, dries up is to say that drought lies like a pall over all the land. The dearth of vegetation means the death of animals and famine and death for humans. Carmel stands also for the northern kingdom, just as Zion stands for the southern kingdom. When the editor was writing, both lay in ruins, the north destroyed by the Assyrians in 722 and the south devastated by the Babylonians in 597 and 587. The exilic editor reapplied Amos's message of doom on Samaria to the divine judgment of Judah in the sixth century. Hence, at the very outset of the Book of Amos, all Israelites of past, present, and future are warned that the Holy One of Israel does not sit comfortably with sin and injustice and that election is no guarantee against divine retribution. The presence of Yahweh in the sanctuary is no natural and automatic source of blessing; rather in the face of injustice and sin Yahweh is prepared to destroy both Yahweh's sanctuary (Amos 9:1-6) and Yahweh's people. Election is not a shield when it comes to accounting for unrighteousness before God.

AMOS 1:3–2:16: ISRAEL AS ONE OF THE NATIONS

Amos 1-2 belongs to the genre "Oracles against the Nations." Something of this genre is found in every prophetic book of the Old Testament except Hosea. There is no common form or structure for these oracles; the only thing they have in common is that they invoke curses or the punishment of Yahweh on those surrounding nations who have interacted negatively or oppressively with God's people (Hayes 1968, 81-92). Of the eight oracles in Amos 1-2, most scholars agree that the oracles against Tyre, Edom, and Judah are secondary and belong to the exilic edition of the book.[3] Teman

---

3. They lack the final "says the Lord" and they shorten the punishments (two instead of four elements, as in the rest). There is a greater focus on motivation, and the guilt is increased by a religious factor. The unit on Judah is entirely religious and corresponds to Deuteronomistic language and theology. The crime of Tyre is a repeat of that of Gaza.

and Bozrah (Amos 1:12) were not incorporated into Edom until the exilic period (Vermeylen 1978, 530). All the oracles are patterned in the manner of the prophetic announcement of disaster, as follows

Thus says the Lord.
For the three crimes, the four crimes of X
I have made my decree and will not relent.
Because ('al, "upon")—[cites some inhumane crime]
I shall send fire . . . to devour the palaces. . . .
I shall destroy . . . the holder of the scepter/deport the king and chief
    men or the whole people.
Says the Lord.

What is noticeable about this arrangement is that the people of God (Israel, and secondarily Judah) have been included within a listing that traditionally names peoples deemed to be enemies of Yahweh! In the mind of Amos, Israel stands before Yahweh on the same level as other nations. Further, Israel is more deserving of punishment when it does injustice: "you alone have I known of all the families of earth, that is why I shall punish you for all your wrong-doings" (Amos 3:2).

Amos was the first person to transform the genre of Oracles against the Nations by turning it against Israel itself. These oracles normally invoked curses on the enemies of God's people, but here Amos includes God's people, for God's people have become God's enemies. The genre castigated the nations for crimes against God's people and invoked punishment on them. God was meant to punish them as a token of salvation for Israel. Here the nations are not punished for crimes against Israel or for the sake of Israel; rather because they have become guilty before Yahweh. Even the crime of Moab against the king of Edom (Amos 2:1) receives just retribution, notwithstanding the fact that Edom is considered the perpetual enemy of Israel in many traditions of the Old Testament.

Except for Judah (Amos 2:4-5), where specific *torah* transgressions are named (and we have seen that the oracle against Judah is secondary) all the crimes are on the level of injustice and unrighteousness in human relations. No positive precept of Yahweh is invoked that the nations might be said to have transgressed. The Arameans of Damascus have threshed Gilead with iron threshing sledges (Amos 1:3). Gilead was a very fertile and luxuriant land and was for long the bone of contention between Aram and Israel. It would seem that in one of their victorious wars, the Arameans ran iron spikes over the bodies of the defeated Gilead soldiers ripping up their flesh, as threshing sleds rip up chaff (Waard and Smalley 1979, 12). Moab burned the bones of the king of Edom to ash (Amos 2:1). Ammon disemboweled the pregnant women of Gilead (Amos 1:13). Gaza exiled an entire population, which they delivered as slaves to Edom (Amos 1:6). Although the Old Testament permitted slavery, it would seem that Amos was appalled at the enslavement of an entire people and thus became the first voice to raise the question of what is permissible in war. There is one element that underlies all these crimes—they are crimes committed against a weaker party that has no other protective institution behind it and no other recourse. All through the ancient Near East of the time, the protection of this category of people was vested in the deity. "The protection of the widow, orphan, and the poor was the common policy of the ancient Near East. . . . Such protection was seen as a virtue of gods, kings and judges" (Fensham 1962, 129; cf. Hammershaimb 1959, 75-101). Amos thus depicts Yahweh as God of the defenseless everywhere—among the nations and even in Israel herself.

The crimes are termed *pešaʿ* ("revolt, rebellion"). Amos was the first to introduce this political vocabulary into the religious language of the time. To commit a crime against fellow human beings is to rebel against Yahweh. One need not invoke the *torah* of Yahweh before guilt can be incurred—there is justice and humaneness for which people everywhere are accountable to Yahweh.

Nations are led by leaders who enter into or command certain acts; these leaders and the nations they represent are accountable before God (cf. Barton 1980, 4.48). National policies are subject to justice and righteousness, and there are no absolute "state rights," whether against individuals or other nations. To say that God punishes a nation is one way of describing national accountability; another and more modern way would be to say that society self-destructs when it abuses the defenseless.

Amos dwelt first on the crimes of the neighboring nations in order to arrest the attention of the audience and secure their approval, a type of *captatio benevolentiae*. They must have felt the rug pulled from under their feet when the prophet finally arrived at his goal—the crimes of Israel (Amos 2:6-16). The prophet begins in the same manner as for the nations, "for the three crimes, the four crimes of Israel," but this time he mentions the four crimes (Amos 2:6-8). They are all crimes of injustice against defenseless fellow Israelites, all crimes committed in order to gain more room and increase one's boundaries. *"They sell the upright for silver and the poor for a pair of sandals"* (Amos 2:6). Borrowers who mortgaged their property surrendered their sandals as pledge (Dearman 1988, 21).[4] Nehemiah 5:1-5 shows creditors selling off pledged land and selling the children of debtors with it. *"They have crushed the heads of the weak into the dust and thrust the rights of the oppressed to one side"* (Amos 2:7ab). The last phrase means literally, "and they twist the way of the weak." It can also be rendered as "they frustrate the life-course of the weak," for

---

4. See also Donald Benjamin, *Old Testament Story* (pre-publication manuscript) 74.

derek ("way") can refer to one's life journey. The grasping rich prevent the weak from attaining fulfillment in life.

"*A son and his father sleep with the same girl thus profaning my holy name*" (Amos 2:7cd). *Naʿărāh* is a young and unmarried girl; by age and status she is dependent and defenseless.[5] In the *torah* itself, a woman's identity is defined in relation to a man, either a husband or the father of the family. Jörg Jeremias (1998, 37) asks whether this might be the rape of a socially dependent person and Robert Martin-Achard (1984, 22) thinks of "residential prostitution." There is no legislation in the *torah* against such ingress of son and father to an unmarried woman, and it is not clear who is considered wronged in this scenario—the girl or one of the men. The traditional ethos in most places, however, considers it an abomination for parents and their children to share the same sexual subject. Amos invokes God's holiness and God's holy name as involved in the social rights of the lowly and downtrodden; contempt for them is contempt for God. To "profane" (*ḥillēl*) is to violate the sacredness of a holy person or thing or to violate a relationship specially protected by God, and this in a context public enough to lead nonbelievers to disrespect for, or the mocking of, God's name. The case in point may even be where Israelites offended against taboos that the nations observed strictly, not unlike the incestuous Christian of Corinth who committed "immorality of a kind that is not found even among gentiles" (1 Cor 5:1). The term "profaning my holy name" is characteristic of Ezekiel (20:39; 36:20-23) and the Holiness Code (Lev 18:24; 19:12; 20:3). It is thus possibly a redactional expansion of the preceding phrase by an editor who understood that phrase as referring to temple prostitution (Mays 1969, 46).

"*Lying down beside every altar on clothes acquired as pledges, and drinking the wine of the people they have fined in the house of their god*" (Amos 2:8).[6] This charge combines a social and a religious crime. If a debtor defaulted on the payment of a debt, a creditor was allowed to seize any possession of the debtor, except what was essential for life; for example, the mantle of the poor may not be kept overnight (Exod 22:26; Deut 24:12). It may be that the rich creditors actually slept in the holy place on mantles taken as pledge from the poor. J. Andrew Dearman (1988, 23) suggests something worse. Taking the verb "spread out" as meaning "to dedicate," he opines that the rich actually dedicated the seized clothes of the poor to the sanctuary. The wine of communion with God that they drank was extorted from the poor; their dedicated offering also was taken from

---

5. The REB rendered *naʿărāh* with "temple girls" and so considered the crime to be that of temple prostitution. The plain sense of the word, however, does not call for this, besides the evidence for Canaanite temple prostitution has worn thin in recent research.

6. The NJPS renders: "in the House of their God" (similar NRSV)— "God" with a capital G refers to Israel's God, Yahweh, and stresses the incongruity of their behavior.

the poor. No wonder Yahweh says that they do all this in the house of "their god" ("god" with small g). Yahweh takes some distance from such warped worship, as if to say that "it certainly is not with me that they are involved."

The basis of oppression in eighth-century Israel was land ownership and unfair distribution of land. The society was in transition from a peasant economy to a market system, and from the patrimonial system to prebendal domain. In the latter, large tracts of land were sequestered and given out to high officials and well-placed persons as prebends or grants. The traditional kinship values that ensured the welfare of the poor were under pressure from the market economy. The ever-widening power of the monarchy and the rise of the merchant class in the ninth century were leading to latifundialization, that is, the combination of smaller holdings into large estates for economic profit. In these estates, vines and olives were planted for export (Amos 5:11: "you have planted pleasant vineyards"), not the staple food (grain) of the peasants. Peasants paid rent on the land, on tools, on seeds, and on water, or they paid through sharecropping— what Bernhard Lang (1985, 97) calls "rent capitalism." Gradually the poor slipped into the condition of serfs who worked the land for the overlord and finally became debt slaves sold in lieu of the debt.

The crimes of the nations mentioned were committed in the quest for territory, for increasing boundaries; those of the elite of Israel were committed in an analogous quest for land. The crimes of the nations were war crimes; Amos depicts the oppression of the poor in Israel as crimes of violence as if at war. Wealth, which prejudices the welfare and rights of others, is analogous to violence (Mays 1983, 14).

The issue for Amos was thus *mišpāt ûṣedāqāh* ("justice and righteousness"), the equivalent of the modern term "social justice." In Amos 5:24, the prophet cries out, "but let justice flow like water and uprightness like a never-failing stream." *Ṣĕdāqāh* is not conformity to any norm, nor is it even legal justice ("giving one what is his/her due"). It is rather the fulfillment of the demands of a relationship (Achtemeier 1976, 80-85). The relationship itself determines what the demands are. If the relationship is one of treaty or covenant, then righteousness is fulfilled when the expectations of these are fulfilled. The behavior of the Israelites against dependent fellow nationals upsets the basic righteousness that cements society together. The crime is made worse when compared with Yahweh's compassion on them and Yahweh's intervention on their behalf in their time of helplessness (Amos 2:9-10). "Salvation history becomes judgment history" as the past acts of Yahweh for the people increase their guilt and become additional grounds for punishment. Forcing fellow Israelites into debt slavery reverses the redemptive act of Yahweh, who had delivered them from the situation of landless slavery and given them the promised land as an inheritance. Israel is not free to organize its society as it likes, for its history with God binds it to a fraternal covenant with the poor and the weak. Compassion in human relations is thus part of Israel's identity. A socioeconomic reorganization without compassion is a denial of that identity and merits the radical no of Yahweh (Huffmon 1983, 115). A corrective intervention by God will clear oppressor and oppressed out of the land and end Israel as a nation (Mays 1983, 176): "the time is ripe for my people Israel; I will spare them no longer" (Amos 8:2 NIV). It is significant that the expression "God of Israel" does not occur in the Book of Amos. God is, for Amos, not God of Israel but God of righteousness. When Israel fails in righteousness it merits the same retribution as other nations.

AMOS 9:7: DO NOT YOU AND THE CUSHITES ALL BELONG TO ME?

Amos 9:7-10 is a theological reflection on the preceding unit, 9:1-4. That unit described Yahweh's retributive intervention in Israel. Yahweh unleashed utter destruction on Yahweh's sanctuary and on the worshipers in it. No survivors were allowed to escape, for Yahweh pursued them to the sea bed and even into exile, promising that "whoever runs away will not run far, whoever escapes will not make good [their] escape" (Amos 9:1). Amos 9:7, which justifies the total destruction in 9:1-4 (Nogalski 1993, 97-99), is now separated from 9:4 by the fragment of a hymn in 9:5-6. It argues that other nations belong to Yahweh as much as Israel belongs to Yahweh. If Yahweh destroyed these nations for their crimes (Amos 1-2), Yahweh would also bring retribution on Israel for its crimes. To this saying are appended three qualifications (9:8, 9, 10) by editors worried about the total destruction of the nation described in 9:1-4 and justified in 9:7.

The first qualification occurs in Amos 9:7a: *"do you not as the children of the Cushites belong to me, children of Israel, says Yahweh."* "Is it not" (*hălô'*) expects a positive response. Beyond this the versions differ. The NJPS has, "to Me, O Israelites, you are just like the Ethiopians—declares the Lord." J. Lindblom understands the verse as a call for punishment:

> Amos was convinced that Israel must perish. Because of their apostasy, they had become to Yahweh like the Ethiopians. But if Yahweh wanted to choose another people as His own, there were other nations at His disposal, such as the Philistines and the Syrians, whose history was likewise directed by Yahweh. (1963, 334)

Lindblom presumes that Yahweh can relate to the Ethiopians only in punishment, but Amos is not of this opinion nor does he hold that Yahweh excludes any nation. Walter Vogels translated *'attem lî* as "you belong to me" and takes it as a shortened form of *'attem lî lĕ'am* ("you belong to me as a people"). Such a phrase expresses the covenant relationship with Yahweh. This may apply to Israel but cannot apply to the other nations, in the opinion of Vogels. Hence, he reads the comparative (*kě*, "as") as introducing a comparison that does not amount to absolute equality. It would allow each nation to belong to Yahweh at its own level. His conclusion (1972, 234): "*ainsi ces bienfaits qui restent différents créent des liens d'apparte-nance qui sont différents*" (thus these deeds that are different create bonds of belonging that are also diverse). All peoples belong to Yahweh, but only Israel belongs as "Yahweh's people." Vogels's argument rests on the presupposition that Yahweh cannot refer to Ethiopia as belonging to Yahweh, but is this true of the thinking of Amos? The surprising thing is that Ethiopia is the principal term of comparison. The phrase goes something like this, "is your belonging to me, children of Israel, not like the belonging to me of the children of Ethiopia?" In other words, Israel belongs to Yahweh as Ethiopia belongs to Yahweh. What Yahweh does for or against one, Yahweh will do for or against the other.

The second qualification of the total destruction announced by the prophet is, "*did I not bring Israel up from Egypt and the Philistines from Caphtor, and the Arameans from Kir?*" (Amos 9:7b). The sense is clearer in the NJPS: "true, I brought Israel up from the land of Egypt, but also the Philistines from Caphtor and the Arameans from Kir." Paul Noble (like Vogels) distinguishes between the exodus event and the granting of a relationship and opines that "by rejecting the law of Yahweh they [Judah and Israel] have reduced [Yahweh's] bringing them out of Egypt to a mere geographical relocation" (Noble 1993, 74). A slight problem with this is that *torah* and covenant are not mentioned in the oracle on Israel (Amos 2:6-16). They are mentioned in the oracle on Judah (2:4-5), but this is a secondary layer in the book. Nowhere else does Amos mention the giving of the law on Sinai. In Amos 2:9-12 the deeds of Yahweh on behalf of Israel are recounted, but nothing is said about the giving of the law on Sinai! It is possible that Amos did not yet know of the Sinai tradition. In the popular mind, the deliverance from Egypt and the exodus were a unique experience of Israel and a unique favor of Yahweh. Amos says flatly that other peoples had their exodus experiences from the same Yahweh. It is significant that Aram and Philistia, the two persistent enemies of Israel in that period, were equally under the active providence of Yahweh. Yahweh has been active in the movements of the various peoples, just as Yahweh has been in those of Israel. If now Yahweh threatens to return the people of Aram to Kir, from which they came (Amos 1:5), then Israel should take notice that Yahweh may as well reverse Israel's entire history.

The third qualification (Amos 9:8) introduces the question of guilt. The punishment of total extermination is only for the "sinful kingdom" (*mamlākāh haḥaṭṭā'āh*). Sinful kingdom can refer to Israel, and if so, the sense is that the destruction of Israel was for sinfulness.[7] It can also refer to any sinful kingdom—any kingdom that sins must expect extermination from Yahweh. An exception has been introduced by an editor: even when the house of Jacob sins, Yahweh will not cut it off totally, but will leave a remnant. The doctrine of the "remnant" appears in Isaiah but not in the authentic sayings of Amos of Tekoa. This qualification goes against the prophet's belief that Yahweh shows no special treatment of Israel vis-à-vis the nations.

The editor of Amos 9:9 transferred the discussion to the individual plane. He also presumed the fact of exile. The house of Israel was already scattered among all the nations. The idea of collective punishment no longer received assent during and after the exile (Ezek 18:2; Jer 32:18-19). It became necessary to transfer guilt to the individual plane. The exile is here seen as a purifying sieve that retains the grain and shakes out the chaff. Individual sinners are the chaff. They are the ones who suffer divine extermination and not the entire people. As clearly stated in Amos 9:10, "all the sinners of my people will perish by the sword, who say, 'disaster will never approach or overtake us.'"

The threat in Amos 9:1 had been that "I will put any survivors to the sword," meaning that there will be no remnant. The editor who wrote 9:10 transferred the threat of total destruction to the sinners and to those who did not believe in the words of the prophet.

CONCLUSION

For Amos, the movements of the nations are under the guidance of Yahweh, just as those of Israel are. He would agree with *Ad Gentes*, the Vatican II Decree on the Missionary Activity of the Church, that "doubtless the Holy Spirit was already at work in the world before Christ was glorified" (no. 4). The 1991 *Dialogue and Proclamation* commented on this as follows, "the firm faith in the religions is an effect of the Spirit of truth operating outside the confines of the mystical body" (no. 26) (Pontifical Council 1991). The affirmation that Israel belongs to Yahweh as much as Ethiopia belongs to Yahweh, and that Aram and Philistia had exodus events under the guiding hand of Yahweh, raises the question of the relation of mission to the preceding actions of God within a people and culture. Yahweh had a "hidden history" with these other peoples, yet such

---

7. Wolff (1977, 348) wishes to understand *mamlākāh* as kingship, in terms of royal house, as opposed to the house of Jacob. Hence it is the sinful royal house that will be exterminated, not the people. In the same way, Andersen and Freedman (1989, 875, 881) interpret "house of Jacob" as the people and identify "sinful kingdom" with "the sinners of my people," both referring to the leaders of the kingdom.

hidden action did not convert them to Yahwism or submerge their histories in that of Israel. Yahweh's participation in their histories was not an exact replica of Israel's narrative. One may thus imagine that they came to know Yahweh in Philistine modes, Aramean modes, and Ethiopian modes (Brueggemann 2000, 98-99).

The dominant message of Amos was that of justice, that is, of ṣĕdāqāh-righteousness as the covenantal relationship of people in society. The identity of Israel consists in reflecting on earth the righteousness of God; when Israel fails in this, it is ready for rejection and destruction. The church itself exists as a society of right relationships of people with God and with one another. In the same vein, the document entitled *Justice in the World* from the 1971 Synod of Bishops declared:

> action on behalf of justice and participation in the transformation of the world fully appear to us as a constitutive dimension of the preaching of the Gospel, or in other words, of the Church's mission for the redemption of the human race and its liberation from every oppressive situation.[8]

Finally, Amos teaches us the dangers of a certain belief in election. God has no favorites. Election is only a call to greater responsibility before God and for the world.

> "The purpose of election is not that the world might serve Israel, but that Israel might serve the world" (Howie 1959, 282).

As Robinson (1953, 69-70) says more extensively,

> Amos sees Yahweh as the vindicator of universal moral laws. [Yahweh] would punish the neighboring tribes, not merely as the patriot-god, for wrongs done to Israel, but for crimes which violated the natural laws of common humanity, whoever the victims might be. Israelite God as [Yahweh] was, [Yahweh] was still more the God of righteousness. [Yahweh's] special relationship to [Yahweh's] own people meant, not privilege to do wrong, but responsibility to do right. It was Israel that must adapt herself to this conception of a universal moral law, not Yahweh, who must consider primarily the mate-

8. Synod of Bishops, *Convenientes ex universo, Justice in the World*, November 30, 1971, "Introduction"; Austin Flannery, O.P., ed., *Vatican Council II*, volume 2, *More Post-Conciliar Documents*, new revised edition (New York: Costello; Dublin: Dominican Publications, 1992, 1998), 696.

rial advantage of Israel. If she failed here, . . . she lost her only *raison d'être*, and, so far from protecting her, Yahweh would [be the one to] ordain her ruin. . . . The real function of Israel amongst the civilized peoples of the world was to work [these supreme laws] out in her common life.

The presence of Yahweh in Yahweh's Zion sanctuary must not be taken for granted. An unjust Israel turns that presence into the roaring of a devouring lion.

Even further, as Brueggemann (2000, 98) points out, something happens to Yahweh when Israel's claim of exclusive belonging to Yahweh is shattered. The formula "I shall be your God" (no other God), "you shall be my people" (the only people of Yahweh) comes in for review; the very notion of "God's elect people," wedding Yahweh to an ethnic community, is under critique (ibid., 100).

DISCUSSION

1. How have scholars analyzed the book of Amos?
2. How did Amos subvert the Oracle against the Nations?
3. Describe the social context within which the prophet Amos preached.
4. Yahweh is God of righteousness, not God of Israel. Discuss.
5. Do you agree with the interpretation of Amos 9:7 in this chapter? Give reasons for your answer.

8

The Protest of Jonah

Why Mission? Because God cares! While Israel is the people of God, the people of God is broader than Israel.

—Terence Fretheim, *Message of Jonah*, 26

The Book of Jonah could illustrate centrifugal mission, but I have placed it here because it is considered more in relation to the nature of Israel's God and thus the nature of Israel itself. I have added a translation of the Hebrew text below as an appendix to this chapter (pp. 89-92). It is based on the New Revised Standard Version, but highlights literary features that add to the meaning and effect.

Jonah is the only prophetic book in the Hebrew Scriptures that is entirely a narrative about a prophet and not a collection of prophetic oracles. Although the word "prophet" does not occur in this book, the prophetic formula for the reception of the word ("the word of Yahweh came to") does, thus indicating the genre of prophecy. The book shares with Isaiah 66:18-21 the distinction of being the only two places in the Hebrew Bible where messengers are actually sent to pagan peoples. The only other possible reference to this motif occurs in the Servant Songs, but scholars are not agreed as to what it means to say of the servant that "he will bring justice to the nations" (Isa 42:1) or that "the coastlands are waiting for his *torah*" (Isa 42:4). I will come back to this in chapter 13, where I argue that these assertions depict an active mission of Israel to the nations.

The Book of Jonah is the fifth book of the Twelve, although Jewish tradition regards the Twelve as a single work. Like other books of the Twelve it has interlinkages with some other books in the collection. For example, Joel 2:13 contains exactly the same fivefold confession of the nature of Yahweh as in Jonah 4:2. Joel is placed before the Book of Jonah to counter Jonah's challenge of these qualities of Yahweh in Jonah 4:2. On the other hand, the Book of Jonah precedes that of Nahum to reaffirm Yahweh's

80

compassion for all peoples, including the Ninevites, before Nahum would gloat over the fall of Nineveh. I consider this reasoning more likely than that of Uriel Simon (1999, xiv), who argues that the placement of Nahum after Jonah signifies that Assyria returned to its evil ways after the short-lived repentance with Jonah. The Book of Jonah can thus be considered an intrabiblical corrective to the apparent xenophobia of the Book of Nahum. In Jonah 4:2, Yahweh insists that Yahweh's compassionate and merciful character is not for Israel only, but extends even to the Ninevites.

APPROACHES TO THE INTERPRETATION
OF THE BOOK OF JONAH

Scholars are not agreed about the exact genre and therefore the interpretation of the book of Jonah.[1] Several genres have been proposed, including *mashal,* parable, and short story. Edwin Good (1965, 41) considers that it is best read as a satire, for "it highlights the attitude of Jonah in order to satirize it. And the satire is through and through ironic. Its basis is a perception of incongruity." Many see the satire operating precisely against prophecy and the prophets. The book is viewed as an affirmation against Jonah that an unconditional message of doom can change if people repent (cf. Jer 18:7-8; Ezekiel 18:21). As Jerome already enunciated while commenting on Ezek 33:1, prophecy "foretells punishment, not to make it happen but so that it may not happen."[2] I agree with Simon (1999, xx) in categorizing the book as a *prophetic tale with theological intent.* But what precise theology is there in the book? Some see the book as moving toward the conversion of Jonah, and so to be really about God's pursuit of the prophet and Jonah's reactions to what is happening (Clements 1975, 16-28). Y. Kaufmann (1960, 285), on the contrary, pronounces that "Jonah is the classic statement of the Israelite idea of repentance." It is pointed out that the Book of Jonah is the Haftarah (with the last three verses of Micah 7:18-20) for the afternoon service on Yom Kippur and is thus used in the Jewish liturgy of repentance of that day. Some see in the book the ongoing tension in Israel between universalism and particularism. Jonah would thus symbolize Israel, Nineveh the gentiles. The true meaning of the election of Israel is that she carries her faith among the nations—thus Rashi and Kimhi. Terence Fretheim (1977, 20) and Simon agree that the Book of Jonah portrays a theological conflict between God and God's prophet. The issue is divine justice and how it can be trusted in the shaping of the moral

---

1. This section is indebted to Simon 1999, vii-xiii.
2. See *Patrologiae cursus completus: Series Latina,* edited by J. P. Migne, 221 volumes (Paris, 1844-64), 25:318: "*non enim praedicit ut veniat, sed ne veniat.*"

order. The prophet argues for strict justice as the bulwark of the certainty of moral order in the world. George M. Landes (1967, 30) sees the key motif of the book as "deliverance belongs to Yahweh" (2:10). In chapter 1, Yahweh saves the pagan sailors. In chapter 2, Yahweh saves Jonah. In chapter 3, Yahweh saves the Ninevites. In chapter 4, the deliverance of Nineveh is used to win the salvation of Jonah if he would repent and change his thinking about the objective of divine mercy. The approach adopted in this chapter is that the book is polyvalent and communicates at different levels of the plot.

Because the story is in a sense fiction, it allows the author ample use of narrative techniques. Interpretation gains by attending closely to the author's use of linguistic and other devices. For example, Jonah is presented as persistently "going down"—down to the ship, down to the hold, and down to the underworld. It is a descent of self-imprisonment that reaches even behind the barred gates of Sheol (Jonah 2:6) before Yahweh would bring him up and back to life. Irony is exploited when Jonah tells the pagan sailors, "I fear Yahweh" (1:9). It is not clear whether this fear is religious or merely psychological. The verb *yārē'*, can mean "religious fear" that leads to worship. We have this fear when the sailors are said to fear Yahweh with a great fear and as a result offered Yahweh sacrifices and vows. But one can hardly attribute religious fear of Yahweh to a prophet who is at variance with Yahweh and in attempted flight from his God!

I attach as an appendix to this chapter the NRSV version of the Book of Jonah, which I have adapted by making it closer to the Hebrew. Some of the linguistic and thematic features are highlighted in italics. The verse numbering will follow this version. I have also replaced "the Lord" with Yahweh, for the narrative is attentive to the distinction between "God" (*El, Elohim*) as the general Semitic name for deity, and "Yahweh" as the particular God of Israel's confession. In the entire chapter 3, which deals with pagan Nineveh, the only divine name used is *Elohim*. When it is said that "the people of Nineveh believed God" it was *Elohim* that they believed in (Jonah 3:5). The use of "Yahweh God" in Jonah 4:6 alerts the reader to the fact that the God in whom the Ninevites believed was actually the Yahweh of Israel. A comparison can be made with Abraham, who "believed Yahweh and this was reckoned to him as righteousness" (Gen 15:6). On that analogy, the belief of the Ninevites won them righteousness before God and reprieve of the threatened destruction of their city.

THE CONTEXT OF THE BOOK OF JONAH

Most scholars place the book in the postexilic period, in the fifth century B.C.E. A prophet named "Jonah, son of Amittai" from Gath Hepher is mentioned in 2 Kgs 14:25 as giving a word of deliverance to Jeroboam II in the eighth century B.C.E. The author of the Book of Jonah used the name of this prophetic figure for his own purposes.

A fifth-century date would make the Book of Jonah contemporary with the work of Ezra and Nehemiah, and the book may even represent a protest against the exclusivistic tendencies of that period. The period witnessed the struggle of the returnees for their ethnic, cultural, and religious identity. Considering themselves as "holy seed" and "true Israel," the returnees refused to associate with the "people of the land," even though these also worshiped Yahweh. They refused them participation in the rebuilding of the temple and forced the divorce of all non-Jewish wives (Ezra 9-10; Mal 2:10-11). Some of these policies were meant to support their struggle with the "people of the land" over the ownership of land. Against such a background, the book of Jonah would represent a stinging rebuke of all types of exclusivism. The author has the Israelite God, Yahweh, send a prophet to Nineveh, the capital of Assyria, which by then had become a symbolic name for the oppressors of Israel. Such a mission shows that no group of people is excluded from the care of Yahweh: *there is mission, because Yahweh cares!* Yahweh argues against Yahweh's prophet that Yahweh has a right to have compassion even on the Ninevites. In Yahweh's exchange with the prophet in Jonah 4:10, it is suggested that Yahweh's concern and commitment had to do with the fact that, unlike Jonah with his plant, Yahweh bore the pains of labor for the Ninevites and made them grow. Also unlike Jonah's plant, which came into being in a night and perished in a night, Yahweh's concern for the Ninevites has had a long history. It is noteworthy that the narrator consistently calls Nineveh "great"; Jonah never. In 3:3, the narrator describes Nineveh as "great to God," as if to say that God also views the city as great. So, "while Israel is the people of God, the people of God is broader than Israel" (Fretheim 1977, 26). The following box illustrates the various points in Yahweh's argument with Jonah in 4:11.

The plant, a small tendril	Nineveh, the great city
The plant is singular	Nineveh has more than 120,000 innocents
You did not grow it	I labored for them and made them grow
You did not work for it	I nurtured them
It appeared and perished overnight	Their birth and nurture took me many years and generations

INTERNAL STRUCTURE AND THEMES
OF THE BOOK OF JONAH

I shall reflect on the internal structure of the book, then on some themes associated with mission. The Book of Jonah starts with "the word of Yahweh came to Jonah" (Jonah 1:1) and ends with the word of Yahweh in Jonah 4:11. This *inclusio* suggests that Yahweh has the upper hand in this narrative and "seeks to persuade the hearers (or readers) about the rightness of what the deity does and will do" (Trible 1994, 224). "The word of Yahweh came to Jonah" (Jonah 1:1) and "the word of Yahweh came to Jonah *a second time*" (3:1) divide the narrative into two parallel diptychs. In the first panel, a captain and his sailors interact with Jonah (chapter 1); then Jonah is left in isolation with Yahweh (chapter 2). This movement is repeated in the second panel, where Jonah interacts with the king, his nobles, and the Ninevites (chapter 3), then is isolated in a booth, with Yahweh trying to persuade him. Such a structure suggests that the theological point of the narrative should be looked for in the tension between Yahweh and Jonah and/or the interaction between them.

Commissioned to "arise, go to Nineveh" in the east (Jonah 1:2) and to "cry out against her, for their evil has come up before me," Jonah arose but set himself to flee with haste, from the presence of Yahweh, to Tarshish in the farthest west. In the delayed information in Jonah 4:2, Jonah himself tells us his motive for fleeing in the first place. If Nineveh is guilty, as Yahweh pronounced, then it merits sure retribution. But he could not trust the compassionate and gracious character of Yahweh when it comes to delivering punishment and doom. Such "mercy undermines the force of justice by detracting from the certainty of punishment" (Simon 1999, 35) and thus contributes to moral confusion and chaos in the world. For, "if God is not going to relate [Godself] to people in ways that are consistent with their conduct, then God is capricious and life is absurd" (Fretheim 1977, 17). There comes a point when Yahweh must act; otherwise the saying of Mal 2:17 would be true, namely, that "everyone who does evil is good in the sight of God." Because of the possibility of divine mercy on pagan and guilty Nineveh, Jonah found his mission intolerable and set himself to flee from the presence of Yahweh. As he was fleeing from Yahweh in a ship, Jonah unintentionally converted the pagan captain and his sailors to the worship of Yahweh (Jonah 1:16).

All through the narrative, pagan peoples are depicted as more open to the word of Yahweh than the prophet and responding to it with alacrity. The narrator deftly sets up contrasts between Jonah and the pagan sailors, contrasts that bear on the theme of mission, for they indicate who is truly for Yahweh and the nature of true piety and worship. When the pagan sailors felt pursued by the furies, they prayed and offered their wares as sacrifice to the pursuing deity. When nemesis caught up with Jonah, he slept, never uttered a word of prayer, but rather asked the sailors to "pick me up and hurl me into the sea . . . for I know that it is because of me that this great storm has come upon you" (Jonah 1:12). Either he felt that death would finally relieve him of a divine mission he loathed, or he genuinely accepted guilt and, according to his theology, also accepted the consequent punishment. In either case, he was at variance with Yahweh. For all he had to do for the storm to stop was to confess his guilt before Yahweh and offer to return to his mission; but that he would not do. The pagan sailors, on the contrary, are shocked that any person should think of fleeing from God (1:10). They themselves became Yahweh worshipers at the unwitting testimony of Jonah and offered Yahweh sacrifices and vows. These pagan sailors tried their best to save the life of guilty Jonah and threw him into the deep only when all their efforts to preserve him proved in vain. Even then, they did so with a prayer to Yahweh not to be held accountable should Jonah be innocent. They showed great concern for life, even the life of a guilty individual, and great concern lest the innocent perish. All this contrasts with Jonah's nonchalance about the life of the citizens of great Nineveh or the perishing of over 120,000 Ninevites, who do not know their right from their left (= are innocent). This narrative contrast between a Jewish prophet and pagan sailors shows that the latter is Yahwistic at heart and the former is locked up in himself against Yahweh, which raises the question of the "circumcision of the heart" and "circumcision of the flesh"—to be dealt with in the next chapter.

When Jonah was cast into the sea, Yahweh appointed a great fish to swallow him and bring him, willy-nilly, to the site of his mission. In the heart of the great fish, Jonah uttered a psalm.[3] He seemed for a moment to have come to himself and to have realized that he had fallen into the hands of Yahweh. In his prayer (chapter 2) he changed and spoke completely differently about God and about himself than he was capable of earlier (Sauter 2003, 150). He reached the insight that "deliverance belongs to Yahweh" (Jonah 2:9)—without any qualifications and limitations. Yahweh is the One who is able and willing to rescue lives from Sheol. Yahweh hears the prayer for deliverance even of disobedient and guilty people like Jonah himself. Yahweh is teaching him that although Yahweh has power to destroy the guilty, Yahweh prefers to deliver and save. Jonah needed to preserve and integrate this insight into his dealings with Nineveh. But already Jonah strikes a jagged note. He boasts that unlike those who worship vain

---

3. For the dispute about whether this psalm is original and/or introduces harmony or dissonance into the narrative see, e.g., Fretheim 1977, 58 (the psalm fits the book well and is not a later addition, even if the author may have used already existing psalm material to compose this psalm); Trible 1994, 157-73 (the psalm is a secondary addition to the narrative and introduces dissonance, yet rhetorical analysis must examine how it functions in the present story).

idols, he, "with the voice of thanksgiving, will sacrifice to you" (Jonah 2:9). In saying this, he introduced the word *ḥesed* ("loyalty, fidelity, faithful love"), which will come into dispute in Jonah 4:2. Here he vaunts his own *ḥesed*; there he challenges the *ḥesed* of Yahweh. He clings to his *ḥesed*; those who worship idols do not. Jonah congratulates himself that it is no idol to whom he prays "for idolatry would be the abandonment of covenantal loyalty (*chesed*, v. 8). Yet that loyalty is precisely what Jonah subsequently abandons, for he has no concept except a rhetorical one that 'salvation belongs to Yahweh'" (Good 1965, 54). The fact is, Yahweh chooses to have mercy on both the idolater and the disobedient. When the commission came to Jonah *a second time* (Jonah 3:1), he arose and went to Nineveh, according to the word of Yahweh. But the narrator omits "according to the word of Yahweh" from Jonah's proclamation, "forty days more, and Nineveh shall be overthrown" (Jonah 3:4). Furthermore, Jonah omits the messenger formula ("thus says Yahweh") that indicates a prophetic message from God. The reader wonders to what extent this message conforms to "the message that I tell you" (Jonah 3:2). The people of Nineveh, however, believed God. They responded with cultic and practical acts of repentance and turning to God. Their king expressed their hope in God, saying, "who knows? God may relent and change [God's] mind" (Jonah 3:9). It is thus suggested that the Ninevites heard the proclamation of Jonah as divine threat and a call to repentance, while Jonah intended it as an announcement of ineluctable doom. They believed that God might relent and change God's mind about a threatened punishment. It may even be that the threat had a double meaning. *Hāphak*, the verb used, can also mean "to be changed" in a positive sense, from something bad to something good. The author may have read the threat as "forty days hence, Nineveh will be a different place" (Good 1965, 49). Hence, "through acts of penance and repentance, Nineveh overturns, as Jonah predicted but not as he intended. From Jonah's perspective, the divine deliverance overturns his prophecy to discredit it" (Trible 1994, 190).

What Jonah feared happened: Yahweh relented and did not bring about the threatened evil. Rather than go home westward, Jonah went out of the city and sat down east of the city, waiting to see what would become of the city (Jonah 4:5). A debate ensued between Yahweh and Jonah about the rightness of sparing Nineveh and how Yahweh might rightly govern the world. When Yahweh got Jonah to delight in a plant and be concerned about its perishing in one day, he made a chink in Jonah's armor and used the occasion to argue with him that concern springs from commitment and love and these lead to compassion. The response of Jonah is not indicated, nor what he did afterwards, but it is at this point that the challenge is thrown to the reader to re-read the entire story in the light of its end. I shall now reflect on some themes associated with mission.

Clements (1975) is somehow right to point out that the book is not "missionary" in the classical sense. Nineveh did not embrace the *torah* or reject idolatry or confess that Yahweh is the only true God. These aspects belong to evangelism, but evangelism is only one aspect of mission. The book is missionary in many other senses. Childs (1958, 61) affirms that the story reveals its kerygma at the end, namely, that God's love is not exclusively confined to Israel. He sees the story as a tale about the hearers, people chosen by God, miraculously saved from death and given another lease on life to proclaim the message of salvation to the heathen. In this reading, Jonah represents Israel in its relation to the nations. If the unwitting confession of a recalcitrant prophet suffices to convert a company of pagan sailors at sea and also great Nineveh, how much more will the conscientious proclamation of the glory of Yahweh achieve!

"Salvation belongs to Yahweh" is like the logo of a missionary's banner. In every chapter of the book, God's deliverance reaches an individual or group without regard to election or merit (Landes 1967, 30). In chapter 1, divine deliverance reaches the pagan sailors. In chapter 2 Jonah, though unrepentant, is delivered from drowning by means of a great fish. The Ninevites who believed God and repented are spared in chapter 3. In chapter 4, Yahweh works to deliver Jonah from his evil (Jonah 4:6). Mission is about God's free gift of deliverance or salvation for all peoples.

The narrative shows that the sincere cry to Yahweh is heard, no matter the ethnic or religious affiliation of the person praying. This has implications for dialogue, an aspect of mission. Prayer belongs in the fourth form of dialogue (dialogue of life, dialogue of action, dialogue of theological exchange, and dialogue of spiritual experience) (*Dialogue and Proclamation,* no. 42). Mission is not only proclamation, for the dialogue of prayer may be a way of mission. In his address to the Roman Curia after the World Day of Prayer for Peace in Assisi in 1986, John Paul II affirmed that "every authentic prayer is called forth by the Holy Spirit, who is mysteriously present in the heart of every person" (ibid., no. 27), Christian or otherwise. And since prayer is usually made according to faith traditions, it follows that the Holy Spirit is present and active in the religious life of the members of other religious traditions. Because the activity of the Holy Spirit is ordained toward Christ, in whom is centered the one plan of salvation for all humankind, mission seeks to gather all these gifts and bring them together under Christ as head (cf. Eph 1:10) (ibid., no. 28).

The fundamental aspect of mission in the narrative of Jonah occurs in the confession of the divine attributes in 4:2: "a gracious God and merciful, slow to anger, and abounding in steadfast love, and ready to relent from punishing." *Ḥannûn* ("gracious") is used of Yahweh alone in the Hebrew Bible and is often paired with *raḥûm*. The root (*ḥnn*) refers to favor manifested by the aspect of the face or the eyes of a superior toward an inferior, especially when that favor transcends the usual limits of law or custom (Freedman and Lundblom 1974, 24). *Raḥûm* (merciful, compassionate) derives from *reḥem* (womb) and refers to the tenderness that a mother feels for her child. Slow to anger is literally "long in breath," and derives from the observation that an angry person snorts and breathes hard and short. The word *ḥesed*, translated as "steadfast love," actually has no English equivalent. It represents the mutual bonds of loyalty and faithfulness of people who have given or received unexpected acts of kindness. All these qualities point to a relationship between Yahweh and people based on grace and not on merit. They are usually invoked in relation to Yahweh's covenant with Israel. It is because Yahweh is a God of this nature that Yahweh gifted Israel with the covenant in the first place. But now they are invoked also in relation to pagan Ninevites. The grace and compassion of Yahweh, as unmerited gift, are universal. They impel Yahweh to enter into relationship with people and to persevere in it despite their infidelity. In the words of Psalm 145:8, "Yahweh is tenderness and pity, slow to anger, full of faithful love. Yahweh is generous to all, [Yahweh's] tenderness embraces all [Yahweh's] creatures." Mission is rooted in divine compassion.

Yahweh originally made this confession of Godself in Exodus 34:6 (see further Dozeman 1989, 207-23) as the basis for forgiving the sin of the golden calf (Exod 32) and renewing the broken covenant of Sinai. To evoke this confession now in relation to the Ninevites means that the nations also live from the mercy of God as much as Israel itself—mission proclaims the compassion and love of God for all peoples. The original confession continued in Exodus 34:7 as follows:

> maintaining his faithful love to thousands, forgiving fault, crime and sin, and yet letting nothing go unchecked, and punishing the parent's fault in the children and in the grandchildren to the third and fourth generation.

This verse came up against the development of doctrine during the exile and needed to be either dropped or modified. By the time of Ezekiel 18:2 and Jeremiah 31:29-30, Israel no longer accepted the notion of inherited guilt. Further, the experience of the exile and the realization of how profoundly Israel depended on the free grace of Yahweh called for the substitution of "yet letting nothing go unchecked" with "ready to relent from punishing." Other texts, such as Exodus 20:5-6; Deuteronomy 5:9-10; 7:9-10, retain the formula of Exodus 34:7 only by making internal adaptations that twist the sense. For example, Exodus 20:5-6 reads, "and I punish a parent's fault in the children, the grandchildren, and the great-grandchildren *among those who hate me*," with the phrase in italics added to safeguard individual responsibility. In the final analysis, God's word to Jonah and the word of mission may be phrased in the words of Ezekiel 18:32: "I take no pleasure in the death of anyone; so repent and live."

> So why should I not be concerned about Nineveh, the great city, in which there are more than a hundred and twenty thousand people who cannot tell their right from their left, to say nothing of all the animals?

DISCUSSION

1. God had the last word, but not quite. Imagine various scenarios for the end of the story.
2. What was Jonah's problem with God?
3. The story of Jonah operates by contrasts or irony. Trace some of these.
4. What is the character of God in the Book of Jonah?
5. Prophecy is God's word to a particular context. Discuss the possible challenges of this story today.
6. How does this book relate to mission?
7. Read the Book of Ruth and analyze it from the point of view of mission.

APPENDIX: THE BOOK OF JONAH
(NRSV base with adaptations to the Hebrew)

1:1 Now *the word of Yahweh came to Jonah* son of Amittai, saying, ² *"Arise! Go to Nineveh*, that *great* city, and *cry out* against her; for their *evil* has come up before me."* ³ And Jonah *arose* but set out to flee to Tarshish from the presence of Yahweh. He *went down* to Joppa and found a ship going to Tarshish; so he paid its fare and *went down* on board, to go with them to Tarshish, away from the presence of Yahweh. ⁴ But Yahweh *hurled* a *great* wind upon the sea, and such a *great* storm came upon the sea that the ship thought it would break up. ⁵ Then the mariners were afraid, and each *cried* to his god. They *hurled* the cargo that was in the ship into the sea, to lighten it for them. Jonah, meanwhile, had *gone down* into the hold of the ship and had lain down, and was fast asleep. ⁶ The captain came and said to him, "What are you doing sound asleep? *Arise, cry out to* your god! Perhaps the god will spare us a thought so that we do *not perish.*" ⁷ The sailors said to one another, "Come, let us cast lots,

so that we may know on whose account this *evil* has come upon us." So
they cast lots, and the lot fell on Jonah. ⁸ Then they said to him, "Tell us
why this *evil* has come upon us. What is your occupation? Where do you
come from? What is your country? And of what people are you?" ⁹ "I am
a Hebrew," he replied. "I *fear* Yahweh, the God of heaven, who made the
sea and the dry land." ¹⁰ Then the men *feared* with a *great* fear, and said
to him, "What is this that you have done!" For the men knew that he was
fleeing from the presence of Yahweh, because he had told them so. ¹¹ Then
they said to him, "What shall we do to you, that the sea may quiet down
for us?" For the sea was growing more and more tempestuous. ¹² He said
to them, "Pick me up and *hurl* me into the sea; then the sea will quiet
down for you; for I know it is because of me that this *great* storm has
come upon you." ¹³ Nevertheless the men rowed hard to *return* the ship
back to land, but they could not, for the sea grew more and more stormy
against them. ¹⁴ Then they *cried out* to Yahweh, "Please, Yahweh, we pray,
do not let us *perish* on account of this man's life. Do not make us guilty
of innocent blood; for you, Yahweh, have done as it pleased you." ¹⁵ So
they picked Jonah up and *hurled* him into the sea; and the sea ceased from
its raging. ¹⁶ Then the men *feared* Yahweh with a *great* fear, and they
offered a sacrifice to Yahweh and made vows. ¹⁷ But Yahweh *appointed* a
great fish to swallow up Jonah; and Jonah was in the belly of the fish three
days and three nights.

2:1 Then Jonah prayed to Yahweh his God from the belly of the fish,
    ² saying,
"I *cried out* to Yahweh out of my distress,
        and he answered me;
out of the belly of Sheol I shouted,
        and you heard my voice.
³ You cast me into the deep,
        into the heart of the seas,
        and the flood surrounded me;
all your waves and your billows
        passed over me.
⁴ Then I said, 'I am driven away
        from your sight;
how shall I look again
        upon your holy temple?'
⁵ The waters closed in over me;
        the deep waters (*tĕhôm*) surrounded me;
weeds were wrapped around my head
        ⁶ at the roots of the mountains.
I *went down* to the land
        whose bars closed upon me forever;

yet you brought up my life from the Pit,
  Yahweh my God.
[7] As my life was ebbing away,
  I remembered Yahweh;
and my prayer came to you,
  into your holy temple.
[8] Those who worship vain idols
  forsake their *true loyalty.*
[9] But I with the voice of thanksgiving
  will sacrifice to you;
what I have vowed I will pay.
  Deliverance belongs to Yahweh!"
[10] Then Yahweh spoke to the fish, and it spewed Jonah out upon the dry land.

3:1 *The word of Yahweh came to Jonah* **a second time,** saying,
[2] *"Arise! go to Nineveh*, that *great* city, and *cry out* to it the message that I tell you." [3] And Jonah *arose* and went to Nineveh, according to the word of Yahweh. Now Nineveh was a city *great* to God, a three days' walk across. [4] Jonah began to go into the city, going a day's walk. And he *cried out*, "Forty days more, and Nineveh shall be overthrown!" [5] And the people of Nineveh believed God; they proclaimed a fast, and everyone, *great* and small, put on sackcloth. [6] When the word reached the king of Nineveh, he rose from his throne, removed his robe, covered himself with sackcloth, and sat in ashes. [7] Then he had a proclamation made in Nineveh: "By the decree of the king and his nobles: No human being or animal, no herd or flock, shall taste anything. They shall not feed, nor shall they drink water. [8] Human beings and animals shall be covered with sackcloth, and they *shall cry* mightily to God. All shall *turn* from their *evil* ways and from the violence that is in their hands. [9] Who knows? God may relent and change his mind; he may *turn* from his fierce anger, so that we do *not perish*." [10] When God saw what they did, how they *turned* from their *evil* ways, God changed his mind about the *evil* that he had said he would bring upon them; and he did not do it.

4:1 But this was a *great evil* to Jonah, and he became angry. [2] He prayed to Yahweh and said, "O Yahweh! Is not this what I said while I was still in my own country? That is why I fled to Tarshish at the beginning; for I knew that you are a gracious God and merciful, slow to anger, and abounding in *true loyalty*, and ready to relent from punishing. [3] And now, O Yahweh, please take my life from me, for it is better for me to die than to live." [4] And Yahweh said, "Is it right for you to be angry?" [5] Then Jonah went out of the city and sat down east of the city, and made a booth for himself there. He sat under it in the shade, waiting to see what would become of the city.

⁶ **Yahweh God** *appointed* a bush, and made it come up over Jonah, to give shade over his head, to save him from his discomfort/*evil*; and Jonah had *great* joy over the bush. ⁷ But when dawn came up the next day, God *appointed* a worm that attacked the bush, so that it withered. ⁸ When the sun rose, God *appointed* a sultry east wind, and the sun beat down on the head of Jonah so that he was faint and asked his soul to die. He said, "It is better for me to die than to live." ⁹ But God said to Jonah, "Is it right for you to be angry about the bush?" And he said, "Yes, angry enough to die." ¹⁰ Then Yahweh said, "You are concerned about the bush, for which you did not labor and which you did not grow; it came into being in a night and *perished* in a night. ¹¹ And should I not be concerned about Nineveh, that *great* city, in which there are more than a hundred and twenty thousand persons who do not know their right hand from their left, and also many animals?"

9

The Primacy of the
Righteousness of God

> The real Jew is the one who is inwardly a Jew, and real circumcision
> is in the heart, a thing not of the letter but of the spirit.
>   —Romans 2:29

This chapter is transitional between the aspect of "community-as-mis-
sion" and that of centripetal mission. It traces the theological foundations
of Israel's eventual decision to invite gentiles into its covenant with God.
The principal text to be studied in this chapter is Jeremiah 31:31-34 in connection with texts on the "circumcision of the heart."

Deuteronomy 10:16 orders as follows, "circumcise your hearts then and
be obstinate no longer." But Deuteronomy 30:6 says, "Yahweh will circumcise your heart and the heart of your descendants, so that you will love
Yahweh, your God, with all your heart and soul, and so will live." This
chapter will examine the trajectory from circumcision as a human work to
circumcision as divine work and gift.

The heart is the center of volition and decision and of the encounter with
God and with fellow human beings. Deuteronomy 10:16 is sanguine about
the ability of the children of Israel to curb the heart and to subject it totally
to Yahweh. Deuteronomy itself abounds in exhortations to repentance and
to keep walking in the paths of Yahweh, so that Yahweh will extend
covenant love to Israel and preserve Israel on the land. Israel can love Yahweh "with your whole heart, with all your soul, with all your strength"
(Deut 6:5). Yahweh's *torah* is doable:

> It is not in heaven, so that you need wonder, "who will go up to
> heaven for us and bring it down to us, so that we can hear and prac-
> tice it?" Nor is it beyond the seas, so that you need wonder, "who will
> cross the seas and bring it back to us, so that we can hear and prac-
> tice it?" No, the word is very near you, it is in your mouth and in
> your heart for you to put it into practice. (Deut 30:12-14)

93

The matter is different when one comes to the second text of the trajectory, Deuteronomy 30:6, which holds out the promise that "Yahweh will circumcise your heart and the heart of your descendants, so that you will love Yahweh, your God, with all your heart and soul, and so will live." Some authors, like Moshe Weinfeld (1976, 35 n. 63), purport to see no significant difference between God circumcising the heart and Israel doing it itself. It seems clear, however, that there is a shift in agency. What the earlier text assigned as a task of the people is in our text taken on by Yahweh: "God promises to give what [God] seeks" (Sarasson 1988, 111 n. 25, Prof. Ronald Hals). Besides, whereas in most of Deuteronomy repentance is the absolute precondition for divine forgiveness and Yahweh's continued relationship with Yahweh's people, this text breathes not a word about repentance. In fact, renewed divine activity is no longer dependent on the disposition of the people, whatever that may be, but on God's own nature and character. I agree with Christian Brekelmans (1981, 348-50) that the school of Jeremiah influenced the later redactions of the deuteronomistic history. I consider that Deuteronomy 30:6 has been influenced by the teaching of the exilic prophets (Jeremiah, Ezekiel and Deutero-Isaiah). Ezekiel (*passim*) expresses the doctrine of divine grace by saying that Yahweh now acts "for my name's sake." As Walter Eichrodt put it,

> Finally, the deepest mystery of true conversion is revealed in the fact that it is solely the work of God, who makes the new heart in which obstinacy is overcome by obedient receptiveness, just as the prophet has experienced within himself, and continually requests for himself. (1967, 468-69)

Deuteronomy is not alone in tracing a trajectory in the matter of the circumcising of the heart, from persons doing it themselves to Yahweh doing it for them. A similar trajectory is traced also in the Book of Isaiah. The Hebrew word pair *mišpāṭ/ṣĕdāqāh* ("justice"/"righteousness"), which, in the Hebrew Bible, stands for social justice, abounds in Isaiah 1-39 (see, e.g., 16:5; 28:17; 32:16; 33:5) but is lacking in Isaiah 40-55. In chapters 1-39, *ṣĕdāqāh* ("justice, righteousness") describes the activity of the people as they strive to live in accord with God's character and the commands of God's *torah*. In chapters 40-55, on the other hand, one meets only the word pair *ṣĕdāqāh/yĕšûʿah* ("righteousness"/"salvation"; cf. Isa 45:8 and 46:12-13), which pair is totally absent from chapters 1-39. *Ṣĕdāqāh* in this section refers to God's own righteousness only, God's faithful performance of God's covenant promises. Though not strictly bound to do so, God had to deliver God's people if God was to act rightly toward them. Both John N. Oswalt (1997, 177-91) and Rolf Rendtorff (1993, 181-89) suggest that Isaiah 56-66 had in mind, as one of the aims of that redaction, to synthesize these divergent views on righteousness in chapters 1-39 and 40-55. The synthesis appears already in 56:1: "act with justice [ṣĕdāqāh], for soon my salvation will come and my saving justice [ṣĕdāqāh] be manifest." In other words, "the righteous living is required but it will now be a gift of God's grace" (Oswalt 1997, 190).

An identical trajectory can be pursued in Ezekiel. Suffice it to mention here the shift from Ezekiel 18:31, "make yourselves a new heart and a new spirit," to 36:26, "I shall give you a new heart and put a new spirit in you." What is commanded in one is freely given in the other.

Between the two poles of the above trajectory supervened what is easily the most defining event for Israel, the catastrophe of the destruction of temple and city and the terrible experience of exile from the land. This experience of exile has so deeply marked the consciousness of Israel that Jacob Neusner (1997, 221) can say that "the paradigm of exile and return contains all Judaisms over all time, to the present." It is a paradigm of "death and resurrection," which makes it clear that the life of Israel was never to be taken for granted but always to be received as gift (ibid., 223). The people of Judah were like lifeless and dry bones lying on the floor of the valley (Ezek 37:4) to which life can come only by the Spirit of God breathing afresh into them the breath of life.

As a bilateral covenant, the Sinai covenant depended on mutual loyalty and faithfulness between Yahweh and Israel. Though Yahweh might remain faithful, the disloyalty of Israel would be enough to invalidate the entire covenant. Should the people reject Yahweh, they would thereby render the covenant invalid for themselves. They would cut themselves off from the promises and blessings of the covenant, beginning with the possession of the land. The fact of the exile of the northern kingdom in 722 B.C.E. and of the southern kingdom in 587 B.C.E. was proof that Israel was now under the curse of the covenant. The warnings of the prophets, including Jeremiah and Ezekiel, had now been realized. Israel was now without a covenant and without the divinely ordained means (temple and sacrifices) of atoning for her covenantal sins. It is true that in the mind of P the covenant was never, and could never be, invalidated, but for P the covenant was the unconditional covenant with Abraham. P has no covenant at Sinai, only the commands for erecting the tabernacle.

At the nadir, the relationship of Israel and Yahweh came down to the question whether and how Israel might have a new existence with Yahweh (McConville 1993, 174).[1] Jeremiah and Ezekiel, who had led the chorus of indictment of Israel before the catastrophe, now became insistent on a new and undreamed-of action of Yahweh, nothing short of a new creation. Deutero-Isaiah would later join the new chorus. The Sinai covenant contained the terms of its dissolution, but not those of its resolution (Raitt

---

1. McConville considers this question the organizing question of the Book of Jeremiah.

1977, 150). As God of the covenant and God above the covenant, Yahweh
had been chafing under the *quid pro quo* logic of the Sinai covenant (ibid.,
99). No less than Israel, Yahweh was struggling with the problem of the
evil of the human heart and the necessity to punish and looking for fresh
alternatives. The solution, as Thomas M. Raitt (1977, 100) notes beautifully, was that Yahweh created new rules and new possibilities, so that
"Israel's defeats are no longer going to be God's defeats." The cycle of disobedience–punishment–return must be arrested. God's act of deliverance
will create both its preconditions and its goals. No longer will there be con-
ditionality about total forgiveness or about the eternal duration of a newly
instituted covenant. As in earlier times, the prior grace of exodus and liberation elicited the adherence of the people to Yahweh, their Savior, so now
a new act of goodwill and grace on the part of Yahweh will elicit the "turning" of the people to Yahweh and their abiding faithfulness to their God.
The trajectory traced above in Deuteronomy and Isaiah actually repro-
duces the shift in Jeremiah and Ezekiel from reposing faith in the people's
repentance as precondition for divine forgiveness to their unbounded faith
in the initiative of Yahweh. For reasons of space, we shall concentrate here
only on the message of God's righteousness in the Book of Jeremiah.

The trajectory takes off from Jeremiah 4:4, which introduces the language of the circumcision of the heart. In that text, circumcision of the
heart is something that people can and should do for themselves: "circumcise yourselves to Yahweh, remove the foreskin of your hearts, O people of
Judah and inhabitants of Jerusalem." Circumcision as the rite of the
removal of the foreskin was a cultural element among the peoples of Palestine, except the Philistines. It became a cultural and religious marker of
Israel during the exile, when the children of Israel were the only circumcised people in their milieu. At the same time, the task of preserving the
religion and the traditions of Israel fell to the family. Symbols that the family could control now came to represent abiding loyalty to the faith and tradition of Israel, namely, Sabbath, circumcision, and food laws. These
symbols now took on importance as religious markers. Within the poly-
theistic context of Babylon, circumcision became the symbol of the total
offering of the person to Yahweh. Some children of Israel in exile assimilated to the foreign culture and abandoned their traditions and faith in
Yahweh. These were circumcised "in the flesh," but not "in the heart." To
be circumcised in heart was to bind one's inner emotions and outward conduct securely to Yahweh and to Yahweh's *torah*.

Jeremiah 3:1-5 had argued that after what Israel and Judah had done,
return to Yahweh was impossible and illegal. Yahweh could not take back
a divorced and remarried bride (cf. Deut 14:1-4). What is more, the guilty
bride remained obstinate in her ways and would not even blush. Yet Yahweh was determined to have the bride back. An appeal went forth from
Yahweh: "come back, disloyal children" (Jer 3:14), "come back disloyal

sons, I want to heal your disloyalty" (Jer 3:22). This was the first indication in the Book of Jeremiah that Yahweh was breaking through the constraints of the Sinai covenant, prefaced as it was on merit. As Raitt (1977, 288) said beautifully, "the Exile was a time for the liberation of God." The appeal of Yahweh stirred the beginnings of a response in the recalcitrant bride:

> we are here, we are coming to you, for you are Yahweh our God. The hills are a delusion after all, so is the tumult of the mountains. Yahweh our God is, after all, the saving of Israel. (Jer 3:22-23)

Jeremiah 4:1-4 now plots the "road map" back to Yahweh. One of the conditions is that Israel should circumcise itself "*for Yahweh*" and remove the foreskin of "*your hearts.*" Israel was urged to fulfill the inward and total gift of self symbolized by the outward rite, and in this manner to be really a people "for Yahweh." Their uncircumcised hearts had made them impervious to divine warnings and instruction. Their ears were uncircumcised (Jer 6:10), and thus they were unable to understand and take to heart Yahweh's word.

The religious distinction between the two types of circumcision appears explicitly in Jeremiah 9:24-25:

> look, the days are coming, Yahweh declares, when I shall punish all who are circumcised only in the flesh; Egypt, Judah, Edom, the Ammonites, Moab, and all the men with shaven temples who live in the desert. For all those nations, and the whole house of Israel too, are uncircumcised at heart.[2]

It would have startled Jeremiah's audience in Judah to find themselves placed on the same level with Edom and Egypt, as far as relation with Yahweh was concerned. The text described them all as *mûl bě'orlāh*. This intended oxymoron is translated literally as "circumcised with foreskin," meaning "circumcised, yet uncircumcised" (Cassuto 1973, 198). The explanation of the pun is that they were all circumcised in the flesh and not in the heart. A second point worthy of note is that Jeremiah applies the saying to the whole house of Israel. All were guilty of covenant disloyalty; all were due for punishment. The physical rite takes its real meaning from the inner disposition of heart that it signifies (Le Déaut 1981, 183); take away this inner disposition and the physical rite lacks all religious meaning. As Paul would articulate it later, "the real Jew is the one who is inwardly a

---

2. LXX Jer 9:26b: "for all the gentiles are uncircumcised in flesh, and all the house of Israel are uncircumcised in their hearts."

Jew, and real circumcision is in the heart, a thing not of the letter but of the spirit" (Rom 2:29). A final point is that the text envisages the possibility of these other nations being circumcised in heart and thus pleasing to God. Peter will draw this conclusion with respect to the house of Cornelius when he says, "God made no distinction between them and us, since he purified their hearts by faith" (Acts 15:9). In the new dispensation, circumcision of the heart is effected through faith in Christ.

The belief that Yahweh will act in the manner depicted above led to a series of illogical statements, what J. G. McConville (1993, 95) terms the "theology of illogical grace." One of these is in Jeremiah 30:15-17. Jeremiah 30:15 is an indictment that complains, "Why cry out about your wound? Your pain is incurable! Because of your great guilt and countless sins I have treated you like this." Then 30:16 rejoins, "*Therefore*, all those who devoured you will be devoured. . . . For I shall restore you to health, and heal your wounds, Yahweh declares." Where one expected an enunciation of (further) punishment, Yahweh promised the divine healing action instead. Yahweh will act for Judah, it seems, precisely because of her inability to escape the consequences of her guilt (ibid.).

Jeremiah 24 narrates the vision of the two baskets of figs—one basket containing excellent figs, the other very bad figs. The time of the vision was soon after the exile of 597 B.C.E. The excellent figs were the exiles with Jeconiah. To them Yahweh promised in v. 7: "I shall give them a heart to acknowledge that I am Yahweh. They will be my people and I shall be their God, for they will return to me with all their heart." The translation of Jeremiah Unterman (1987, 79) better underlines the point at issue: "I will give them a heart to be obedient to me because (*kî*) I am Yahweh." For Israel to return to Yahweh with all her heart, it was necessary for Yahweh first to make a gift to Israel of a heart wholly devoted to Yahweh! Jeremiah felt acutely the problem of the inconstancy of the heart of humankind: "the heart is more devious than any other thing and is depraved; who can pierce its secrets?" (Jer 17:9). In fact, just as the Ethiopian cannot change his skin nor the leopard his spots, Israel cannot do right, being so accustomed to wrong (Jer 13:23). The wound of the children of Israel is incurable (Jer 30:12-13; cf. 14:17; 15:18), and nothing but divine "heart surgery" (the phrase is Jacob Milgrom's) will cure it. That surgery is promised in 31:31-34, which pledges that "within them I shall plant my Law, writing it on their hearts" (v. 33). Raitt (1977, 116-19) outlines a series of elements that characterize this radical deliverance being promised by Yahweh. Deliverance is always in tension with judgment, which is never forgotten. No conditions are attached, however; God gives to people or creates in them a new capacity to respond to God. God's initiative ("I will") precedes human initiative.

Jeremiah 31:23-40 functions as the prose conclusion to the poetic unit in chapters 30-31, usually called the Book of Consolation. The concluding prose unit of 31:23-40 is linked by the repetition of the phrase "the days are coming" (vv. 27, 31, 33, 38) and the element of "reversal" in each of the subunits. *No longer* will people say, "the fathers have eaten unripe grapes, the children's teeth are set on edge" (v. 29), rather from now on personal responsibility before God will replace collective retribution. The new covenant will *not be like* the "covenant I made with their ancestors" (v. 32), which they broke. Rather, it will never be broken. *Never again* will the rebuilt city be destroyed or demolished (v. 40), for the whole city, including the Kidron Valley, which used to be desecrated by burning corpses, will be consecrated to Yahweh forever. Within this context of reversals, Jeremiah 31:31-34 depicts a "new covenant" as the sole action of Yahweh. Not once is this action of Yahweh grounded in human repentance or any prior work of Israel; rather the promise is totally unconditioned. It is not even mentioned, as in Isa 40:2, that Israel's guilt has been atoned for, Israel having received from the hand of Yahweh double punishment for all her sins. Yahweh outlines a series of divine actions that will make possible continued relations with Israel. "I shall forgive their guilt and never more call their sin to mind" (v. 34). The verb used is *sālaḥ*; which always has God as subject. Yahweh changes the strategy in dealing with people. First, divine forgiveness will precede the people's act of return to God and the giving of the new covenant. "God does not forgive them because they are clean; rather, they are clean because [God] forgives" (Shead 2000, 40). Second, guilt will no longer lead to destruction, as it did under the Sinai covenant. Andrew Shead (2000, 41) raises the question whether this forgiveness will be once-for all or ongoing. The answer would seem to be in the action of Yahweh to follow. Yahweh promises that "within them I shall plant my Law, writing it on their heart" (v. 33). W. L. Holladay (1989, 198) says that the singular "their heart" refers to the corporate will and intention of the people. Jeremiah 32:39 says the same thing in another way: "I shall give them singleness of heart and singleness of conduct, so that they will always fear me." In 17:1, "the sin of Judah is written with an iron pen, engraved with a diamond point, on the tablet of their heart and on the horns of their altars." God now replaces the heart of sin and rebellion with a heart that is pliable and totally open to God and to God's will. This promise appears equivalently in Deut 30:6 in the image of God circumcising the hearts of the children of Israel. Ezekiel 36:26 uses the image of the stony heart: "I shall remove the heart of stone from your bodies and give you a heart of flesh instead." As said earlier, the heart in Hebrew thinking is the center of volition and decision and of the discerning encounter with God. In the light of all this, what Yahweh promises in the texts we have just seen is nothing short of the re-creation of humanity in such manner that humans will be totally and consistently faithful to Yahweh. What the *torah* commanded from outside will now be the very object of the desire of the human heart! The result will be human beings who delight in what God wills. Because all will strain from within after devotion to Yahweh and service of Yahweh, the teaching office will prove otiose. The new covenant will never be broken, and God will really and forever be their God and they God's people. The exile will never happen again, for Israel will forever prove to be faithful and loyal covenant partners of Yahweh. It is noteworthy that 31:31-34 focuses exclusively on the spiritual relationship between Yahweh and Israel/Judah and contains no promises of the repossession of the land, as in 32:37, 41. As such, all peoples and nations may discover themselves in this text.

The oracle of Jeremiah 31:31-34 was originally addressed to "the house of Israel," but in the aftermath of the events of 587 B.C.E. the addressees have been expanded to include "the house of Judah." Talk of the "ancestors" in v. 32 makes it clear that the children of Israel were being directly addressed. It is clear, however, that the promise is not exclusive to them. The "ancestors" were linked with the broken covenant, whereas God is now doing a new thing. There is nothing in the promise of the new covenant that may not apply to other nations. The promised action of Yahweh is not grounded, as often elsewhere, in Yahweh's covenant fidelity to Israel or the divine promise or oath to the ancestors of Israel. The focus is uniquely on the nature and character of Yahweh and on Yahweh's unconditioned mercy. Such a focus opens the horizon of the text indefinitely and implicitly universalizes the promised action of God. Thus, the words of Yahweh in our text call to mind the text of Wisdom 11:24-25: "you love all things that exist, and detest none of the things that you have made. . . . You spare all things, for they are yours, O Lord, you who love the living."

In the tradition of the Old Testament, the eschatological times will be a time of gathering together of all nations unto Yahweh (Zech 14:9). Eschatological "Israel" will embrace the whole world, as already depicted in Jeremiah 3:14-18. In the words of Shead,

> the cleansing of Israel will make her the nation of God in the middle of [God's] creation, to which—as the book's frame indicates—the nations will flow, merging into the eschatological nation which is called Israel but is made up of all peoples. Thus Israel continues, but her continuation is bound up with God's purposes for the whole cosmos. (2000, 42-43)

CONCLUSION

What has been treated in this chapter underlines two aspects of mission. First, mission is all God's work (*missio Dei*) in which we share. Paul would later say of God's action in Christ that "God was in Christ reconciling the world to himself, not holding anyone's faults against them, but entrusting to us the message of reconciliation" (2 Cor 5:19). The fact is that God has been at the work of reconciliation already from the beginning of creation.

The second is that mission is a service of thanksgiving to God. Where the prior justifying action of God is recognized and acknowledged, mission necessarily follows as the outburst of joy and thanksgiving in the service of proclaiming and sharing the mighty deeds of God.

Israel needed the realization of the primacy of God's righteousness before she could open her doors to gentiles and invite them to share in her covenant with God. The process of Israel's opening the covenant to gentiles will be traced in the chapters to follow.

DISCUSSION

1. Discuss the theme of the "circumcision of the heart."
2. Argue for the validity of the usual Jewish interpretation of Jeremiah 31:31-34.
3. As a Christian, try to show the validity of your interpretation of Jeremiah 31:31-34 to a person of the Jewish faith.
4. What is the *torah* that Yahweh will put in the hearts of recreated humanity?
5. What is new in the "new covenant"?

10

"Sing to Yahweh all the earth"

Psalm 96

Then the glory of Yahweh will be revealed and all humanity will see
it together.

—Isaiah 40:5

The ultimate goal of mission in Orthodox Christianity is that the glory
of God may fill the universe (Stamoolis 1986, 49, 52). When the glory of
God encounters human beings, it draws forth praise. The glory and praise
of God are thus the single aim of mission. Praise is confessional (Mays
1994a, 65-66). Other religions enthrone the icon of their gods in their sanctuaries, and thus people can go there "to see the face of god." But Israel's
God is "enthroned on the praises of Israel" (Ps 22:3 NRSV). Israel has no
icons of Yahweh but only its praise in which to present to itself and all the
world the person and character of its God. Israel does this by telling abroad
what its God has done for it and been for it, and how this God is in Godself. Israel's praise thus assumes an evangelical function: "it witnesses to the
present and coming reign of the Lord. It finds in its very content the motive
for its openness and outreach" (Mays 1994a, 68).

Psalm 96 constitutes, with Psalms 93-100, the editorial center of Book
IV of the Psalter, and Book IV is itself the editorial center of the Psalter.[1] Its
perspective is universalistic. Common to these psalms is the theme of the
universal reign of God, which is to be realized primarily through justice
and righteousness. Books I-III of the Psalter are dominated by personal
lament. With Book IV begins the crescendo of praise that finds completion
in Psalm 150, where Yahweh is praised with every instrument by all people and all things in the universe. Books I-III constitute the messianic
Psalter in that the hope in them is focused mostly on the Davidic dynasty.

---

1. For much of this last section, see Gerald H. Wilson (1992, 129-42).

Books IV and V constitute the theocratic Psalter in that they transpose the hopes for deliverance onto God. After the hopes in human kingship and the covenant with David have been dashed (Ps 89), Psalm 90 and the following psalms begin to point Israel away from reliance on inadequate human kings and kingdoms to the adequacy of Yahweh, the rock of refuge available even before the monarchy. Psalms 93, 96-99 thus celebrate the kingship of Yahweh, who, unlike human kings, rules forever. All these psalms agree that Yahweh's future reign is a world empire encompassing all nations (Gunkel and Begrich 1998, 69). And they turn the hopes of Israel toward this coming universal reign of Yahweh and the pilgrimage of the nations to Yahweh in Zion.

Psalm 96 summons all the earth to come and worship Yahweh on Yahweh's holy mountain and to tremble before Yahweh, that is, to submit to Yahweh's rule emanating from Zion. Isaiah 40:5 promised that "then the glory of Yahweh will be revealed and all humanity will see it together" (Isa 40:5). In P, Yahweh's glory (*kābôd*) means the effulgence of Yahweh's divine presence, which is manifested in a bright cloud covering the temple. Here, however, the manifestation of Yahweh's glory refers to the public accomplishment and acknowledgment of Yahweh's power and deeds (Rendtorff 1968, 46). The prophet of the exile referred in particular to the imminent restoration of God's people to their land, a deed that will reveal Yahweh's power and glory as the unique God of all the earth. Though the marvelous works are done on behalf of Israel, they manifest the inner nature of Yahweh in a manner that attracts the nations also. Psalm 19:1 asserts that "the heavens declare the glory of God, the vault of the heavens proclaims [God's] handiwork." So, not only history but also nature and its courses manifest something of Yahweh and invite all peoples to the praise of God.

Psalm 96 is subtle in the way it depicts the onward march of praise. This psalm actually consists of two psalms, vv. 1-6 and vv. 7-13, that have been joined together. Verses 1-6 are a typical hymn, with the call to praise and the motive for praise. Verses 7-13 have the elements of a psalm of enthronement of Yahweh. The pattern repeated in each section of the composite psalm is as follows. "All the earth" or the "families of nations" are first called upon to praise Yahweh; then Israel is summoned to publish among them the content of this praise. In v. 10 this takes the form of inviting Israel to "say among the nations, 'Yahweh is king.'" Israel becomes the medium of praise of Yahweh by the nations. The families of nations can confess Yahweh because Israel has verbally professed and visibly demonstrated her God's unparalled character (Marlowe 1998, 451).

In vv. 1-6, all the earth is called upon to sing a new song to Yahweh (v. 1), Israel's God. A new song is needed when the old songs no longer suffice. In African villages a new song is composed to enshrine the memory of particularly significant events and persons. The word "new" in Yahweh's relations with Israel is a feature of the period of the exile. Second Isaiah sang of the "new things" that will replace the "former things" (Isa 43:19; 48:6). Jeremiah 31:31-34 sang of the "new covenant," and Ezekiel 36:26 of a "new heart and new spirit." What is "new" in the psalm is a deed of salvation by Yahweh (v. 2): "proclaim his salvation day to day (v. 2). The salvation is achieved on Israel's behalf—hence the TEV translation, "proclaim every day the good news *that he has saved us*" (italics mine). The verb used is *baśśĕrû*, the verb behind the New Testament verb *euangelizomai*; it means "to proclaim good news." Israel is thus called upon to proclaim the "gospel" to all the earth. The good news is twofold, namely, Yahweh is Savior and Creator of the heavens and everything (v. 5). From Yahweh's deliverance of Israel the nations can see the results of Yahweh's reign and submit to Yahweh, "who by the deliverance of Israel re-establishes the disrupted world order—before the eyes of all nations" (Zenger 2000, 174). But it is not only for Israel that Yahweh does deeds of salvation. Yahweh also does "marvels for every people" (v. 3).

The second section, vv. 7-13, calls upon the families of the nations to give Yahweh glory and power, the glory due Yahweh's name (v. 7). Following the pattern described above, it then summons Israel to publish among the nations that "Yahweh is king" (v. 10). The kingship of Yahweh is founded on the same twofold fact of creation and salvation (in chiastic order) as above. Yahweh set the world firm, so that it cannot totter, and Yahweh will judge the nations with justice (v. 10). The nations are given a new reason for praise—Yahweh means to rule over all, and this rule of Yahweh means justice for all.

The phrase *Yhwh māl'āk*, can be rendered "Yahweh is king" or "Yahweh has become king." The latter is the acclamation at the accession of a new king (2 Sam 15:10). In the process of enthronement of a new king, the new ruler was anointed at a holy site by a priest and was crowned. Then in celebratory parade he ascended the throne and seated himself. All present prostrated before him and kissed his feet. There was joy in the entire kingdom; trumpets announced the fact of accession, and a herald carried the message all through the land: "he has become king." All who heard it clapped and applauded (Gunkel and Begrich 1998, 67). In the creation myths, the assembly of the gods so acclaimed Marduk, when, having subdued his enemies, he built himself a temple and palace and sat on his throne.

First Chronicles 16:23-33 includes much of Psalm 96 within a liturgy ushering the Ark into the temple. The Ark was considered the throne of Yahweh, and so the enthronement of the Ark in the temple would represent the enthronement of Yahweh. The exclamation *Yhwh māl'āk*, would thus have been heard in the liturgy as "Yahweh has become king"—in the very liturgy itself. It is not clear that there was ever an annual festival of the enthronement of Yahweh, but the enthronement psalms were probably influenced by the Babylonian pattern of the annual enthronement of the king who represented the rule of Marduk.

Yahweh is coming to judge and rule the earth in righteousness and faith-fulness. *Šāphaṭ* can mean both "to judge" and "to rule," and both senses are to be understood here. By judgment, Yahweh removes every evil; by jus-tice, Yahweh vindicates the righteous and the oppressed poor. The new government that Yahweh is establishing requires a new orientation, a new power structure, and a new value center (Brueggemann 1984, 144-46). The families of nations are invited to affirm Yahweh's glory and power (v. 7). Yahweh's power consists in righteousness (*ṣedeq*) and faithfulness (*'ĕmûnāh*). Faithfulness derives from the root *'mn* ("to be stable, stead-fast"). It is the inner attitude of steadfastness in doing good and the con-stancy toward others in a relationship with oneself. All through its history, Israel has found that it could depend on Yahweh. Psalm 96 declares that in Yahweh's coming and universal rule the nations too will find Yahweh steadfast and constant in their favor. The coming and rule of Yahweh are focused on Yahweh's courts in Zion, but they are of universal import: the "coincidence of cultic and cosmic coming and appearing [means that] from the particularity of the elect Israel, Yahweh emerges in universal revela-tion" (Kraus 1989, 255).

The world is set firm; it cannot be moved (v. 10). Creation was in fact the first act of redemption. For in the beginning the "many waters" of chaos threatened to engulf the universe. But Yahweh intervened and estab-lished the universe on firm foundations (Ps 93:4). Historical persons and events may seek to clothe themselves in the garments of primeval chaos and to challenge this creative act of Yahweh, but they will never prevail against Yahweh, creator and ruler of the universe. The families of nations have nothing to fear, for they are assured security under Yahweh. They should therefore abandon their gods, who are mere idols, unable to guarantee their salvation (v. 4).

The salvation of God is not only for humans, but includes the entire ecosystem. "Let the heavens rejoice and earth be glad! Let the sea thunder, and all it holds! Let the countryside exult, and all that is in it, and all the trees of the forest cry out for joy" (vv. 11-12). The wholeness of all creation belongs to the vision of the reign of God, and it is to this reign that the church witnesses in its mission to preach the gospel to every creature (Ruether 1999, 121).

The marvelous works that the families of the nations have witnessed pose the question of who truly is God, who truly controls nature and his-tory. The deeds of Yahweh expose the inanity of the gods of the peoples. These are now shown up as *'ĕlîlîm*, (*'ĕlîl* is the diminutive of El/god) "little nothings." They are worthless and ineffective. They have no control over history or over people's fate. The families of nations are thus invited to turn from their idols to the praise and worship of the One whose rule will mean stability and equity for all peoples. They will thus come to a realization that was already the possession of the "children of God" in Psalm 29, namely, that Yahweh is enthroned over the flood (*mabbûl*), enthroned as king forever (Ps 29:10). The *mabbûl* referred to the waters over which God sat on God's heavenly throne. Enthroned over the heavenly ocean, Yahweh's authority in the heavenly sphere is acknowledged by all the heavenly beings. Psalm 29 ended with Israel in the temple taking up the chorus of glory to God intoned by the heavenly choir. Psalm 96 picks up the chorus and extends it to all families of the earth. God's name is to be hallowed on earth as it is in heaven!

Praise finds completion in worship. The peoples of the earth, who so praise God, need to profess their allegiance and loyalty in act. Having recognized the power and glory of Yahweh in Yahweh's deeds for Israel and marvels on their own behalf, they are invited to contemplate Yahweh in Yahweh's sanctuary abode. They are to put on the special dress worn on holy occasions and for entry into hallowed space. Here I read with the NAB, which has "worship the Lord in holy attire." They are to come into the temple precincts with their offering (*minḥāh*), which is the tribute of a subject people. There is ample evidence that gentiles participated in temple worship in Jerusalem (Vermes and Millar 1979, 309). Sacrifice was offered by and for gentiles as attested by the fact that one of the first acts of the Jewish Revolt in 66 C.E. was to declare that no more sacrifices were acceptable from gentiles (ibid., 310). Already 1 Kings 8:41-43 spoke of the foreigner who would come from a distant country to pray in the temple because he was attracted to Yahweh's name. Josephus (*Wars of the Jews* 5.1.3) speaks of the temple as "esteemed holy by all [hu]mankind" and its altar as "venerable among all [people], both Greeks and Barbarians" (Whiston 1987, 697).

The psalmist calls on Israel and the nations to be united in the worship of the one God, Yahweh. The gentiles may be restricted only to the "courts," that is, the courtyards of the temple, which are open to non-Jews, yet the "wall of separation" has begun to crumble, if not in fact, surely in the religious imagination.

The praise and worship of the nations, which the prophets predicted of the eschatological future, are transferred to the present in our psalm (Gunkel and Begrich 1998, 25).

The coming of Yahweh is, first of all, *liturgical*: the royal glory and power of Yahweh are made manifest to the worshipers, who accordingly prostrate in obedient submission to their King. The very assembly of praise enacts the reign of God, for the assembly thereby recognizes itself as servants coming into the presence of their lord to acknowledge Yahweh's rule and to declare their fealty to Yahweh (Mays 1994a, 64). As Walter Brueggemann affirms, "liturgy is not play acting, but is the evocation of an alternative reality that comes into play in the very moment of the liturgy"

(1984, 144). The alternative reality is that of a society that has been made right under God—true worship leads to true society. Liturgy is the beginning of the dismantling of the old order of injustice and faithlessness (ibid., 146). Insofar as Israel and the families of nations participate in the worship of Yahweh they are sharing in the dismantling of the old order and the emergence of the new order under Yahweh.

But the coming of Yahweh is at the same time *eschatological*. Cultic gatherings at the temple anticipate the gathering of the nations and peoples of the earth to the shrine of Israel's God, who is over the nations (Willis 1997, 302). The eschatological promise is that all the earth will also enjoy the just effects of the rule of Yahweh.

In a subtle manner, Psalm 96 merges the praise of "all the earth" and that of Israel. The Israelite who makes such an "oratorical outreach" (Marlowe 1998, 451) is being invited to pull down the wall of separation that continued to keep apart fellow worshipers of Yahweh.

CONCLUSION

The twofold theme of proclamation in this psalm is Yahweh as creator and savior. As creator, Yahweh made the heavens and both founded the earth and secured it. Psalm 100:3 will describe this fact more fully when it has Israel and the families of nations who have come to worship say that Yahweh "made us, we belong to [Yahweh], his people, the flock of [Yahweh's] sheepfold." As savior, Yahweh has done deeds of deliverance for Israel and marvels for every people (v. 3). Mission proclaims the marvelous deeds of God on behalf of creation.

Psalm 96 proclaims loud and clear that "the kingdom of God is near" (Mark 1:15). Yahweh, the only creator and savior of the world, has taken up active rule over Israel in Zion. Israel is the people of Yahweh who acknowledge Yahweh's rule in life and worship and in so doing reveal Yahweh to the nations. The rule of Yahweh over Israel is the harbinger of Yahweh's universal rule over all creation. It is the duty of this people to proclaim Yahweh's rule among the nations and to bring them into subjection to it. Mission is in the service of the universal reign of God.

The coming and universal reign of God is designated as one of justice and equity. It will equally benefit material creation, even the trees of the forest. It therefore envisages both the salvation of human societies and the wholeness of creation. The church's mission of redemption cannot therefore be divorced from justice in society and the healing of the wounds wrought by an exploitative human industrial system (Ruether 1999, 111).

The psalm links the glory of God with acts of salvation for Israel and for all creation. Justice and faithfulness define the rule of Yahweh; hence, all have cause for joy, including the trees of the forest. The ultimate goal of mission is that the glory of Yahweh may fill the universe. By worship and praise and by modeling a community of justice and righteousness, Israel plays some part in extending the glory of God. But this is not enough, for God's glory can be fully realized only when the families of nations share fully together in the worship of Yahweh and in life with Yahweh. The internal dynamism of the psalm moves toward this future reality. The families of nations are invited to renounce idolatry (v. 4). They are to come with the tribute of a subject people to worship Yahweh, the king of the universe (v. 8). Perhaps the psalm already envisaged the acceptance of "god-fearers," and the members of the families of nations may thus worship Yahweh in that category. But if the psalm was written before Isaiah 56:1-8 (see chapter 12), they would not have been able to enter the Holy Place to worship Yahweh on the same terms as Israel. Chapter 12 will trace how this became possible.

How did the psalmist see the universal rule of Yahweh as one of justice and equity for all peoples? One possible answer is furnished in the next chapter, where the nations refer their quarrels to Yahweh for adjudication. Streaming to Zion, the seat of Yahweh, the nations learn Yahweh's *torah* and learn to walk in Yahweh's ways, with the result that they beat their swords into ploughshares.

DISCUSSION

1. Locate Psalm 96 within the structure of the Psalter.
2. Describe the pattern and context of the enthronement psalms.
3. How is praise of Yahweh evangelical and missionary?
4. What could "Yahweh has become king" mean in the context of this psalm?
5. Liturgy evokes an alternative reality (Brueggemann). Discuss this dictum in relation to Psalm 96.

11

Zion, Center for World Peace and Moral Center of the World

Isaiah 2:2-5

The nations are attracted to Zion, the spiritual center, because the teaching that goes forth from that source appeals to the deepest human longings for *shalom* (peace, welfare).
—B. W. Anderson, "A Worldwide Pilgrimage to Jerusalem," 16

The last chapter ended with the announcement of a universal rule of Yahweh in justice and faithfulness. But this raised the question of how Yahweh's just rule over the families of nations might be realized. Isaiah 2:2-5 depicts one possible scenario. It is also the classical text for centripetal mission in the Old Testament.

THE UNIT AND ITS CONTEXT

Isaiah 2:2-5 is usually called the "pilgrimage of the nations to Zion." The unit is found, with divergent conclusions, also in Micah 4:1-5. It does not serve our purposes to enter into the debate as to which is primary or whether both depend on a common tradition. We shall rather examine the text of Isaiah 2:2-5 within its own context. Some scholars end the unit at v. 4, but v. 5, though secondary, seems to serve as a transition. It is meant both to conclude the unit and, through the phrase "house of Jacob," to link up with the next unit, Isaiah 2:6-22.

Isaiah 2:1 is obviously the superscription for a collection that stretches from Isaiah 2 to 12, a collection framed with words of hope and salvation for Zion (2:2-4 and 12:1-6). Isaiah 1 is generally understood as programmatic for the entire book of Isaiah, which is focused on the fortunes of Zion (Judah and Jerusalem), the judgment on Zion (Isa 1:21-25), and the hopes for Zion's redemption (Isa 1:26-28). The judgment on her is interpreted as a "purging" already in Isaiah 1:25, so that Zion will again become the "faithful city" (1:28). It is of such a purged and faithful Zion that the "vision" of 2:2-5 speaks. It is a vision for the end-time, a time of lasting salvation for Zion.

Scholars are equally divided as to the dating of this unit. Gerhard von Rad (1966, 233) considers the unit authentic and says that "this is the first and also the earliest expression of a belief in the eschatological glorification of the holy mountain and of its significance for the redemption of the entire world." It may be the earliest expression of a belief in the eschatological glorification of Mount Zion, but a convergence of indications suggests the exilic or postexilic period. The entire thought world of the unit has no parallel in parts of the Book of Isaiah that definitely derive from the eighth-century prophet (Wildberger 1957, 66). Rather, they occur in prophetic books or parts thereof that clearly belong to the exilic period and after. The idea of universal peace and reconciliation, even with the animal world, does appear in Isaiah 11:6-9 and 65:25, but most scholars do not attribute these units to the eighth-century prophet. One may mention other indications of exilic or postexilic authorship. The idea of temple and Zion as not uniquely for Israel but also for the nations, the idea of the religious instruction of humanity and of Yahweh as teacher (as contrasted with Lord and Sovereign of the world)—these are usually considered late. Add to these the use of באחרית הימים (at the end of days), usually considered postexilic, and of the late wisdom term, ארח ("path") (Wildberger 1957, 66).

The unit probably derives from the final stages of the edition of Isaiah. The entire book of Isaiah is framed with words of hope. In doing this, the editors reshaped the prophet Isaiah from a prophet of doom to a prophet of salvation for Zion. The book as a whole moves toward the eschaton, which is depicted as a new cosmos centered on a new Jerusalem/Zion (Webb 1990, 68). It thus unfolds the process of Yahweh's worldwide sovereignty based in Zion. Purified Zion becomes the center for Yahweh's worldwide rule, the locus of revelation to Israel and all the nations (Sweeney 1996a, 64).

THE CULTURAL BACKGROUND

The myth of the "cosmic mountain" (Clifford 1972) was a worldview current in the ancient Near East of which Israel was a part. For example, Psalm 48:1-2 (NIV) describes Mount Zion as "beautiful in its loftiness, the joy of the whole earth. Like the utmost heights of Zaphon is Mount Zion, the city of the Great King." In actual elevation, Mount Zion is dwarfed by the Mount of Olives. Yet in the myth it becomes Mount Zaphon, a holy mountain in the northern Syrian-Palestinian border that was considered the highest of the mountains. In Ugaritic poems, this mountain was considered the mountain of the gods, where they assembled and issued decrees for the government of the world (see Lipinski 1974, 435-43). In the myth, Mount Zion replaced Mount Zaphon as the seat of divinity. In the earliest tradition of Israel, Yahweh was God of Sinai (Exod 19). But with the establishment of the Ark in Solomon's temple, Yahweh became the one "who dwells on Mount Zion." Thus

> Zion became the prime locus of theophany, the home of YHWH, the seat of [Yahweh's] government, from which [Yahweh] promulgated decrees and at which Israel renewed her partnership in covenant with [Yahweh]. (Levenson 1985, 187)

The cosmic mountain lies at the center of the world, and everything takes its bearing from it (Levenson 1985, 115). Ezekiel 5:5 evoked this myth when it said of Jerusalem, "this is Jerusalem, which I have placed in the middle of the nations, surrounded with foreign countries." Ezekiel 38:12 speaks of the Israelites gathered from the nations as living "at the Navel [*tabbûr*] of the World."[1]

MOUNT ZION AS THE HIGHEST OF THE MOUNTAINS

"In the final days" (*bĕ'aḥărît hayyāmîm*). Some scholars see the Hebrew phrase as the equivalent of "later" or "next," like the Akkadian *ina aḥrât ūmī*. They argue that it did not refer to the end-time until Daniel 2:28; 10:14 (that is, in the early second century B.C.E.). However, the cessation of all wars and all training for war and strategizing about it posits a new and definitive world order. It is thus a vision for the end-time, the final days.

The exaltation of the mount of Yahweh's house symbolically presents Mount Zion as Olympus and Yahweh as supreme above all the gods of the nations. The sacral center of the world has shifted to Mount Zion. Shrines were usually erected to the gods on hills and elevations. Because of the importance of this practice, in low-lying Babylon the ziggurat was built to imitate a hill, and on it a shrine was erected. What our unit says through symbols and images, Psalm 97:9 says explicitly: "for you, O Lord, are the Most High over all the earth; you are exalted far above all gods." Baruch J. Schwartz (1998, 14) suggests that the mount is elevated not spiritually

---

1. In an article in Hebrew in *Tarbiz* 45 (1976):163-77 (cited in Levenson 1985, 116), Shemaryahu Talmon argues that *tabbûr* did not mean "navel" until postbiblical times, under influence of the Greek *omphalos* (navel); rather it originally meant "high plain." But this has not won much following.

but physically, so that it can be seen from afar.[2] The nature of this elevation, however, is indicated in v. 3. The nations stream to the mountain of Yahweh's house because they have been captivated by the *torah* coming out of Zion. The elevation is therefore more moral than geographical.

"*It shall stand firm*" (*nākôn*, NJPS). Psalm 93:2 uses the same root, *kûn* ("to be firmly set") of both the earth and Yahweh's throne in Zion when it says that "the world is indeed set firm (*tikkôn*), it shall never be shaken; your throne is set firm (*nākôn*) of old, from all eternity you exist." The earth was originally watery and thus shifting, but Yahweh exerted power to establish the universe on firm foundations. It was from the earthly throne of Yahweh on the holy mount that the universe was secured.

"*Then all the nations will stream to it.*" The verb *nāhărû*, is the denominative of *nāhār* ("river, stream"). Jeremiah 51:44 uses the same verb also about a pilgrimage of the nations to Bel in Babylon: "in the future, the nations will stream to him no more" (*wĕ lō' yinhărû 'ēlāyw 'ôd*). The NJPS reads "and all the nations shall gaze on it with joy," interpreting the root *nāhār* from *nĕhārā'* ("light," in Aramaic, cf. Job 3:4 and Dan 5:11, 14) (see also Schwartz 1998, 15).

MISSION BY ATTRACTION

In some traditions, Zion is where Yahweh destroys the armies of the nations. In Psalm 48, the kings of the earth joined forces, but at the very sight of Zion trembling seized them, and "you destroyed them like the ships of Tarshish shattered by an east wind" (Ps 48:7 NIV). Joel 4:2, 12 summon the nations to battle at the Valley of Jehoshaphat, for Yahweh to shatter their weapons and slaughter them and thereafter usher in salvation for Israel (see also Zech 14:2). Isaiah 2:2-5 stands out in subverting the language of the conquest of the nations. It is not Yahweh who shatters the weapons of the enemies trying to storm the city of God. Rather, the peoples do it themselves after they have been instructed by Yahweh on Mount Zion (Wildberger 1991, 93).

The focus on Mount Zion is uniquely moral and spiritual. It is not conceived of as the national center of Israel, but as the "mountain of Yahweh's house." In alignment with this idea, the house of Jacob is in v. 5 depicted as covered with the light of Yahweh. The nations of the earth come to the mountain of Yahweh's house of their own volition, pulled toward it by *torah* issuing from there. They exhort one another, saying, "Come, let us go up to the mountain of Yahweh, to the house of the God of Jacob." In

---

2. The NJPS seems to agree with this when it has the nations gazing on the mount with joy.

the words of Bernhard W. Anderson (1992, 16), the nations are attracted to Zion, the spiritual center, because the teaching that goes forth from that source appeals to the deepest human longings for *šālôm* ("peace, welfare"). Mission is at its best when it brings something to a people that responds to their deepest desire and quest.

TORAH FROM ZION

But what is the *torah* that shall go out of Zion? The root meaning of *torah* is instruction. The root is *yārāh,* which means "to teach" and which also underlies the phrase "that he may teach us" (*yōrēnû*). The phrase "for the *torah* will issue from Zion," is in synonymous parallelism with "and the word of Yahweh from Jerusalem" (v. 3). *Torah* in this context is thus rightly translated as "instruction."

Schwartz (1998, 20) argues that the instruction refers to the legal tradition of Israel and precisely that of the centralized high court of arbitration legislated in Deuteronomy 17:8-11. He writes that

> when the peoples of the world follow Israel's social example, they too will enjoy, on the international level, the tranquility that the Israelite population has been blessed with in the domestic sphere thanks to its perfect, divinely revealed, system of justice. If the prophet's call for repentance in Isa 1 is heeded, Zion will become God's flagship city. (1998, 25)

Our unit does demand that the house of Jacob somehow model for the nations the behavior expected of them in order to walk in the paths of Yahweh. But in question is apparently more than a legal system of justice. World peace is not secured by legal instruments alone, but needs internal dedication to the ways of peace and reconciliation on the part of all. In Isaiah, *torah* is not a legal instrument but the instruction (teaching, decree) of God mediated through the prophet. Isaiah 1:10 thus has the word of Yahweh in parallelism with *tôrat ʾĔlōhēnû* (the *torah* of our God), which in context refers to the words of the prophet. Marvin Sweeney reached the same conclusion after a close study of the twelve uses of *torah* in Isaiah (1:10; 2:3; 5:24; 8:16, 20; 24:5; 30:9; 42:4, 21, 24; 51:4, 7). He writes:

> *torah* is the teaching of YHWH, expressed by the prophet, which stands as the norm for proper conduct by both Israel and the nations, and which stands as the norm for order in the created world. (1996a, 63)

In Deuteronomy 17:11 *torah* is parallel to *mišpāṭ* (a decision pronounced by judges): "you will abide by the decision (*torah*) which they give

you, and by the sentence (*mišpāṭ*) which they pronounce." Hans Wildberger (1991, 91) thus correctly argues that the "word of Yahweh" and
"his paths" in Isa 2:3 refer not to religious instruction but to authoritative
judgments that Yahweh renders through an oracle when the nations come
to settle their disputes. Thus, "the nations come not to be proselytized into
the Hebrew religion . . . but to learn from God" (Childs 2001, 30).

YAHWEH ADJUDICATES BETWEEN THE NATIONS

*"Then he shall judge between the nations, and arbitrate between many
peoples."* The verb translated "and arbitrate" is *hôkîaḥ*, which the NAB
renders as "and impose terms on many peoples." The verb can mean "to
convict" or "to reprove." Yahweh not only judges between one nation and
another but also unveils the machinations of the powerful and imposes
terms upon them (Wildberger 1957, 80). In judging justly and teaching the
nations Yahweh secures world peace.

The writer of the unit has given up on traditional hopes for a Davidic
world empire based in Zion. In that tradition, the Davidic king was given
an iron scepter to break the kings of the nations and to bring them into
submission to Yahweh (Ps 2:9). Here it is Yahweh who directly achieves the
submission of all nations to Yahweh's rulings. But Yahweh's arbitration is
not an imposition. The nations are taught by Yahweh and really internal-
ize this teaching so as to walk in the paths of Yahweh in justice and peace.
They return home and hammer their swords into ploughshares. Weapons
of war and death are turned into implements that nourish life. The art of
war is banished from among the nations. No longer will they learn war
anymore. Zion becomes the universal center of peace and reconciliation.

THE MISSION OF THE HOUSE OF JACOB

Isaiah 2:5 is an editorial insertion the purpose of which is to round off
the unit and link it up with what follows. That this is the case is suggested
by the different ending of the unit in Micah 4:4: "but each [person] will sit
under [their] vine and fig tree with no one to trouble [them]. The mouth of
Yahweh Sabaoth has spoken." The nations encouraged one another saying,
"Come let us go up to [*lĕkû wĕna'ăleh*] the house of the God of Jacob, that
he may teach us his ways so that we may walk in his paths" (Isa 2:3). The
editor now exhorts Israel saying, "O house of Jacob, come, let us walk
[*lĕkû wĕnēlĕkāh*] in Yahweh's light" (Isa 2:5).

This editorial joint in fact causes a profound rereading of the unit, for it
associates the house of Jacob's walking in the light of Yahweh with the
nations' walking in the paths of Yahweh. To the "going up" of the nations

to learn to "walk in Yahweh's paths" must correspond the "walking" of the house of Jacob in Yahweh's light. The expression "light of Yahweh" occurs only here in the Old Testament, but in Isaiah 10:17 the "light of Israel" is in synonymous parallelism with "its Holy One," namely, Yahweh. The light of Yahweh could refer to the word of Yahweh, as in Psalm 119:105, "your word is a lamp for my feet, a light on my path." "Your word" in this late psalm refers to the *torah* ("law") of Moses. Here *torah* is not just "instruction" but the law that regulates the entire life of Israel. The house of Jacob would thus be invited to walk steadfastly in the Law of Moses and in so doing model for the nations the walking in the paths of Yahweh. "Only when [the *torah*] begins to give light there can the Zion-torah go forth from Israel into the world of the nations" (Lohfink 2000, 40). The *torah* that issues from Zion is thus related to the *torah* of Moses from which Israel derives light for life.

The editor of Isaiah 2:5 reinterprets the vision of Isa 2:2-4 also in the light of Isa 60:1-3. Light is one of the motifs that run through the Book of Isaiah (see Clements 1997a). It stands for salvation, joy, enlightenment, life in full. Isaiah 60:1-3 contrasts the darkness covering the peoples with the light that shines over Jerusalem. The nations come to Jerusalem's light and kings to its dawning brightness (Isa 60:3). The light over Jerusalem is none other than the glory (*kābôd*) of Yahweh (Isa 60:1). The glory of Yahweh covers the new Jerusalem as if she were the very temple of Yahweh. *Kābôd* is the effulgence that makes the presence of Yahweh manifest to humans. Its light symbolizes the presence of God and God's deliverance, but it also flows from a way of life grounded in justice and righteousness: "Light and divine effulgence (*kbwd YHWH*) are metaphors of salvific deliverance which suggest a social order of justice and righteousness which are also established by divine action" (Polan 2001, 62). Zion's light is the divine light. Nevertheless it can in a real sense be called Zion's light (Lohfink 2000, 55). Yahweh has reconstituted the community and established justice and righteousness in her. The glory of Yahweh now rests over the community as effulgent light shining in the darkness, giving light to all nations who have been in darkness. But Israel is not totally passive in this thought, for Israel must let the light of Yahweh's glory shine in her. For the nations to come to Israel's light, it is imperative that the house of Jacob walk in the light of Yahweh, that is, live in justice and righteousness, in peace and reconciliation.

Jeremiah 3:17 carries further the tradition of a Zion graced with the effulgence of Yahweh. The Ark was kept in the holy of holies and symbolized the presence of Yahweh, but it was probably lost during the Babylonian invasions of 597 and 587. The editor of Jeremiah 3:17 affirmed that it will not be missed, for "Jerusalem will be called the Throne of Yahweh, and all the nations will converge on her, on Yahweh's name, on Jerusalem and will no longer follow their own stubborn and wicked inclinations." The

Ark will not be missed because the entire city of Zion has become the holy of holies! The expression "stubborn and wicked inclinations" is elsewhere in the Old Testament used only of Israel. The nations too have learned to obey Yahweh religiously and will stream to Jerusalem, which has become a shrine wholly dedicated to Yahweh.

CONCLUSION

Reconciliation and conflict resolution have become significant works of mission in our strife-torn world. The Israelis and the Palestinians both press their claims on Jerusalem. Other nations and groups are in mortal conflict because of their counterclaims. Isaiah's vision of Zion as the center for world peace and reconciliation gives hope to many to sustain activity for reconciliation and peace in our world. Mission today must contribute to justice, peace, and reconciliation among peoples.

The nations are attracted to Zion, the spiritual center, because the teaching that goes forth from that source appeals to the deepest human longings for šālôm ("peace and welfare") (Anderson 1992, 16). Mission must respond to the deepest longings of the peoples.

We posited a first reading of Isaiah 2:2-4 before the editorial insertion in v. 5 would suggest rereadings that would move in the direction of a more religious interpretation of the passage. The original unit of Isaiah 2:2-4, however, contains a number of reversals of normative Israelite tradition. The nations do not give up their national identity and political independence. They are not aggregated into Israel, in contrast to Psalm 87, which accredits as Israel's children the many nations coming to Israel. They are not portrayed as going to Zion to offer gifts and sacrifices or to prostrate in worship before Yahweh.[3] Nor is it said expressly that their encounter with Yahweh led to their religious conversion to Yahweh. We miss the type of confession of Yahweh usually put in the mouths of foreigners who convert to Yahweh, for example, the confession of Jethro in Exodus 18:11, "Now I know that Yahweh is greater than all other gods." It is not said that in bringing themselves under the arbitration of Yahweh the nations have given up their national cults. Nothing is said explicitly about a "da'at Yhwh," the religious knowledge Yahweh (Wildberger 1957, 80). "Let us go up" ('ālāh) is language of pilgrimage. "That he may teach us his ways, so that we may walk in his paths" would normally suggest induction into covenantal torah. In Deuteronomy, such a phrase would be completed by

---

3. Schwartz rightly objects to the term "pilgrimage" on the grounds that this always involves appearing before Yahweh with gifts, prostrating in worship, sharing sacrifice in the presence of Yahweh, as part of the celebration of a clan or national festival (1998, 16).

"and to love him" (Deut 10:12) or "and to cleave to him" (Deut 11:22). None of this is in evidence in the coming of the nations to Yahweh in Isaiah 2:2-4. Walking in the ways of Yahweh has not meant for the nations an explicit religious conversion to Yahweh. The mission of reconciliation and peacemaking seems a goal in itself without its having to take on the aspect of proselytization.

DISCUSSION

1. Can there be authentic mission without proclamation and invitation to conversion?
2. Explain the mythic background of the elevation of Mount Zion.
3. What is the *torah* that shall go out from Zion?
4. Describe mission according to Isaiah 2:2-5.
5. What is the role of Israel vis-à-vis the nations in this text?
6. How did the editorial insertion in Isaiah 2:5 cause a rereading of the whole unit?
7. What dimensions are added when Isaiah 2:2-5 is read together with Isaiah 60:1-3?
8. In some traditions, Zion is object of desire of the nations, while in others it is where Yahweh will shatter the armies of the nations. How would you interpret these in relation to each other?

12

The Inclusive Covenant

It is the *world* that turns out to be Yahweh's *chosen people.*
—Walter Brueggemann, *Isaiah 1-39,* 166

Four texts will be studied in this chapter: Isaiah 19:16-25; Zechariah 14; Isaiah 56:1-8; and Isaiah 66:18-24. All the texts mark a decisive stage in the relation of Israel and the nations, for they envisage the inclusion of gentiles in Israel's covenant with Yahweh. Two of them, Isaiah 56:1-8 and 66:18-24, depict centrifugal mission.

Isaiah 56:1-8 is particularly important for mission in the Old Testament. It seems to be the earliest attestation of the religious conversion of gentiles to Yahweh. It opened Judaism up to the inclusion of gentiles. Morton Smith remarked:

> Judaism became, legally, a condition open to anyone able to satisfy the requirements for admission, and these requirements might be matters of practice or belief, not ancestry or territorial origin. Thus "Judaism" could become a world religion, capable of indefinite extension by conversion of all peoples. (1984, 269)

ISAIAH 19:16-25

Isaiah 19:16-25 is part of the Oracles against the Nations in Isaiah 13-23. The unit is linked by the catchphrase "in that day." Verses 16-17 play the role of transition from doom to deliverance. They speak of the plan that Yahweh has against Egypt. Isaiah speaks often of the "plan/counsel of Yahweh." Yahweh's design is to humble all that is high and proud and to overcome the "plan and design" of anti-Yahweh forces in the world (see Brueggemann 1997, 31). In our text, the plan is somehow linked with the land of Judah and the terror that will come upon Egypt when Yahweh raises Yahweh's threatening hand against Egypt. But the Yahweh who strikes Egypt in these verses will also heal Egypt in v. 22! Verses 18-25 proclaim salvation for Egypt and Assyria, not in isolation but in intimate relation to Israel. The unit is broken up into four smaller units, vv. 18, 19-22, 23, 24-25, each captioned by "in that day" (*bayyôm hahû'*). It is unclear whether they derive from the same pen or the same period. Most scholars think that these verses do not come from the pen of the eighth-century prophet or someone from his period, but rather much later. They see them as belonging to that "apocalyptic rendering of the Isaiah tradition" (Anderson 1988, 17-38) that characterizes the editorial process of that tradition. The four smaller units of "in that day" have been tagged onto what preceded as successive reinterpretations of the prophetic word of doom on Egypt. Many scholars are comfortable with a date under the Persians in the fifth century B.C.E.[1] There is evidence that Jews regarded the Persian conquest of Babylon, the return of the exiled Jews to Jerusalem, and the restoration of the Jerusalem temple as manifestations of Yahweh's worldwide rule (Sweeney 1996a, 57, 59).

In prophetic literature the expression "in that day" (*bayyôm hahû'*), generally signals late, scribal prophecy. The primary reference is less to coming historical events than to a day referred to earlier in the text or a future day that is taken for granted as known to the hearers/readers. Claus Westermann (1991, 257) opines that the phrase was understood as "in that day, the coming of which the prophets have announced." It is the day of Yahweh, the day in which Yahweh's universal sovereignty over creation will be manifested. The "city of the Sun"[2] (v. 18) is Heliopolis, the city of Ra, the sun-god. Even this epicenter of Egyptian religion will join four other cities in adopting both the Hebrew language and the worship of Yahweh as its city religion. What has led to this conversion of the Egyptians is not stated, but the text presumes some contact with Yahweh worshipers. A Jewish military settlement with its own (syncretistic?) Yahweh temple is attested in Elephantine from the fifth century B.C.E. The "Letter of Aristeas" 12-13 says that Ptolemy III (246-221) "removed from the land of the Jews into Egypt up to one hundred thousand people, from whom he armed about thirty thousand men and settled them throughout the land in the forts."[3] It also says that before this a fair number of Jews had entered Egypt with the Persians, and that before them other confederate troops, though not as many as those brought over by Ptolemy, had been dispatched to fight

---

1. Otto Kaiser (1974, 110) dated it to the time of the peace of Apamea (118 B.C.E.), but this dating is almost universally taken as too late. Marvin A. Sweeney (1996b, 163-76) argues for the period of Manasseh (687-642), but not many scholars side with him.

2. The MT actually reads "the city of destruction" (*'îr haheres*), while the LXX reads "city of righteousness," perhaps with the underlying thought of the Diaspora of Egypt as the rightful recipient of the promises of salvation (see Sawyer 1986, 63, citing Seeligmann).

3. "Letter of Aristeas," in James Charlesworth, ed., *The Old Testament Pseudepigrapha* (New York: Doubleday, 1985) 12-13.

with Psammetichus against the king of the Ethiopians. It is not clear whether the reference is to Psammetichus I (663-609) or Psammetichus II (594-589). Our text presumes that the Jewish Diaspora in Egypt would be faithful enough to Yahweh to provoke questions by would-be proselytes. In this they would be unlike the Judean remnant of Jeremiah 43-44 who settled in Tahpanhes on the border with Egypt and who insisted on continuing to offer incense to the Queen of Heaven.

The high priest Onias IV, who fled to Egypt and asked Ptolemy VI Philometor (181-145 B.C.E.) for permission to build a temple in Leontopolis, cited in support the words of the prophet in Isaiah 19:19, as follows:

> I desire, therefore, that you will grant me leave to . . . build there a temple to Almighty God, after the pattern of that in Jerusalem, and of the same dimensions. . . . For the prophet Isaiah foretold that there should be an altar in Egypt to the Lord God; and many other such things did he prophesy relating to that place. (Josephus, *Antiquities,* 13.67-68, cited from Whiston 1987, 339).

The altar at the center and a pillar (*maṣṣēbāh*) at the frontier of Egypt, all dedicated to Yahweh, are tokens of the overlordship of Yahweh that is about to be actualized. Isaiah 19:4 had stated, "I shall hand Egypt over to the clutches of a cruel master, a ruthless king will rule them." Isa 19:20 now says that when this happens the Egyptians[4] will cry out to Yahweh and Yahweh will send them a savior and leader to deliver them.[5] As Brueggemann (1998, 163) remarks, the exodus experience of Israel itself is replicated. The Egyptians under hard service are to be saved by Yahweh just as Yahweh rescued the Hebrews who were also under hard service. Yahweh will do for Egypt what Yahweh has done for Israel. Israel's exodus is paradigmatic; it pertains peculiarly to Israel, but not exclusively. Just as Yahweh is for Israel the God who strikes and heals, so Yahweh will also be for the Egyptians. By first striking and then healing them, Yahweh will reveal Godself to the Egyptians and they will know Yahweh. The verb *yāda'* ("to know"), connotes both acknowledgment and commitment expressed in the submission of one's life. Egypt will convert to Yahweh and will worship Yahweh with sacrifices and cereal offerings, with vows and their fulfill-

---

4. Kaiser (1974, 108) is one of the few scholars who take the verse as referring to oppressed Jewish communities in Egypt. He writes, "by sending to his faithful, oppressed by the Egyptians, as it were a second Moses to be a savior and to conquer the oppressors, he will impart to the Egyptians the certainty that Yahweh is God, so that they are converted to him." This interpretation seems linked to Kaiser's seeking of the historical referents of the oracle within the Seleucid-Ptolemaic politics of the late second century B.C.E.

5. The NRSV has Yahweh doing the work of deliverance: "he will send them a savior, and will defend and deliver them," reading *wĕrāb* instead of the MT *wārāb*.

ment. This cultic worship of Yahweh is presumed to be offered in Egypt itself, perhaps localized at the altar in the center of Egypt in v. 19. Apparently, the Deuteronomistic strictures against an altar to Yahweh outside Jerusalem (Deut 12) are not deemed to apply. Whether and to what extent our text has been influenced by the temple of Onias in Leontopolis, which was destroyed by the Romans in 73 C.E., is not clear.

All the wars and unrest in the Fertile Crescent have been unleashed because of the rivalry and imperial ambitions of Egypt and the various kingdoms of Mesopotamia. Israel was often a pawn between the two powers, and the prophet Isaiah had a hard time persuading the kings of Judah to desist from alliances with either power, but rather to trust in Yahweh alone. Now the one worship of Yahweh[6] will unite the entire Fertile Crescent, with Israel attaining the status of the erstwhile superpowers. A highway (*mĕsillāh*), which reminds us of the highway across the desert on which the exiles are to return home in Deutero-Isaiah, will go from Egypt to Assyria,[7] and people will travel freely and safely on this highway. Peace in the Fertile Crescent from Egypt to Assyria is tantamount to a universal world peace. Hitherto, the roads connecting Egypt and Assyria had served the armies of both empires in their attempts to overcome and rule the other. Now they serve for reconciliation and peace between the parties. The blessing of Abraham for all the families of the earth (Gen 12:1-3) now reaches its term. Egypt stands with Israel and Assyria as blessing in the midst of the earth. The primacy of Israel in the history of salvation is retained—Israel is still "my inheritance." But Israel somehow attains the goal of its election when its prerogatives are shared with Egypt and Assyria, the two poles of

---

6. The MT of v. 23 is ambiguous: *wĕ'abdû miṣrāyîm et-aššûr* can be translated as "the Egyptians will serve Assyria," a reading adopted by the LXX. NJB translates: "Egypt will serve with Assyria," which retains the ambiguity somewhat. But since the verb *'ābad* has been used in the religious sense of "worship," most modern versions translate the verse in the manner of the NRSV: "the Egyptians will worship with the Assyrians" [with Yahweh understood or stated explicitly as the subject worshiped].

7. Kaiser (1974, 110) thinks that the context is that of the situation following the peace of Apamea in 118 B.C.E., which allowed free passage between the kingdoms of the Seleucids and the Ptolemies. He opines that the Seleucid kingdom is given the code name "Assyria." Other scholars think that this dating may be too late or that the text represents prophetic imagination, not actual reality. Sweeney (1996b, 263-76) dates the cooperative relationship between Egypt, Israel, and Assyria—with Assyria as the dominant partner, during the period of Manasseh of Judah (687-642), who sent troops to support Assurbanipal's Egyptian campaigns. The seventh-century editor of Isaiah 19:1-25 portrays Manasseh's policies in relation to Egypt as fulfilling Isaiah's condemnation of Egypt. But when these nations came under Persian suzerainty in the late sixth century, the fifth-century editor, who saw Persian activities as acts of Yahweh, reinterpreted the conquest of Egypt by Cambyses in 525 as the fulfillment of Isaiah's oracle, demonstrating Yahweh's intention to subdue the nations while establishing sovereignty throughout the world (ibid., 273).

the Fertile Crescent, the extremities of the then known world. Egypt becomes "my people" and Assyria "the work of my hands" (v. 25). It is Israel's Yahwistic faith that is now embraced by Egypt and Assyria. Her calling, as defined in Genesis 12:1-3, is now shared with others (Wilson 1966, 81). What is said of Egypt, Israel, and Assyria means that "together they form a single new and permanent people of God" (Kaiser 1974, 111).

ZECHARIAH 14

Zechariah 9:1, 12:1, and Malachi 1:1 each begins with *maśśā'* ("a proclamation"). The three are anonymous collections that now end the Book of the Twelve. Zechariah 9-14 is usually called Deutero-Zechariah. Zechariah 14 develops four themes (see Cunliffe-Jones 1973, 18-24). The first is that of God's victory over evil. Evil is personified by all the nations who gather to attack Jerusalem and whom God vanquishes. Since v. 16 speaks of the "survivors of all the nations," it is to be understood that God's defeat of the nations left a remnant, just as God's elimination of evil among God's own people left a remnant (Zech 13:7-9). The purposes of God will triumph in the end.

The second is the transformation of nature under God's rule. Living waters issue from Jerusalem (v. 8), the entire country becomes a plain, except for Jerusalem, which retains its preeminence (v. 10). Jerusalem lives in peace and security, and the curse of destruction is banished (v. 11). This scenario leads to the third theme, namely, the worship of Yahweh in Jerusalem by all the nations, who now join the remnant of Israel every feast of Shelters (v. 16). Zechariah 8:22-23 already spoke of the nations seeking to go to Jerusalem "to seek Yahweh Sabaoth and entreat Yahweh's favor." Finally, the secular is swallowed up in the sacred—every cooking pot in Jerusalem and every bell on the horses in the streets will be holy to Yahweh (vv. 20-21). "Consecrated to Yahweh" was the inscription on the flower attached to the turban of the high priest (Exod 39:30-31). That every cooking pot in Jerusalem and every bell on the horses in the streets will be holy to Yahweh means that every utensil in Jerusalem has become holy and may be used in the worship of Yahweh. This means, in effect, the abolition of the laws of pure and impure and of the limits on the access of gentiles to Yahweh's temple. Holiness is redefined to include all true worshipers of Yahweh, be they of Israel or of the nations.

ISAIAH 56:1-8

Isaiah 56:1-8 shares so many themes with Isaiah 66:15-24 that most scholars are of the opinion that they are meant to frame chapters 56-66.[8]

---

8. W. A. M. Beuken (1991, 204-21) argues further that Isaiah 66:7-14 concludes Trito-

They share many common themes, as pointed out by Joseph Blenkinsopp (2003, 132): the servants of Yahweh (56:4 and 66:14), Yahweh's imminent intervention in salvation and judgment (56:1 and 66:15-16), preceded by the gathering in of all nations (56:8 and 66:18, both using the verb *qbṣ*). Other common themes are "my holy mountain" as the symbolic center (56:7 and 66:20, both using *har qodšî*), foreigners qualified to serve (using verb, *šrt*) as cultic ministers (56:6 and 66:21), and Sabbath observance as the confessional marker of the Jewish faith (56:2, 4, 6 and 66:23). Isaiah 49-55 focused on Zion/Jerusalem; "my holy mountain" begins to appear only in Trito-Isaiah—the phrase occurred already in Isaiah 11:9, but many scholars think this is late. The Israel defined by this term is more religious than a national and geographical group. The one defining characterization of the group is its relationship to the Holy One who inhabits "my holy mountain."

Isaiah 56:1-8 is framed by the authoritative word of Yahweh. The author is conscious of the fact that some stipulations of the Law of Moses are being abrogated and that the new order thus needs divine backing. Just below the surface of the text one can hear polemics about the nature of temple worship and who may have charge of it; there was also a question about how the identity of the community may be defined.

Verse 1 uses *ṣĕdāqāh* in two different senses: do *ṣĕdāqāh*/righteousness for my *ṣĕdāqāh*/deliverance is about to be revealed. In Isaiah 1-39, *ṣĕdāqāh* is mostly paired with *mišpāṭ* ("justice") to signify what in modern terms is called social justice, hence act of humans. In Deutero-Isaiah (Isa 40-55), *ṣĕdāqāh* is mostly paired with *yešûaʿāh* ("salvation, deliverance"). Scholars such as Rolf Rendtorff and John Oswalt[9] have commented that the particular usage of *ṣĕdāqāh* in two diverse senses in Isaiah 56:1 is intentional and is meant to link the preceding collections with Trito-Isaiah. All is not just human activity or pure grace: justice and righteousness are to be done *because my salvation* is at hand. In other words, obedience is to be lived out as response to divine grace and salvation (Oswalt 1998, 455). The text means to say that the promises of Deutero-Isaiah have not proven false; rather the delay in deliverance has been occasioned by disloyalty to Yahweh on the part of some in the community. Verse 2 is in the form of a macarism and outlines four criteria for membership among the servants of Yahweh. They hold fast to my promised deliverance and persevere in doing righteousness. They refrain from doing evil and keep the Sabbath and do not profane it. "Profane" (*ḥillēl*) recurs in Exod 31:14 (anyone who profanes [the Sabbath] shall be put to death).

Isaiah, 66:15-20 concludes Deutero-Isaiah and Trito-Isaiah together, and 66:22-23(24) concludes the book as a whole, but this has not yet found consensus among scholars.

9. See chapter 8.

It is a common term, especially in Ezekiel, for the profanation of the name of Yahweh. Such usage shows that the Sabbath had become the principal confessional marker of Israel. It had become simply the covenant or the sign of the covenant with Yahweh. Circumcision, which in Genesis 17 was the covenant, is not even mentioned here. In line with the confessional importance of the Sabbath in postexilic times, Nehemiah 13:18 regarded desecration of the Sabbath as the chief reason for the exile and the destruction of Jerusalem. The origins of the Sabbath are obscure,[10] but scholars tend toward the opinion that it was not derived from the Babylonian *shapattu*, which signified a day of rest on the full moon and on the fifteenth of the month. The weekly Sabbath appears already in Amos 8:5 as a day marked by the absence of work, but it attained confessional status during the exile. The sequence of *ḥag* (annual feast), new moons, and Sabbaths is unknown outside Israel (Hasel, 850).

Isaiah 56:3-6 begins and ends with the foreigner, but within the verses the case of the eunuch is treated. This suggests that both groups are aligned together and that the specifications given in vv. 7-8 apply to both. The *ben hannēkār* is an immigrant foreigner as distinct from a *gēr* or *tôšāb* (resident alien). Such a foreigner, who would fulfill the conditions given above, is to be included among God's people. And even if such persons were Ammonites or Moabites, peoples excluded by Deuteronomy 23:4, they would still be admitted. Their fear that Yahweh might separate them from God's people is laid to rest. The verb used for "to separate," *hibdîl*, is a word used by P for the separation of pure from impure, of things that should never go together. The eunuch is more likely a male who has been sexually mutilated for imperial service, for castration was not practiced in Israel, either for court or harem officials or as judicial punishment, as elsewhere in the ancient Near East (Blenkinsopp 2003, 137). Deuteronomy 23:2 places the eunuch at the head of the list of those excluded from the assembly of Yahweh. Our text may be a case where the prophetic voice uses divine authority to abrogate elements of the *torah*. It authorizes eunuchs to be admitted to the assembly of Yahweh and promises that Yahweh will give them a good and permanent standing in the community. Foreigners and eunuchs may offer acceptable sacrifices to Yahweh, contrary to Leviticus 22:25, which prohibited the acceptance of sacrificial animals from foreigners. Their prayer will be equally acceptable, for "my house shall be called a house of prayer for all peoples." To call the temple a house of prayer is to reinvest it with spiritual values gained during the exile, when there were no sacrifices and prayer and repentance were the sole means of access to Yah-

---

10. H. H. Rowley argues for a Kenite origin in "Moses and the Decalogue," *Bulletin of the John Rylands Library* 34:81-118.

weh (see the prayer of Solomon in 1 Kgs 8:41-43). The verb *šrt* (v. 6) can mean "to serve" or specifically "to minister" in the cult. The latter meaning is clearer in Isaiah 66:21. The authority behind the new arrangements is given in v. 8 as the Lord Yahweh who gathers the exiles of Israel and who purposes to gather "others" besides. In context, the "others" must be the foreigners spoken of earlier. In the prophecies around the period of the exile and after, the verb *qbṣ* ("to gather"), always presumes the prior divine act of scattering (the exile) and Yahweh's hoped-for restoration to the land. For example: "I shall restore your fortunes and gather you in from all the nations and wherever I have driven you. . . . I shall bring you back to the place from which I exiled you" (Jer 29:14). Since the foreigners and the "others" in our text had not been driven from Yahweh's land, the idea of gathering to "my holy mountain" is being used analogically and must not be seen in terms of possession of the land, but rather in the spiritual terms of bringing them close to Yahweh in worship and righteous living. The Israel of God is constituted by Yahweh through Yahweh's gathering of the pious and righteous, from Israel and from among the nations.

Isaiah 56:1-8 opened the door to the admission of gentiles into Israel through religious conversion. The P final editors of the Pentateuch completed the process by redefining the word *gēr*. *Gēr* was originally a sociological concept that referred to the resident alien. The editors moved the concept of *gēr* from the sociological plane to the religious plane. It now referred to the proselyte who has become "Jewish" through religious conversion and who was bound to keep the whole law. Another word, *tôšāb*, now served to designate the resident alien as a sociological status (Kuhn 1964, 729; Smith 1984, 269). It was thus that "in the Persian period the word [*gēr*] comes to be applied to foreigners (men of other than Jewish descent) who join themselves to [Yahweh], or to Israel as the worshippers of [Yahweh]" (Moore 1971, 328). The LXX appropriately translated *gēr* in its newly acquired religious sense as *prosēlytos* ("proselyte").

ISAIAH 66:18-24

Isaiah 66:18-24 opens with Yahweh[11] coming to gather every nation and every language to "my holy mountain, Jerusalem" (v. 20). As in Jeremiah 3:17 (see the last chapter), the entire city has become Yahweh's temple, where Yahweh is now enthroned as king, where all peoples come for continuous worship, and where nothing that is unholy or impure may

---

11. The MT actually has the feminine *bā'āh*, for which the NJPS supplies "time"; hence, "the time has come to gather all nations and tongues."

abide. Hence, the Book of Isaiah ends with the contrast between the mountain and the valley, between everlasting worship in the temple and everlasting annihilation (Westermann 1969, 428). The line cuts through Israel herself and the nations. The theological center of the Isaiah tradition has been the prophet's encounter in the temple with the "Holy One," who was seated on a high and lofty throne with the seraphs shouting to each other, "Holy, holy, holy is Yahweh Sabaoth. His glory fills the whole earth" (Isa 6:1-3). The entire Book of Isaiah has relentlessly pursued the humbling of all that is high and exalted before the majesty of Yahweh. It traced the redemption of Zion from faithless city (Isa 1:21) to "city of Saving Justice, Faithful City" (Isa 1:26). It has seen the glory of Yahweh rise over Zion and the nations come to Zion's light (Isa 60:1, 3). The transformation of Zion is the key to both the formal and the thematic structure of the book of Isaiah as a whole (Webb 1990, 6). Both God's glory and God's holiness are always recognized simultaneously. Only someone who knows of Yahweh's holiness can also recognize Yahweh's glory (Kaiser 1974, 79). The glory of Yahweh is Yahweh's majesty as king of the universe, ruling in righteousness and redeeming the faithful who walk in Yahweh's ways.

It is not clear who the "survivors" are, but v. 16 speaks of Yahweh executing judgment by fire on all peoples. It is possible that this act of judgment is the sign that Yahweh will set among the nations (see v. 19). From among the survivors of the nations,[12] who apparently have seen the glory of Yahweh in some deed or manifestation of Yahweh, Yahweh sends messengers all over the world to declare Yahweh's glory among those "that have never heard of me or seen my glory" (v. 19). This is one sure and certain mention of mission as we today employ the term—the sending of individuals to distant people in order to proclaim God's glory among them (Westermann 1969, 425). The sending of Jonah to the Ninevites (see chapter 8) would be another, the activities of the Jewish Diaspora in Egypt mentioned above would be a third. The messengers sent "will proclaim my glory to the nations" (v. 19). The offerings brought by members of the nations will be pure and pleasing to Yahweh. In addition, Yahweh will confirm the new order introduced in 56:1-8 by establishing some people as priests and Levites, functions that hitherto had not been accessible to all Israel, but only to some families by heredity. A scribe has not thought well of this largesse of Yahweh in respect of the members of the nations, and so has inserted v. 20, which reinterprets the ministering of the nations.

---

12. Some scholars argue that the survivors sent must be Jews of the Diaspora or at least proselytes among the nations, for the task assigned them requires prior knowledge of Yahweh. But the grammatical referent of *mēhem* ("from them") is the nations mentioned in v. 18.

Now their offering consists of Israelites of the Diaspora whom they bring back in horses and chariots. Those whom Yahweh will appoint as priests and Levites are now made to be these returned Jews (Westermann 1969, 427).

> Israel is not to be separate so that it can revel in its separateness, but so that its faith can survive to be declared (Oswalt 1998, 691).

But the last word belongs to Yahweh: "from New Moon to New Moon, from Sabbath to Sabbath, all humanity will come and bow in my presence." It becomes clear that the enduring promises of Yahweh are given not to a particular people but to those of all flesh who worship God from month to month and Sabbath to Sabbath. Israel is not to be separate so that it can revel in its separateness, but so that its faith can survive to be declared (Oswalt 1998, 691).

CONCLUSION

Three motifs of mission appear in Isaiah 56:1-8 and 66:18-21 together. The first is the shift from focus on the nation to focus on the individual: Judaism had become a confessional community in which belonging is by individual choice. This means a radical change in the idea of the chosen people. Membership ceases to be based on birth and now depends on resolve, the resolve to take as one's god the God of Israel (Westermann 1969, 305). Paul will later stand on this tradition to transfer the notion of election from nation to individual. He will also argue for a distinction between the Israel of the flesh and the "Israel of God" (Gal 6:16) constituted by faith in and obedience to Christ. The second is precisely this division that cuts across the people of God, with the result that the erstwhile promises to the nation are now inherited by a faithful remnant, called the servants of Yahweh or those who tremble at Yahweh's word. In the end the remnant is defined not in national or ethnic terms but in confessional terms. Being Israelite does not guarantee inclusion in the remnant, and being foreign does not entail exclusion from it (Webb 1990, 79). Foreigners who confess Yahweh are included in "Israel" and are even allowed ministerial positions, while Jews who do not adhere to Yahweh are excluded. Finally, our texts, especially Isa 66:18-21, proclaim the universal worship of Yahweh on "my holy mountain" as the worldwide response to the effective sovereignty of Yahweh. Mission will reach its term in the universal acknowledgment and worship of Yahweh on Yahweh's holy mountain.

DISCUSSION

1. Discuss the Exodus themes in Isa 19:20.
2. Do you think that Isa 19:18-25 portrays the conversion of Egypt and Assyria or is the reference to Jews of the Diaspora? Give reasons for your answer.
3. What themes do you discover in Zech 14?
4. What is prescribed in Isa 56:1-8 and what is its novelty?
5. The survivors sent to proclaim Yahweh to the nations are Jews of the Diaspora. Argue for and against this proposition.
6. How did this chapter advance the argument of the book?

13

A Light to the Nations

Deutero-Isaiah and Mission

I shall make you a light to the nations so that my salvation may reach the remotest parts of earth.

—Isaiah 49:6

In Antioch in Pisidia Paul read Isaiah 49:6 as a command of the Lord for mission to the gentiles when he said, "we turn to the gentiles, for this is what the Lord commanded us to do when he said, 'I have made you a light to the nations, so that my salvation may reach the remotest parts of the earth'" (Acts 13:46-47). When Simeon took the child Jesus in his arms, he sang his *Nunc Dimittis,* content to die in peace for, said he, "my eyes have seen the salvation which you made ready in the sight of the nations; a light *of revelation* [italics mine] for the gentiles and glory for your people Israel" (Luke 2 :30-32). These and other texts of the New Testament concur in reading the text of Isaiah 49:6 as mandate for the gentile mission. But is Isaiah 49:6 a mandate for mission to the nations in its Old Testament context? Scholars differ on the matter. The problem is that Deutero-Isaiah (Isaiah 40-55, to which some scholars add Isaiah 60-62) does not seem to present a coherent doctrine of the nations or of mission. Many of these texts hardly envisage mission to the nations, to say the least. For example, in an apostrophe, Zion/Jerusalem is asked to put on her finest clothes "for the uncircumcised and the unclean will enter you no more" (Isa 52:1). The context does make it clear that the reference is to the hostile entry of armies for conquest. The text means to say that conquering armies will no longer enter renewed Zion/Jerusalem. But how language is used matters, for it also depicts the attitudes and viewpoints of the speaker. The language of "uncircumcised" and "unclean" depicts a religious attitude toward the nations that is other than that of mission. Another text in this mold is Isaiah 45:14. It says of the peoples of Egypt, Cush, and Seba that they will be struck by Yahweh's deeds on behalf of Israel and "will come over to you and belong to you. They will follow you, *walking in chains* [italics mine], they will bow before you, they will pray to you, 'with you alone is God, and there is no other!'" These peoples will profess Yahweh and will come over to belong to Israel, but in chains, that is, as a captive people. In line with this scenario, Isaiah 60:12 says that "the nation and kingdom that will not serve you will perish, and the nations will be utterly destroyed." Such texts seem to envision a world empire of Israel based in Jerusalem, not a moral and religious universe in which all gladly worship Yahweh on equal terms.

Scholars of the theme of Israel and the nations in Deutero-Isaiah are divided. H. H. Rowley (1944, 53, 64) asserted that nowhere in the Old Testament as in Deutero-Isaiah do we find so clear a call to active missionary effort. The Servant is both Israel, the whole community called to be a missionary community, and also and supremely a figure in the future. A. Gelston (1992, 391) finds that in Deutero-Isaiah the nations are "invited to experience [Yahweh's] saving and liberating interventions for themselves," in a manner comparable to, but not identical with, that of Israel. The salvation of the nations in context may be of a political and possibly military nature (390). We must not assume, however, an inner consistency in the prophet's sayings, for at times he sank back to a more traditional and superior attitude toward the nations. D. W. van Winkle (1985, 457) concluded that the nations receive salvation in the worship of Yahweh and by living in a world in which Yahweh's justice is manifest. Salvation for them, however, includes submission to Israel. Davies (1989, 93-120) posits *successive developments of a theme* by different writers. With the Zion material, he sees the theme of the nations contributing to the unity of the book of Isaiah. The book is now framed by 1:2-2:4(5) and 65-66, which present the Zion temple as central but as a place for Yahweh's word (rather than sacrifice), a place where justice and righteousness dwell and where the exiles of Israel and the nations gather to hear Yahweh's word and behold Yahweh's glory. Roy Melugin (1997, 260) argues that "recognition of Yahweh's glory is the central purpose of divine activity" in Deutero-Isaiah and that Yahweh's actions toward Israel and the nations are subservient to this more basic concern. The nations receive both salvation and servitude to Israel, and the two are left in unresolved tension (ibid., 262). If justice is connected with Yahweh's creation and lordship of the world, then Genesis deals better with the issue of relationships between Israel and the nations, and Deutero-Isaiah cannot be legitimately called the "high-water mark" in biblical testimony on the subject (ibid.).

The concern in this chapter is twofold—how are Deutero-Isaiah's statements on the relation of Israel and the nations to be correlated and whether the prophet envisages a missionary task of Israel in relation to the nations that would bring them into full and equal religious subjection to Yahweh. The chapter will be developed in three sections. The first section examines what Deutero-Isaiah really means when he says that the nations will acknowledge Yahweh or bend the knee to Yahweh or that Yahweh's salvation will reach the ends of the earth. The second section examines the role of Israel vis-à-vis the nations outside the Songs of the Servant. The third examines the role of Israel vis-à-vis the nations in the Songs of the Servant. The Songs of the Servant are treated apart following the slight majority of scholars who consider them later than Deutero-Isaiah.

THE SALVATION OF THE NATIONS AND
THEIR ACKNOWLEDGMENT OF YAHWEH

Two texts are considered. The first is Isaiah 44:1-5, which gives reasons for the demographic expansion of Israel. The unit is an oracle of salvation addressed to "Jacob, my servant." Jacob/Jeshurun fears national extinction because of the paucity of numbers. He is told not to be afraid, because Yahweh will pour out Yahweh's spirit and blessing on his descendants. As water poured out on thirsty ground causes vegetation to flourish, so shall the pouring out of Yahweh's spirit on Jacob's descendants cause a speedy repopulation of the land. The oracle is coherent up to this point. But then follows verse 5, which says, "One person will say, 'I belong to Yahweh,' another will call himself by Jacob's name. On his hand another will write 'Yahweh's' and be surnamed 'Israel.'" Who are these persons? If they are returnees, they are presented as apostates returning to Yahweh. Brevard Childs (2001, 342) believes so and affirms that the reference is to the returnees who now rededicate themselves to Yahweh. But there are reasons to think otherwise.

The unit is preceded by a dispute between Yahweh and Israel in which Yahweh accuses Israel of not having invoked Yahweh and of having grown weary of their God. That was then. But now, Yahweh will wipe away Israel's transgressions "for my own sake and not call their sins to mind" (43:25). Yahweh will restore to them the blessing of Abraham, the blessing of numerous progeny. The spirit of Yahweh will be poured out and, like water causing green grass to sprout, will cause the repopulation of the land. The pouring out of Yahweh's spirit is a miracle sufficient for the increase of the people. Verse 5 is thus an additional reason for the repopulation and may be an insertion. People from among the nations will convert to Yahweh and aggregate themselves to Jacob. Branding oneself on the hand or head was a symbol that indicated ownership or group identity. By so doing, these people will indicate their belonging to Yahweh. The verse explains the enormous demographic expansion of the Jewish people in the later Old Testament period by the influx of proselytes (see Blenkinsopp 2002, 234). Zechariah 2:15 refers to the same phenomenon when it says, "On that day many nations will be converted to Yahweh. Yes, they will become [Yahweh's] people, and they will live among you." Isaiah 44:5 is to be interpreted in terms of the inclusion of gentiles in "Israel" and belonging to Yahweh.

The second text is Isaiah 45:22-25. The question is, what is meant by saying that the nations will acknowledge Yahweh or bend the knee to Yahweh or that Yahweh's salvation will reach the ends of the earth. The poetic words are fluid in meaning. I lay out the texts of the NRSV and the NJPS.

Isaiah 45:22-25 (NJPS)	Isaiah 45:22-25 (NRSV)
[22] Turn to Me and *gain success*, All the ends of earth! For I am God, and there is none else. [23] By Myself have I sworn, From My mouth has issued *truth*, A word that shall not turn back: To Me every knee shall bend, Every tongue swear loyalty. [24] They shall say: "Only through the LORD Can I find *victory* and might. When people trust in Him, *All their adversaries* are put to shame. [25] It is through the LORD that all the offspring of Israel have vindication and glory."	[22] Turn to me and *be saved*, all the ends of the earth! For I am God, and there is no other. [23] By myself I have sworn, from my mouth has gone forth *in righteousness* a word that shall not return: "To me every knee shall bow, every tongue shall swear." [24] Only in the LORD, it shall be said of me, are *righteousness* and strength; *all who were incensed against him* shall come to him and be ashamed. [25] In the LORD all the offspring of Israel shall triumph and glory.

The addressees are the "survivors of the nations" (v. 20). Some scholars (e.g., Hollenberg 1969, 32) see these as crypto-Israelites who had fled to the nations to escape the catastrophe that befell Israel. Such scholars generally align "the ends of the earth" (*'aphsê 'āreṣ*) with the *qĕṣê hā'āreṣ* (the remotest parts of the earth from which Israelites are to be gathered home) in Isaiah 43:6. But the immediate context of Isaiah 45:20-21 suggests that the addressees are non-Israelites. They are those who "pray to a god that cannot save" (v. 20). The author engages their gods in a trial dispute to present their case and say whether they foretold the deliverance and repatriation of Israel.

Christians are quick to understand the root "salvation" soteriologically, but this is not always the case. The word being translated is וְהִוָּשְׁעוּ, the *niphal* of the root *yš'*, which means "to save." According to the NJPS, what the nations gain by turning to Yahweh is *success*; according to the NRSV it is *salvation*. But "salvation" in context may take on a sociopolitical or a religious and soteriological sense. The NJPS almost consistently translates this root in a sociopolitical sense wherever it occurs in Deutero-Isaiah. For example, in Isaiah 52:10 it renders *yĕšû'at 'Ĕlōhênû* by "the victory of our God," while the NRSV reads "the salvation of our God." For the NJPS the salvation in question is God's victory over the gods of the nations resulting in the national deliverance and vindication of Israel. What the ends of the earth see is this victory of God on behalf of Israel.[1]

Other scholars detect some tension between v. 22 and v. 25, and I join myself to them. In v. 22 the "ends of the earth" are invited to turn to Yahweh and be saved, while in v. 25 the unit ends with "justice and glory" for Israel and with Yahweh putting to shame all those who used to rage against Yahweh (v. 24b), namely, the very nations. D. E. Hollenberg (1969, 30, 32) maintains that in Deutero-Isaiah salvation and covenant are not for the foreign nations but only for Israel. God's deeds for Israel will bring the nations to the acknowledgment of Yahweh as the only true God and to prostration before Israel. The call to "turn to me and you will be saved" is not a call to conversion to Yahweh but to the universal recognition of Yahweh's power.[2] It goes too far to say that in Deutero-Isaiah salvation and covenant are not for the foreign nations, for some texts clearly say so, even if some may be editorial rereadings (e.g., Isa 44:5, considered above, and 45:14, where the peoples of Egypt, Cush, and Seba, though coming in chains, profess "with you [Israel] alone is God, and there is no other. The gods do not exist"). Rather, we should admit that the text is at some variance with itself. It both calls the nations to acknowledge Yahweh and focuses on the glory and triumph of Israel. It invites the nations to abandon their gods, whose inanity has been proven by the event of the deliverance of Israel. They should give up their gods and acknowledge the power of Yahweh as the only one who controls history and human destiny. But acknowledging the power of Yahweh is not the same as joining Israel in the worship of Yahweh. When it is said that the Egyptians shall know that I am Yahweh (Exod 7:5 and passim), the acknowledgment of the power of Yahweh does not necessarily lead to faithful obedience. Israel eventually developed the system of "god-fearers," that is, gentiles who accepted monotheism, imageless worship, and certain moral norms (cf. Vermes et al. 1986, 165), without entering fully into the covenant. I conclude that the present text of Isaiah 45:22-25 is not an invitation to religious obedience and inclusion in the covenant with Yahweh, even if it may invite the nations to acknowledge the power of Yahweh, give up their gods, and be prepared to live in a world subject to Yahweh.

---

1. But the editors of the NJSB (2004, 877) nevertheless comment that "Israel's vindication leads other nations to worship the Lord as well. The mixture of nationalism and universalism here is noteworthy: a universalist outcome results from a particularist victory." This comment hardly coheres with the interpretation chosen.

2. In similar strain is Robert Martin-Achard (1969, 16-30) who maintains that the prophet's task was to comfort his brothers and sisters and not to make them responsible for the conversion of the nations. The nations assist in the salvation of Israel without benefiting from it; they are witnesses to God's rehabilitation of God's people, with no consideration of conversion. He points out the significant fact that two-thirds of the oracles in Deutero-Isaiah are oracles of salvation for Israel in response to the complaints of the exiles.

THE ROLE OF ISRAEL VIS-À-VIS THE NATIONS
OUTSIDE THE SONGS OF THE SERVANT

Outside the Songs of the Servant, Jacob/Israel is called "Servant" in various texts of Deutero-Isaiah (Isaiah 41:8, 9; 42:19; 43:10; 44:1, 2, 21, 26, etc.). C. R. North (1956, 183-85) already noted that Servant/Israel is the passive recipient of salvation, while in the Songs of the Servant (42:1-4; 49:1-6; 50:4-9; and 52:13-53:12) the Servant clearly has an active mission. I shall examine two possible exceptions that seem to posit an active role for Servant/Israel.

The first is the vocation of Israel as Yahweh's witnesses in Isaiah 43:10, 12; 44:8. Israel is witness to Yahweh in two senses. In her very existence and in the deeds of Yahweh on her behalf, Israel is living witness to the universal sovereignty of Yahweh, her savior. Such passive witnessing will nevertheless lead the nations to acknowledge Yahweh as the sole deity (North 1964, 19). But Israel is also an active witness to Yahweh in Yahweh's assize against the gods of the nations. An example is Isaiah 43:10: "You yourselves are my witnesses, and the servant whom I have chosen."[3] Israel can testify to the fulfillment of the prophetic predictions of her current deliverance and thus confirm Yahweh's argument that it is only Yahweh who controls history and destiny.

The second text to be considered is Isaiah 55:1-5, particularly the subunit of vv. 3-5. Isaiah 55:3-5 reckons with Persian hegemony and the demise of the Davidic dynasty. The ideology of Psalm 2, which consigns the world under the Judean king, now rings hallow. Deutero-Isaiah sees that the true vocation of David in the original theological purpose of God was not to rule but to witness to God's wonders among the peoples. In fact, Childs (2001, 435) posits that Deutero-Isaiah already fused the function of the Servant and that of the messianic Davidic rule, seeing that the Isaianic corpus has a common vision of the ultimate rule of Yahweh in justice and compassionate love. Yahweh made David a witness to the peoples, a leader, and a lawgiver to them. As "witness to the peoples," David proclaimed the might and greatness of Yahweh to the peoples in his empire, as well as being prince and ruler over them (Eissfeldt 1962, 202). The covenant with David and the divine promises to him in 2 Samuel 7 are transferred to Israel as a whole. The result is that the people now enter into David's (reinterpreted) role of witnessing to Yahweh. Another term given to David was that of a מְצַוֵּה. The NJPS (also NRSV) renders this as "commander of peoples," but the NJB renders it as "lawgiver to peoples." Norbert Lohfink (Lohfink-Zenger 2000, 52) rightly points out that the participle מְצַוֵּה occurs

---

3. NJPS: "My witnesses are you—declares the *Lord*—My servant, whom I have chosen." This reading comes from omitting *wĕ* ("and") from *wĕ'abdî* ("and my servant").

almost exclusively in Deuteronomy and is there connected with the proclamation of the *torah* through Moses. He concludes by asking,

> Is this the way Israel is to be "witness," by interpreting the "Davidic"
> position of ruler over the nations that it has attained to mean that it,
> Israel, Moses-like, proclaims the torah to them?

He answers this question in the affirmative. Israel "will summon a nation
unknown to you" (Isa 55:5). The summons here is a missionary invitation
to participate in Israel's worship of and covenant with God. What is
described here is a priestly function and rejoins the promise in Exodus
19:5-6 of a "holy nation" and a "kingdom of priests" (see chapter 6). This
text corresponds to the scope of the final editing of Isaiah, which, according to Marvin Sweeney, points to a priestly community restored in Zion as
the "servants of Yahweh." As such,

> the people of Israel will continue to represent YHWH's eternal
> covenant in the world at large as a priestly people who serve YHWH
> at Zion. . . . Zion will serve as the holy center or sanctuary of
> YHWH's new creation and the people of Israel will serve as the
> priesthood to the nations in relation to the establishment of YHWH's
> sovereignty over the entire world. (1997, 43)

THE ROLE OF ISRAEL VIS-À-VIS THE NATIONS
IN THE SONGS OF THE SERVANT

Ever since Bernard Duhm's 1892 *Commentary on the Book of Isaiah*,
the Servant Songs (Isa 42:1-4; 49:1-6; 50:4-9; and 52:13-53:12) have been
isolated as a unit. The Songs received later additions in Isaiah 42:5-9; 49:7-
9 (12); and 50:10-11. Scholars usually point out that in the Songs the Servant is an agent of Yahweh's salvation, but outside them Servant/Israel
seems mostly a passive recipient of salvation. Further, the Songs when
taken together increasingly suggest that an individual is being spoken of,
but with Servant/Israel, one is never beyond the realm of personification.

We are warned that "the question of identity is at the present time an
enigma beyond resolution" (Brueggemann 1998, 109). Jacob-Israel is several times called Servant outside the Songs (e.g., Isa 41:8; 44:1), but also
within them, in Isaiah 49:3.[4] Claus Westermann (1969, 20-21, 93) warns
against a single and consistent line of interpretation to the exclusion of others and that exegesis should not be controlled by the question Who is the
servant? but by what the texts make known about what transpires or is to
transpire between God, the servant, and those to whom his task pertains. I

---

4. All manuscripts of the Hebrew contain this reference to Israel, except Kennicot 96. It is
also in 1QIsa[a], though lacking in 2QIsa[d]. It is read by both the LXX and the Targum.

interpret both Servant/Israel and the Servant of the Songs as figures bearing the ongoing vocation and mission of Israel. I examine the first, second, and fourth Songs.

The first Song is Isaiah 42:1-4. Yahweh presents Yahweh's servant and outlines his task and manner of accomplishing it. The Servant will accomplish Yahweh's goals on earth. His primary vocation is to the nations (vv. 1, 4) and the coastlands (v. 4). The coastlands and islands, first mentioned in Isaiah 41:1, stand for the far distant isles that were considered the extremities of the earth. Three times the task of the Servant is related to the word *mispat* (vv. 1, 3, and 4) and once to *torah* (v. 4). These words have been rendered in diverse senses in the versions, also in Isaiah 51:4 where the task is assumed by Yahweh.

Isaiah 42:1

> He shall teach *the true way* to the nations (NJPS).
> He will bring *forth justice* to the nations (NRSV).
> He will *bring fair judgment* to the nations (NJB).

Isaiah 42:3

> He shall bring forth the true way (NJPS).
> He will faithfully bring forth justice (NRSV).
> Faithfully he presents fair judgment (NJB).

Isaiah 42:4

> Till he has established *the true way* on earth; and the coastlands
> shall await his teaching (NJPS).
> Until he has established *justice* in the earth; and the coastlands wait
> for his teaching (NRSV).
> Until he has *established fair judgment* on earth, and the coasts and
> islands are waiting for his instruction (NJB).

Isaiah 51:4

> For teaching [*torah*] shall go forth from Me, *My way* for the light
> of peoples (NJPS).
> For a teaching will go out from me, and *my justice* for a light to the
> peoples (NRSV).
> For a law will come from me, and I shall make *my saving justice* the
> light of peoples (NJB).

The versions are thus split. *Mišpat* is the "true way" according to the NJPS, or "justice/judgment" according to the NRSV and NJB, while *torah* is "teaching" (NJPS, NRSV) or "law" (NJB). In the one set, the task of the Servant is that of moral and religious instruction of the nations in the true way—the way of Yahweh. In the other, his task is rather in the field of law or politics.

Torah derives from the root *yrh* ("to teach") and refers basically to instruction. It was the instruction of priest or prophet concerning the concrete will of Yahweh and came to mean "ordinance" or "law"; in biblical usage it stood for the law of Moses. Isaiah often uses the phrase "word of Yahweh" as parallel to the *"torah* of our God," both referring to the word of the prophet. *Mišpaṭ* operates in the field of justice and is usually the judgment or legal decision pronounced by a judge or ruler *(šōphēṭ)*. But it may also refer to the order or ordinance promulgated by a ruler. It is so used in a few passages to refer to the divine law, for example, Jeremiah 8:7: "but my people do not know Yahweh's laws" *(mišpaṭ Yahweh)*. See also Isaiah 58:2 and Jeremiah 5:4, 5, where *mišpaṭ ᵓĔlōhênû* ("the law of our God") is in parallelism with *derek Yahweh* ("the way of the Lord"). But *mišpaṭ* in itself does not refer specifically to the law of God, only when it is used with the name of God. In Isaiah 42:1 the Servant will cause to go out *mišpaṭ (yōṣîᵓ mišpaṭ)*, a phrase that seems to refer to proclaiming some decree or giving an authoritative speech. The speaker may be judge, prophet, or king. It should be noted that the word of the prophet may be a political act, effective also in the social and political order.

It is my contention that the task of the Servant in the Songs cannot be interpreted without reference to their rereading in Isaiah 51:4-5, which transfers to Yahweh the task earlier assigned to the Servant. Isaiah 51:4 links intertextually to Isaiah 2:3, where the nations stream to Zion, from which *"torah* will go forth [using the same verb, *tēṣēᶜ*, as Isa 51:4] and the word of Yahweh from Jerusalem." In Isaiah 51:4, Yahweh publishes abroad among the nations Yahweh's *torah* and *mišpaṭ* as light for them, light being salvation and well-being in either the spiritual or social order. For Israel, there is no sharp distinction between the two, for a righteous social order was always founded on the *torah* or law of Yahweh. The light Yahweh will bring the nations is characterized as follows: "I will bring near my deliverance swiftly, my salvation has gone out and my arms will rule the peoples" (NRSV). The reference is to the universal rule of Yahweh, which was also what the Servant was called to realize and which the nations of earth will experience as one of justice. When Isaiah 42:1-4 is read in relation to Isaiah 51:4-5, *torah* and *mišpaṭ* seem to point to the task of establishing the universal sovereignty of Yahweh and consequently ordering the world society in justice and righteousness. A more religious interpretation is given to this task in 42:6, which speaks of "light to the nations," a phrase borrowed from 49:6, which is the next text to be considered.

The second Song is Isaiah 49:1-6. The unit is an address of the Servant to the coastlands. The Servant is designated in v. 3 as Israel (see n. 4 above), even though he is given a mission to Israel in v. 5. Several solutions have been advanced to unravel this enigma. One recent attempt is that the mission given to Cyrus or Servant/Israel in Isaiah 40-48 is from Isaiah 49:3 consigned to the prophet himself. The prophet's mission to Israel becomes a paradigm for the mission of Israel to the nations (Wilcox and Paton-Williams 1988, 91, 99). Yahweh widens the task of the Servant, making him a light to the nations. A later insertion adds another task, namely, that of being *bĕrît 'am* (Isa 49:8; see also 42:6). What does this phrase mean? The versions diverge in the rendering of Isaiah 49:8, as follows:

Isaiah 49:8
> And appointed you a covenant people—restoring the land, allotting anew the desolate holdings (NJPS).[5]
> And given you as a covenant to the people, to establish the land, to apportion the desolate heritages (NRSV).
> And have appointed you to be the covenant for a people, to restore the land, to return ravaged properties (NJB).

Isaiah 42:6
> And appointed you a covenant people, a light of nations (NJPS).
> I have given you as a covenant to the people, a light to the nations (NRSV).
> I have made you a covenant of the people and light to the nations (NJB).

The meaning *of bĕrît 'am* is obscure, and the expression "give as *bĕrît*" occurs nowhere else in the Hebrew Bible (Westermann 1969, 100). The expression hardly means "a covenant people," as in the NJPS[6] version, for this would be *'am bĕrît*. The correct translation should be "a covenant of/to the people." In Isaiah 49:8 the people are Israel, for the expression is followed by an infinitive of purpose, "to restore the land, to return ravaged properties." The appearance of *bĕrît 'am* in Isaiah 42:6 is secondary and depends on its use in 49:8. I judge the combination of "covenant of the people" and "light to the nations" in Isaiah 42:6 a succinct summary of the task of the Servant as given in 49:6. As such, "covenant of the people" is not in synonymous parallelism with "light to the nations." Were this so, "people" (*'am)* would parallel "nations" and would refer to humankind.

---

5. The NJPS has Yahweh as subject of the verb and renders as follows: "it is too little that you should be My servant in that I raise up the tribes of Jacob and restore the survivors of Israel."

6. The editors of the NJSB (2004, 867) so explain the rendering: "the nations of the world will witness God's faithfulness to the covenant when Israel is redeemed. Consequently, the people will be the tool through which God becomes known to all nations as mighty, just, and reliable. In these passages, the Israelites are a light to the nations by virtue of what happens to them, not because of what they do."

Rather, it retains its usual reference to the people of Israel. As "covenant of the people," the Servant becomes the bearer of God's covenant with Israel and is God's agent in restoring Israel to the land in peace and well-being. But he is also to be "light to the nations." What this may mean is discussed next.

Norman H. Snaith (1967, 147) insists that "light to the nations" does not depict a mission of the Servant on behalf of the nations. Rather, "the Return is the prophet's dominant theme, all else is subservient to it." The salvation/news that is to reach the ends of the earth is Yahweh's salvation of Israel, with which the prophet is primarily concerned. For Harry M. Orlinsky (1967a, 411) it is sheer eisegesis to make "a light to the nations" mean that Israel was in exile to bring redemption to the world (internationalism). Rather, here as elsewhere, the prophet was nationalistic. The Servant is Israel and through him God's victory (thus *yešu'â* should be translated as "victory" rather than "salvation") in restoring God's people to their homeland becomes a world phenomenon. Martin-Achard (1959, 29) concurs and affirms that the text on the "light to the nations" does not include a mission of the Servant to the gentiles. For, it is rather by giving life to God's people that the God of Israel makes of them the light of the world (*c'est en accordant la vie à son peuple que le Dieu d'Israël en fait la lumière du monde*).

Light is a motif that runs throughout the book of Isaiah (Clements 1996, 57-69), appearing first with the call of Isaiah in 6:1-13. The prophet's mission is to make the people blind and deaf! The darkness intensifies in 8:22, but is to be removed by the deliverer-king in 9:1: "the people who walked in darkness have seen a great light." Light is wholeness; it is the realization of the saving will of Yahweh. Isaiah 60:1-3 both develops and transforms the image when it says, "arise, shine out, for your light has come and the glory of Yahweh has risen on you" (see chapter 11). Renewed Israel's light is a reflection of the glory of Yahweh. Israel becomes a community that radiates the righteousness and holiness of Yahweh and the well-being that flows from it. To such an Israel, the nations will come in pilgrimage ("the nations will come to your light" [Isa 60:3; cf. 2:1-5]). It seems that Isaiah 49:6 implies an active mission to the nations. The nations do not come to Israel; rather, the Servant brings "light" to them. What the Servant brings to the nations is similar to what he is commissioned to bring to Israel. In Isaiah 49:5, his commission is both "to bring Jacob back to [Yahweh] and to reunite Israel to [Yahweh]." That task to Israel is at once political and spiritual. It involves both the returning of Israel to Yahweh and restoring them to the land. So also is the Servant's task as "light to the nations" both sociopolitical and spiritual. Israel's mission as God's servant was to "achieve the vision and knowledge of YHWH for itself and put an end to that dark ignorance of God which characterized idolatry not only in Israel but in distant lands as well" (Stern 1994, 231). The full meaning of "light to the nations," when interpreted in relation to Isaiah 60:1-3 and the focus of the final editing of the book of Isaiah on a transformed Zion from which both justice and righteousness radiate, is that of missionary evangelization among the nations. When Paul cited Isaiah 49:6 in the synagogue of Pisidia, he was rooting the Christian mission to the gentiles on Old Testament foundations.

Isaiah 52:13-53:12 is the final text to be considered. David J. A. Clines (1976, 61) calls attention to the use of only the pronouns I, he, we, they and warns that "the poem is free to do its work by its very lack of specificity, its openness to a multiplicity of readings." The "he" stands in the center of relationships—what transpires in the poem is the breaking in of a new vision of the Servant and of the nexus of relationships that engulfs him. The unit has a threefold structure (Childs 2001, 411), with the confession of a group that designates itself as "we" framed by divine speeches:

52:13-15   First divine speech—assures that the servant will be exalted
53:11a   Confession of a chorus of "we"—humiliation of the servant
53:11b-12 Second divine speech—endorses and exalts the servant

Yahweh introduces a figure whom Yahweh calls "my servant" and assures the audience that he will succeed and be exalted. Then a chorus of persons appears and confesses that they had imagined the figure as stricken by God but now realize that the punishments he bore have brought them forgiveness of sin and removal of their punishment. They now see the pains of the Servant as from Yahweh's own hand and that through him the purpose of Yahweh shall be accomplished (Isaiah 53:10). They express the hope that he shall see offspring and prolong his days. Yahweh adds the assurance that "the righteous one, my servant, shall make many righteous, and he shall bear their iniquities" (Isa 53:11 NRSV).[7] In v. 12a, Yahweh gives another assurance, the rendering of which varies in the versions, as follows:

NJPS	NRSV	NJB
Assuredly, I will give him *the many*[8] *as his portion*. He shall receive *the multitude as his portion*.	Therefore I will allot him *a portion with the great*, and he shall divide the *spoil with the strong*.	Hence I shall give him *a portion with the many*, and he shall share the *booty with the mighty*.

---

7. Westermann (1967, 267) argues that the arrangement of words in the Hebrew rules out this translation. He rather follows Sigmund Mowinckel in seeing *yaṣdîq* as internal *hiphil* and thus rendering, "my servant will show himself righteous and [so stand] as righteous before the many."

8. The Hebrew text has הרבים (*hārabbîm*, "the many") in synonymous parallelism with *ʿaṣûmîm* ("the strong" or "mighty," but can also be read as "the multitude," hence the NJPS rendering). A synonymous parallel to *ʿaṣûmîm* would be *hārabbîm* ("the great," hence the NRSV rendering).

According to the NJPS, the reward of the Servant will be the repatriation and repopulation of Israel in the land;[9] the other versions simply say that the reward of the Servant will be great. North (1956, 176) argued that "the many" included the nations and kings of Isaiah 52:15, and thus the horizon of the text extended beyond Israel; in fact, he considered the text as a prophecy of someone to come. W. A. M. Beuken (1972, 28) also read the "we" as the nations and kings and affirmed that the death of the Servant was salvific both for Israel and for the nations. However, the expression "the many" does not necessarily mean "all." It recurs in Daniel 12:2-4, 10 as a term for the faithful, and at Qumran as a designation of the Qumran covenanters. It may even have also been a self-designation of the early Christian community (cf. Mark 14:24; Rom 5:15). The "many" probably referred to the disciples of the Servant, who are heard in Isaiah 53:1-11a (cf. Blenkinsopp 2002, 350). The suffering and death[10] of the Servant do have universal import, but through the action of Yahweh on the "the many." Through him Yahweh's purpose *(ḥēpheṣ)* will be achieved (Isa 53:10). Yahweh's purpose (cf. Isa 49:6; 51:4-5) is that of bringing *torah* and justice as light to the nations and having Yahweh's arms rule the peoples (Isa 51:5 NRSV). It includes the return of Israel to Yahweh, restoration of the land, and the ushering in of an order of justice and well-being (light) for the world. In Isaiah 44:28 Cyrus was to carry out this purpose of Yahweh by saying to Jerusalem, "you will be rebuilt" and to the temple, "you will be refounded" (see also 46:10; 48:14). But all references to Cyrus drop after Isaiah 48. The role is assumed by the Servant of Isaiah 49:1-6, who is both to "restore the tribes of Jacob and bring back the survivors of Israel" but also and even more to be "a light to the nations so that my salvation may reach the remotest parts of earth" (Isa 49:6). But in this last Song of the Servant, Yahweh achieves these aims through the route of the suffering of the Servant.[11] The sufferings were at first misconceived by the chorus as punishment for guilt. But when it was revealed to them that the power of Yahweh was working in and through the Servant (Isaiah 53:1), they came to see that "ours were the sufferings he was bearing, ours the sorrows he was carrying" (Isaiah 53:4). This contrite group in Israel will later, in Isaiah 56-66, be designated as the offspring of the Servant announced in 53:10 ("he will see his offspring and prolong his life"), and will be characterized as the "servants of Yahweh" (54:17; 65:8; 65:13-15)

---

9. The NJSB editors thus see the "resurrection of the Servant as probably a metaphor for the renewal of the nation at the end of the exile" (2004, 892).

10. The MT has an obscure *nega' lamō* ("there was a blow to him"? "to them"?), which many correct to *nugga' lamawet* ("he was smitten to death") with the LXX which has *echthē eis thanaton* ("he was done to death").

11. Orlinsky (1967b, 55) remarked that "nowhere in the Hebrew Bible did anyone preach a doctrine . . . which allowed the sacrifice of the innocent in the place of and as an acceptable substitution for the guilty."

or those who tremble at Yahweh's word (66:2, 5). These inherit "my holy mountain" (65:9; 66:20) from which the proclamation of the glory of Yahweh will go out to all nations (66:19). It is this nucleus that will merge with those summoned to Yahweh from among the nations to form the "new heavens and new earth" (65:17) that Yahweh is creating for the time to come. Once again, the purification of Zion is in function of salvation to the ends of the earth. We can fittingly end this chapter with Brueggemann's assertion (1998, 144) that both Jews and Christians see in their history the capacity and willingness of God to do something new through suffering: "newness through suffering is the gospel that attests to the *power of God* at work *through human weakness* to bring to fruition God's intention for the world."

CONCLUSION

Deutero-Isaiah does not present a coherent doctrine of mission. The central concern seems to be recognition of the universal might and rule of Yahweh and the consequent rejection of idols as nothings (Melugin 1997). The universal rule of Yahweh secures the deliverance and well-being of Israel but also includes the nations somewhat in a manner rife with unresolved tensions. But there are texts that envisage the inclusion of the nations in Israel's covenant with Yahweh (e.g., Isa 44:5). The call to the ends of the earth to "turn to me and you will be saved" (45:22) is at some variance with itself, for it both calls upon the nations to acknowledge Yahweh and yet focuses on glory and triumph for Israel. Such texts may have been at the origin of the system of "god-fearers" that arose in the later Persian period. The role of Servant/Israel outside the Songs of the Servant differs from that of the Servant in the Songs. For one thing, Servant/Israel outside the Songs is the passive recipient of salvation, while the Servant in the Songs clearly has an active mission to the nations. But Servant/Israel seems to have an active role in at least two texts outside the Servant Songs. In Isaiah 43:10 Israel is to be Yahweh's active witness in the assize against the gods of the nations. In Isaiah 55:3-5, the prophet transfers God's covenant with David to the entire people. And David's original role is reinterpreted such that Israel becomes a "witness to the peoples" and a "lawgiver to peoples." As a priestly people (cf. Exod 19:5-6), they receive the missionary function of inviting the peoples to Yahweh's covenant and *torah*. The primary vocation of the Servant in Isaiah 42:1-4 is to universal mission. His task toward the nations is that of *mišpaṭ* and *torah*. Both terms point to the task of establishing the universal sovereignty of Yahweh and consequently ordering the world society in justice and righteousness. Isaiah 49:1-6 (see also the later addition in 42:6) adds the task of "light to the nations." It was concluded that the full meaning of "light to the nations," when interpreted in relation to 60:1-3 and the focus of the final editing of the book of Isaiah on a transformed Zion from which both justice and righteousness radiate, is that of missionary evangelization among the nations. The Servant (explicitly designated as "Israel" in v. 3) is to achieve the vision and knowledge of Yahweh for itself and so to enlighten the nations. In so doing, the Servant will bring them into Yahweh's reign and to the benefits that accrue from it. In Isaiah 52:13-53:12, Yahweh takes over the Servant's mission and executes the purpose to bring justice and *torah* to Israel and the nations. But this time, Yahweh is able to produce newness and to prepare the "new heavens and new earth" through the suffering of the Servant.

DISCUSSION

1. Discuss some of the problems of the theme of Israel and the nations in Deutero-Isaiah.
2. How is Israel or the Servant "light to the nations"?
3. Is there mission in Deutero-Isaiah?
4. Discuss the theme of the glory of Yahweh in Deutero-Isaiah.
5. What concretely does Yahweh's "salvation" mean for the nations?

14

"I am creating new heavens and a new earth"

Isaiah 65:17-25

God creates a new heaven and a new earth which, by interpretive allusion within Isaiah, are equated with Zion and Jerusalem, the Lord's holy mountain—they are the goal of the new exodus.
—Peter Miscall, "Isaiah: New Heavens, New Earth, New Book," 52

Isaiah 65:17-25 is in a certain sense the apex of Old Testament revelation on the election of Israel. In equating the new heavens and the new earth with Jerusalem/Zion, it is the world that turns out to be Yahweh's chosen people (Brueggemann 1998, 166). On the surface it appears to represent centripetal mission. But the deeper reality of this unit is that the dichotomy of Israel/the nations has been bypassed and Zion has in fact become a symbol of humanity dwelling with Yahweh in reconciliation

I assume, despite some voices to the contrary, that Isaiah 65:17-25 form a unit. With Joseph Blenkinsopp (2003, 285) I take the initial *kî* ("for") as a connective particle that functions here with no particular subordinating force and is the start of a new unit, something that happens often in Isaiah 40-66. Two verses are in parallelism, both using the participle of *bārā'* ("to create"). "For look, I am creating new heavens and a new earth" (Isa 65:17) is a parallel construction to "for look, I am creating Jerusalem to be 'Joy'" (Isa 65:18). This parallelism is an argument against removing v. 17 (with v. 25) as if these were later attempts to give the unit an apocalyptic character. And even if this were so, one would still have to interpret the text as it is.

Claus Westermann (1969, 411) argues that, as in Isaiah 60-62, 65:16b-25 is addressed to the whole nation and there is no suggestion of a cleavage among the people. The context of Isaiah 65-66, however, makes it clear that there has been a division among the people of God. Ever since Isaiah 53:10 raised the hope of "seed" for the servant, the question has been, "in whom is the seed promised the Servant in 53:10 realized?" (Beuken 1990, 68). The answer begins in Isaiah 54:17, where Zion becomes the inheritance not of the entire people but of the "servants of Yahweh." The Israel addressed as a whole in Isaiah 40-48 is being redefined in terms of a nucleus within it. From this point in Isaiah we hear no more of the servant (in the singular), but of these "servants of Yahweh" in the plural. They are "my chosen ones" (Isa 65:9, 15), "those of my people who have sought me" (Isa 65:10), and those "who tremble at my word" (Isa 66:2, 5).[1] It is from this nucleus that Yahweh will in due course bring into existence a new Israel to inherit both temple and land. The people as a whole are now like a bunch of grapes that should be destroyed but for the fact that it contained a blessing (Isa 65:8). The blessing corresponds to "those of my people who have sought me" (65:10) in contrast to "those of you who abandon Yahweh." The heritage of Jacob, "my mountains from Judah," now belongs exclusively to the former: "my chosen ones will own them, and my servants will live there" (65:9). Similarly, after describing the adulterous ways of some of the people, Isaiah 57:13 ends with the promise, "but whoever trusts in me will inherit the land, they will own my holy mountain." The earlier hope had been that "your people, all of them upright, will possess the land forever" (Isa 60:21). But now some of the people have proved to be obstinately disloyal to Yahweh. They have oppressed and even excommunicated the "servants of Yahweh" who tremble at Yahweh's word (66:5).[2] Yahweh now intervenes on behalf of the oppressed servants and distinguishes between true Israel and disobedient Israel. Isaiah 65:13-16 lays out five coming reversals in the fortunes of the two groups. Five blessings of the servants of Yahweh are juxtaposed to five curses of the opposing group. The blessings point forward to the condition of the blessed in Isaiah 65:19-22. The five antitheses read as follows:

You will see my servants eating while you go hungry,
You will see my servants drinking while you go thirsty,
You will see my servants rejoicing while you are put to shame;
You will hear my servants shouting for joy of heart, while you shriek
    for sorrow of heart and howl with a broken spirit

---

1. The word הַחֲרֵדִים ("the tremblers") occurs elsewhere in the Hebrew Bible only in Ezra 9:4 and 10:3. In Ezra this group trembled at the law of God. In both Ezra and Isaiah 66, the "tremblers" are opposed by people addicted to non-Yahwistic cults or to marriage with women outside the community. It is strongly suggested that these "tremblers" and the "servants of Yahweh" are identical and that they consider themselves as having taken over the identity and mission of the larger social entity (Blenkinsopp 1997b, 171).

2. "Your brothers who hate you and reject you because of my name, have said, 'let Yahweh show [Yahweh's] glory.'" The verb used is *śn'* ("to hate"), which at Elephantine was used for divorce.

> And you will leave your name behind as a curse for my chosen ones
> . . . but to his servants he will give another name. (Isa 65:13-15)

The distinction is no longer between groups defined by national boundaries, but splits across the nation. This means that it is no longer the entire
nation that is recipient of Yahweh's salvation or judgment word. Rather the
line cuts through the one nation (Hanson 1979, 150).

Isaiah 65:17-25 equates "new heavens and new earth," "Jerusalem,"
and "my holy mountain." They interpret each other as symbols of God's
promised new creation. Already Isaiah 56:6 had "foreigners who adhere to
Yahweh to serve him . . . and cling to my covenant" equally finding a home
on Yahweh's holy mountain. Hence,

> in the end the remnant is not defined in national or ethnic terms, but
> in confessional and behavioral terms. Being Israelite does not guar-
> antee inclusion in the remnant, and being foreign does not entail
> exclusion from it. (Webb 1990, 79)

Expressed in Pauline language, the Israel of the flesh has given way to the
Israel of God (Gal 6:16) characterized solely by obedience to Yahweh. The
mystery of the election of Israel is finally disclosed. Israel embodied and
manifested the saving activity of God in the world as center of, and pointer
to, God's activity among all the nations. In the words of Peter Miscall,
"God creates a new heaven and a new earth which, by interpretive allusion
within Isaiah, are equated with Zion and Jerusalem, the Lord's holy mountain—they are the goal of the new exodus" (1992, 52). The equation of
new heavens/earth with Jerusalem shows that all along God was not
focused uniquely on Israel and her history. Rather,

> Israel's own history is neither a substitute for the order of God's
> world to which it points, nor is it the full actualization of this order
> on earth. Israel's historical institutions did not replace Yahweh's cre-
> ation and sustenance of the world. They were supposed to point to
> that realm of Yahweh's domination. (Knierim 1981, 100)

Our unit is defined by the contrast between the former things
(*hāri'šōnôt*) and the new things. In Isaiah 43:18-19, the former things
referred to the prodigies that Yahweh wrought in the past in Israel's history,
especially in the exodus. In the rest of Deutero-Isaiah the "former things"
may refer also to recent prophecies in the process of fulfillment, especially
those bearing on the early victories of Cyrus. The "new things" are the
events about to happen, namely, the overthrow of Babylon, the return from
exile, and the restoration of Zion, in short, the new exodus (Anderson
1962, 187). In our passage, however, the "former things" are reinterpreted

to refer to the past troubles of the righteous group (Isa 65:16) and the "new things" to be the new heavens and new earth that Yahweh is creating for them. Isaiah 57:1 gives us some idea of the past troubles of the servants of Yahweh when it says that "the upright person perishes and no one cares. The faithful is taken off and no one takes it to heart." The reversals in the antitheses of Isaiah 65:13-16 also afford a glimpse of what their condition was like. As the former situation is summed up in sorrow and a broken spirit, so the reversed situation will be one of joy and gladness (65:18). Yahweh will recreate Jerusalem as quintessential "Joy." The "I" of Yahweh is stressed as the one who ushers in the new creation on behalf of Yahweh's servants. The verb *bārā'* ("to create") always has God as the subject, but it does not yet mean creating out of nothing. This verb was introduced into Old Testament literature as a theological idea for the first time in the exilic period (Bernhardt 1975, 245). Deutero-Isaiah uses it several times for God's activity in molding history and creating a change of fortune for the exiles. God's creative acts belong to the history of salvation, whether performed in *Urzeit* (Isa 51:9) or at the time of the new creation (Isa 45:8; 48:7): "[God's] redemptive acts are acts of creation, and [God's] creative acts are acts of history" (Anderson 1962, 185).

"And I shall be joyful in Jerusalem, and I shall rejoice in my people" (Isa 65:19). Yahweh's joy in Yahweh's new creation recalls the joy of the creator in Genesis 1:31 when the creator saw everything that the creator had made and behold it was very good. Finally, Yahweh is able to relate to Yahweh's creation as Yahweh had intended at the origins. Aspects of the joy of God and people are described. There will be no weeping. Weeping (*běkî*) is heard at bereavements. The righteous will live out their days, and infant mortality will be forgotten. Whoever fails to reach a hundred years will be considered accursed by God! Before the advent of belief in the resurrection of the dead in the later part of the Old Testament (Dan 12:1-2, second century B.C.E.), the goal of life was to live to an accomplished and ripe old age and to die with honor surrounded by children and grandchildren. The "sound of a shriek" (*qôl zě'āqāh*) is cry for redress from violence (*ḥamas*). In Exodus 3:9 Israel's cry for help (*ṣě'āqāh*, a cognate of *zě'āqāh*) reached Yahweh, and Yahweh came down to rescue the Israelites from the clutches of the Egyptians. No sound of a shriek means that there will be no violence, from outside or from inside—no oppression within and no conquests from without. Verse 25 expresses this hope poetically when it says that "the wolf and the young lamb will feed together." The futility curse is canceled: they will not toil in vain, nor bear children for disaster (Isa 65:23). No more will their children die in combat or the produce of their labor be under impress by agents of empires and other oppressors.

The coming governance of Yahweh will radically transform both bereft "nature" and disabled "history" (Brueggemann 1998, 275). One of the blessings of covenant obedience in Lev 26:6 is the promise that "I shall rid the land of beasts of prey." In Ezekiel 34:28 foreign oppressors are represented as beasts of prey, and the children of Israel are promised that no more will the wild animals of the country devour them. Israel always remembered that God's original intention was for all living beings (*nepheš hayyāh*), which includes humans and animals, to eat vegetables (Gen 1:29) and not kill others for food. The corruption of God's intention was indicated in Genesis 6:13, when it was said that all flesh was full of violence (*hamas*). God had to bow to necessity when God conceded to human beings the killing of animals for food, but God put the restriction that "you must not eat flesh with life, that is to say blood in it. And I shall demand an account of your life-blood, too. I shall demand it of every animal, and of humans" (Gen 9:5). The tradition, however, retained the hope that creation would go back to God's original intention. It is this hope that is fulfilled in the promise that "the wolf and the young lamb will feed together, and the lion will eat straw like the ox" (Isa 65:25). In Isaiah 11:7 this hope of peace in the animal world reposes on Yahweh's anointed, while in our text it is the result of divine action in establishing the new heavens and new earth as a place of peace and reconciliation between God, humans, and all creation. The serpent will be content with dust (as the curse in Gen 3:14) and will no longer be a danger to God's righteous people. Later texts carry forward the idea of the solidarity of human beings and the animal world. The *Syriac Apocalypse of Baruch* (2 Baruch) 73:6 (ca. 100 C.E.) says that "wild beasts shall come from the forest and minister to humans, and asps and dragons shall come out of their holes to submit themselves to a little child."

"In all My sacred mount, Nothing evil or vile shall be done" (v. 25 NJPS). The *hiphil* verb *hišḥît* refers not only to violence and destruction but to acting perversely or corruptly. Hence, in Genesis 6:12 "God looked at the earth and it was corrupt, for corrupt were the ways of all living beings on earth." The literal reading is, "all flesh had corrupted [*hišḥît*] its way on the earth." Not only will there be no violence, human or bestial, but human beings will no longer behave in ways displeasing to Yahweh. *2 Baruch* 73:4-5 fills out the picture:

> and law suits and accusations and contentions and revenges, and murder and passions and envy and hatred, and all things like these shall be done away and go to their condemnation. For it is these things that have filled this world with evils, and it is because of these that the life of man has been so troubled.[3]

---

3. Cited from Mitchell G. Reddish, ed., *Apocalyptic Literature: A Reader* (Peabody, Mass.: Hendrickson, 1995).

There will be no confiscation of the fruits of one's labor, either by occupying armies or by the wicked and powerful among the people. In fact, as in Isaiah 2:1-5, what is described here is a world without war, in which God's people live in security and peace/*šālôm*. Deuteronomy 28 details covenant promises and curses for keeping or failing to obey the voice of Yahweh. Deuteronomy 28:30 expresses the "futility curse" when it says, "build a house, you will not live in it; plant a vineyard, you will not gather its fruit." The promises of Isaiah 65:21 thus mean that the curse that resulted from breaking the covenant is annulled: "they will build houses and live in them, they will plant vineyards and eat their fruit." In the Deuteronomistic conception, covenant fidelity issues in peace and abundant life for Israel, for it calls down the blessing of Yahweh and this produces overall well-being, both social and spiritual.

In the new creation access to God will again be opened. In Isaiah 65:1 Yahweh made Yahweh-self available to a nation that did not seek Yahweh. Yahweh had "said 'here I am, here I am' to a nation that did not invoke my name." Now the reverse will be the case, for "before they call I shall answer, before they stop speaking I shall have heard" (Isa 65:24). "My holy mountain" is the temple abode of Yahweh. This home of Yahweh had to be recreated after the atrocities of Isaiah 66:3, so that now it is home only for those who tremble at the word of Yahweh and who are attentive to the holiness of God's abode. These people have been under oppression and have been excluded by the powerful and unfaithful people. Yahweh comes to their aid and re-creates the social order for them in such a manner as to effect a reversal of their fortunes (Isa 63:13-16). God transforms the universe in transforming Zion: "The transformation of Zion is the key to the transformation of the cosmos, and the emergence and eventual perfection of a faithful remnant is the key to the transformation of Zion" (Webb 1990, 81). Transformed Zion is not for the "servants of Yahweh" alone. Yahweh has other servants also, whom Yahweh has taken from the nations (Isa 56:6; 66:19) and who equally inherit "my holy mountain." Unlike the new heavens and the new earth of Revelation 21:1-4, in which death will be no more, the new heavens and new earth of Isa 65:17-25 retain a foot in the present world reality. Houses are still built, vineyards harvested, and death still comes, even if at a ripe old age. What our text describes can be called the "consummation of creation" in the sense of the perfection of the existing world order, its rejuvenation or renewal (Knierim 1981, 104). The earth has again become paradise. It is interesting in this connection that Ezekiel 28:13-14 identifies "Eden, garden of God" with the holy mountain of God. But our text also describes an "existence between the times": it announced the new creation as the child of the earth but also as the bride of heaven (Mauser 1982, 184). Israel lives in this world but is not defined by this age. Israel belongs wholly to the age to come. When the entire history of Israel and God's dealings with it are focused on God's holy mountain, it means that what defined Israel all along was not land or blood ties, but the covenant relationship with its God. Israel exists to draw the entire creation into God's holy presence. "In the end, it is the world that turns out to be Yahweh's chosen people" (Brueggemann 1998, 166).

DISCUSSION

1. In what ways does this text reveal the ultimate meaning of the election of Israel?
2. "In the end, it is the world that turns out to be Yahweh's chosen people" (Brueggemann). Comment.

Conclusion

And all the people of the whole earth will be converted
and will reverence God with all sincerity.
All will renounce their false gods who have led them astray into error,
and will bless the God of ages in uprightness.

—Tobit 14:6

This book has pursued two lines of research: first, how and when Israel opened up its covenant with Yahweh to the gentiles; and, second, what the theological foundations for such a development might be. It is now time to pull the threads together. The investigation will turn on how and when the movement toward mission traced all through this book came to full term and Israel became effectively missionary.

By way of recapitulation, here is a summary of the method used in this book (for full details, see chapter 1). Four approaches were applied to the material of most of the chapters. The text was considered in its literary context and in its function within the larger complex and the whole. Attention was given to possible layers in the text, particularly in prophetic literature, where the later strata often comment upon and adapt the earlier ones. Historical analysis was applied to the text insofar as this was called for or was possible. The reception of the text within the Old Testament, and sometimes into the New Testament, was investigated with the aim of elucidating the text's total field of meaning. Texts in diverse contexts but with similar content were compared. Such comparison often manifested the variety of points of view on particular subjects and issues within the Old Testament tradition itself. The method was thus attentive both to context and to rereadings and intertextual linkages. The aim was always to understand a particular theme of mission in the Old Testament in light of the full development of that theme in the tradition.

Mission being part of the identity of any faith community, it cannot be defined without reference to the particular community. A definition of mission formulated with respect to traditions outside the Old Testament tradition, for example, with a view to the New Testament, may not fit the reality of Israel, where mission was in a certain tension with election. Accordingly, four faces of mission in the Old Testament were discerned as both a heuristic tool and an instrument for the organization of the chapters to follow (see chapter 1 for details). The first face of mission in the Old Testament was identified as the aspect of universality—universality of salvation and universality of righteousness before Yahweh. Chapters 3-5 explored this first face of mission. The second face of mission in the Old Testament was designated as "community-in-mission." It is the awareness that Israel's very existence is bound up with the knowledge and glory of Yahweh among the peoples and that Israel's election serves this glory of Yahweh. Because Israel was meant to be a pattern for individual and social life that will draw all humanity to Yahweh, a primary aspect of Israel's mission is to be fully the Israel that God has desired it to be, a revelation of God to the nations. This aspect of mission in the Old Testament may correspond to what Walter C. Kaiser (2000, 9) called "centrifugal witnessing." Chapters 6 to 8 developed this face of mission. Chapter 9 was a transitional chapter that investigated the theological foundations that made possible Israel's inclusion of gentiles in the covenant with Yahweh. Then the face of mission that scholars generally call "centripetal mission" was investigated. It formed the material of chapters 10-11. Finally, chapters 12-14 investigated texts that mostly portrayed "centrifugal mission."

One overriding purpose of Yahweh throughout the biblical tradition, especially in Isaiah, is that of the establishment of Yahweh's universal reign on Mount Zion. Such universal rule of Yahweh is anticipated and celebrated in the liturgy of the Psalms of Enthronement (Pss 47; 93; 96-99; see chapter 10 above). In quest of this goal, Yahweh commissioned servant-Israel as light to the nations (Isa 49:6). Israel's mission as God's servant was to achieve the vision and knowledge of Yahweh for itself and put an end to that dark ignorance of God that characterized idolatry not only in Israel but also among the nations (see chapter 13). Gradually the later texts of the Hebrew Bible began to concentrate the hopes of Israel and of the world on Yahweh's holy mountain. This began already in Exodus 15:17-18 (which many scholars consider a later addition to the text) when in the hymn of triumph after the crossing of the Reed Sea the goal of the exodus was given as follows:

> You will bring them and plant them on the mountain which is your heritage, the place which you, Yahweh, have made your dwelling, the sanctuary, Yahweh, prepared by your own hands. Yahweh will be king for ever and ever.

The mountain of the temple of the Lord is portrayed as the seat of Yahweh's universal and everlasting rule. Redeemed Israel is to be the agent of Yahweh's universal rule. For the nations to walk in the way of Yahweh, it is necessary that Israel walk in the light of the Lord. Isaiah 2:2-5 portrays purified Zion as the center for world peace and for the instruction of the nations in the way of Yahweh. The nations stream to Zion to be taught by Yahweh and return home to hammer their swords into ploughshares (see chapter 11). The expression "my holy mountain" begins to appear in Isaiah 11:9, a layer many consider late. No hurt or harm will be done on "my holy mountain" for the land shall be wholly righteous and full of the knowledge of Yahweh as a result of the work of the shoot of Jesse. In Isaiah 56:7 Yahweh promises to lead foreigners and eunuchs who adhere to Yahweh and to Yahweh's covenant (the Sabbath) to "my holy mountain" and to "make them joyful in my house of prayer . . . for my house will be called a house of prayer for all peoples." Yahweh self-introduces as the one "who gathers the exiles of Israel" and promises that "there are others I shall gather besides" (Isa 56:8). Since the "others," that is, gentiles, had not been driven away from the land ("to gather" is the opposite of "to drive away") Yahweh's gathering of these others must be seen analogically as a gathering unto Yahweh in worship and righteous living (see chapter 12). By Isaiah 65:17, 25 "my holy mountain" merges with the new heavens and new earth (see chapter 14). It no longer symbolized Israel as a whole, for a split had occurred in that Israel. It now became the abode of the righteous, both of Israel and from among the nations. Yahweh will send missionaries to the nations, for "I am coming to gather every nation and every language. They will come to witness my glory" (Isa 66:18). Yahweh's missionaries will "proclaim my glory to the nations" (66:19). And of the peoples gathered from among the nations, Yahweh will make some of them Levites and priests.[1]

In Isaiah 55:3-5, Israel's consciousness of mission is portrayed when the text reinterprets the Davidic covenant and transfers it to the entire people. Yahweh made David a witness to the peoples, a leader and lawgiver to them. As witness, David proclaimed the might and greatness of Yahweh to the peoples in his empire and brought them under Yahweh (see Eissfeldt 1962, 202). Israel is to "witness" by proclaiming the *torah* to the nations in the manner of Moses (see chapter 13). Missionary Israel "will summon a nation unknown to you, a nation unknown to you will hurry to you" (Isa 55:5). Israel assumes the function foreseen in Exodus 19:5-6 of a "holy nation" and "kingdom of priests," that is, a nation that ministers to other nations on behalf of Yahweh (see chapter 6).

On the question of the admission of gentiles into Yahweh's covenant with Israel, Ezra-Nehemiah presents a double voice. In Ezra 9-10 Ezra forced a covenant on the community of returnees to send away their foreign wives and their children. The reason given was that through such marriage, "the holy race has been contaminated by the people of the country"

---

1. In chapter 12, I argued that the reference is to the gathered gentiles and not to Jews of the Diaspora, whom the nations return as an offering to Yahweh in Isaiah 66:20.

(Ezra 9:2). And Nehemiah 13:3 says that "having heard the Law, they excluded all foreigners from Israel." The law that was heard was Deuteronomy 23:4-6, which read as follows:

> No Ammonite or Moabite is to be admitted to the assembly of God, and this is for all time, since they did not come to meet the Israelites with bread and water, and even hired Balaam to oppose them by cursing them. (Neh 13:2-3)

On the surface it appeared that the conversion of foreigners to the Yahweh religion was not an option. But a report in Ezra 6:21 says that "the Israelites who had returned from exile and *all those who had renounced the filthy practices of the people of the country to join them in resorting to Yahweh, God of Israel* [italics mine], ate the Passover." The renunciation of idolatry and the immorality connected with it would qualify foreigners to join Israel for the Passover. Ever since the first Passover in Exodus 12:1-28 the celebration of the Passover has been a mark of Jewish identity. This shows that Ezra's concern was less racial segregation than to establish the *torah* at the center of the restored community (Sweeney 1997, 59). In Ezra 9:4 and 10:3 the group around Ezra is called the "tremblers." Ezra 9:4 says that "all those who trembled at the words of the God of Israel gathered round me, when faced with the infidelity of the exiles." The same term appears in Isaiah 66:2, 5. Yahweh proclaims that "my eyes are drawn to the person of humbled and contrite spirit, who trembles at my word" (Isa 66:2). These "tremblers" at Yahweh's word were persecuted by the wicked and excommunicated from the community (Isa 66:5; and see chapter 14). Joseph Blenkinsopp (1997b, 170-71) points out that in both Ezra 9-10 and in Isaiah 66 the "tremblers" are characterized by strict adhesion to the *torah* and are opposed by those who practiced non-Yahwistic cults. They formed an entity distinct enough to be excommunicated en bloc. He thus suggests that these "tremblers" and the "servants" of Isaiah 65-66 were identical. Both regarded themselves as having taken over the identity and mission forfeited by the larger social entity, but both were open to receiving foreigners who adhered as closely to the *torah* as themselves.

The hero of the Book of Ruth is a Moabite woman, who even became the ancestress of David, although Moabites were supposed to be excluded from Israel, according to Deuteronomy 23:4. Her action is characterized as taking refuge under the wings of Yahweh (Ruth 2:12). Later in the rabbinic period, conversion would be characterized as "taking refuge under the wings of the Shekinah."

The final edition of the Pentateuch should be dated around 400 B.C.E. It opens with eleven chapters of universal history. This history is prefaced with the P account of creation (Gen 1:1-2:4a), in which God sets up human beings as God's own image and likeness on earth, that is, God's vice regents. Humanity is given the mission to "fill the earth and to subdue it" (Gen 1:28). Stewardship over God's creation is part of the mission of humanity. God rested on the seventh day and set the Sabbath as a sign of God's sovereignty over creation. The Sabbath subverts the present order of master and slave and of humankind's wickedness to animals (see chapter 3). When God's experiment with humanity ended in grief, God called Abram and promised to make him a blessing, so that "in you all the families of the earth shall be blessed" (Gen 12:3 NRSV). The promise of blessing to Abraham contains an internal and creative tension. Abraham is the physical progenitor of Israel, and in blessing Abraham God is conferring the blessing on his descendants, that is, Israel. Yet God surprisingly links this blessing to blessing for all families of the earth. It means that the blessing of Israel consists precisely in being blessing for all families of earth. The special favors of God to Abraham and to his descendants are in view of making them agents of blessing for all of humankind (see chapter 5).

The final edition of the Pentateuch also met the issue raised in Ezra-Nehemiah by developing the legal concept of conversion (Smith 1984, 269). The editors did this by transforming the sense of the Hebrew word *gēr* ("resident alien"). Like the *metoikos* in a Greek *polis*, the *gēr* did not acquire landed property in his place of residence. The status of the *gēr* was, thus, a sociological concept. But the *gēr* was being gradually integrated into the Jewish community. In Exodus 20:10 and 23:12, the *gēr* must keep the Sabbath. Deuteronomy 5:14 and 29:9-14 draw the *gēr* into the religious festivals. What the P final editors of the Pentateuch did was to complete the process of the religious integration of the *gēr* by moving the concept of *gēr* from the sociological plane to the religious plane. They now used another word, *tôšāb*, for the former sociological reality of *gēr* (Kuhn 1964, 729; Smith 1984, 269). The result, as pointed out by George F. Moore, is that "in the Persian period the word [*gēr*] comes to be applied to foreigners (men of other than Jewish descent) who join themselves to [Yahweh], or to Israel as the worshippers of [Yahweh]" (1971, 328). D. Kellermann (1974, 446-47) illustrates this fact by examining some of the laws in P concerning the *gēr*. Like the Israelite, the *gēr* is forbidden to eat blood (Lev 17:10, 12, 13) and is subject to the laws of purification. The laws on permissible degrees of relationship in marriage and on sexual intercourse (Lev 18) apply also to the *gēr*. The law on the Passover in Numbers 9:14 states that the same statute shall apply to the native and the *gēr*. When Exodus 12:45 excludes the *tôšāb* from the Passover, while Exodus 12:48 includes the *gēr*, if he is circumcised, it seems taken for granted that the *gēr* was distinct from the *tôšāb*, was circumcised, and was thus a full participant in Israel's life and cult. Smith (1984, 269) underlines the importance of this move by the later strata of P in the Pentateuch·

Judaism became, legally, a condition open to anyone able to satisfy the requirements for admission, and these requirements might be matters of practice or belief, not ancestry or territorial origin. Thus "Judaism" could become a world religion, capable of indefinite extension by conversion of all peoples.

The LXX translated the Hebrew word *gēr*, which had become a purely religious category, with the word *prosēlytos* ("proselyte"; Kuhn 1964, 728 n. 2). This word occurs only in Jewish and Christian writings and was probably coined by the synagogues of the Diaspora. In the Greco-Roman Diaspora "proselyte" became a technical term for someone who has crossed over fully to Judaism through circumcision. The LXX confirms that by around the mid-third century B.C.E. converts to Judaism were being admitted in the Diaspora, but we have no historical records to gauge the extent.

The Book of Esther (175-150 B.C.E.) was the first book to describe the actual conversion of gentiles to Judaism. Esther 8:17 says that upon Ahasuerus's edict of rehabilitation of the Jews, many of the country's population became Jews since now the Jews were feared. The term used was *mityahădîm*, literally, "making themselves Jews." The Hebrew text did not explicitly mention circumcision, but the LXX mentioned this when it rendered the text as *perietemonto kai ioudaizon* (were circumcising and Judaizing themselves). The first Hebrew text explicitly to mention circumcision in the making of a proselyte was the account of the conversion of Achior the Ammonite in Judith, a book usually dated to the mid-second century B.C.E. Judith 14:10 says, "Achior, recognizing all that the God of Israel had done, believed ardently in him and, accepting circumcision, was permanently incorporated into the House of Israel."

The oldest historical example of a proselyte in the sense above is the house of Herod in Idumea, which was forcibly converted to Judaism through circumcision by John Hyrcanus (134-104 B.C.E.). After the victorious Maccabean resistance against the effort to ban circumcision, circumcision became the most important mark of Jewish faithfulness (Hyatt 1962, 629).

To what extent was Judaism "missionary" in the Hellenistic period? We already mentioned the lack of historical records of early Jewish proselytism. But in the Diaspora, especially in Alexandria, a large body of apologetic and "missionary" literature arose during the Hellenistic period. These documents originated from Jews who had received a Hellenistic education and who sought thereby to present Jewish faith and practice in a manner attractive to people of Hellenistic culture and also to defend Judaism against various charges. Some of this literature sought to prove the religious and moral superiority of Judaism. Scholars differ in their evaluation of such literature as to what light it can throw on Jewish proselytism. For example, some regard *Joseph and Aseneth* as depicting active Jewish mission. Genesis 41:45 recounted that Pharaoh gave Joseph Aseneth, daughter of Potiphera, priest of On, to be his wife. *Joseph and Aseneth* was written in Greek probably between the first and second centuries C.E. to recount the conversion of Aseneth to Judaism. Scot McKnight argues that Judaism, even as late as the first century C.E., was not missionary. He agrees with C. Burchard, who held that *Joseph and Aseneth* was not written in order to promote Jewish prose-lytism, rather that "Judaism is not depicted as mission-minded in *Joseph and Aseneth*. Proselytes are welcomed, not sought, and conversion certainly is not an easy affair" (McKnight 1991, 62).[2]

I tend to agree with Louis H. Feldman (1993, 293, 323), however, who argues that the Jewish attitude toward proselytism changed from a passive to a more active approach in the Hellenistic period. He thinks that the fact that we do not know the names of any Jewish missionaries of this period nor a single extant proselytizing tract of the period may be because the mission was carried out by individual Jews rather than as a concerted effort, as the later Christian mission was to be (Feldman 1993, 289, 332). Among other proofs of Jewish proselytism in the Diaspora in the Hellenistic period, Feldman adduces the dramatic increase in Jewish population at this time, an expansion that can be explained only through the accretion of converts. Further, Jews were expelled from Rome in 139 B.C.E. and also in 19 B.C.E. The reason for the expulsion of 139 B.C.E. was "because they attempted to trans-mit their sacred rites to the Romans" (ibid., 293-304).

In the Roman period (inclusive of the New Testament), there is abun-dant evidence of gentiles attaching themselves to Jewish synagogues, but without full religious aggregation to Judaism. Such were called *sebomenoi* or *phoboumenoi ton theon* ("god-fearers"). That they differed from pros-elytes can be shown from the fact that in the Jewish catacombs in Rome proselytes were buried with other Jews, while god-fearers were buried with gentiles (Kuhn 1964, 733). There apparently was no uniform religious requirement or expectation of god-fearers. It would seem that they gener-ally undertook to observe monotheism and imageless worship and some moral norms (Vermes et al. 1986, 165). Not all god-fearers were monothe-ists. For in Acts Cornelius showed his piety by prayer and almsgiving (Acts 10:2), others by association with the synagogue (Collins 1985, 184). Jose-phus (*Contra Apionem* 2.282) spoke of the widespread adoption of Jewish observances, especially the Sabbath:

> Nay, farther, the multitude of [hu]mankind itself have had a great inclination of a long time to follow our religious observances; for there is not a city of the Grecians, nor any of the barbarians, nor any

---

2. Cited from C. Burchard, "Joseph and Aseneth," in *The Old Testament Pseude-pigrapha*, edited by James Charlesworth (New York: Doubleday, 1985) 1:195.

nation whatsoever, whither our custom of resting on the seventh day hath not come, and by which our fasts and lighting up of lamps, and many of our prohibitions as to our food, are not observed. (cited from Whiston 1987, 811)

Eventually the Mishna (200 C.E.) stipulated three requirements for the conversion of males to Judaism, namely, circumcision, immersion baptism with public witnesses, and a sacrifice in the temple[3] (this last ceased with the destruction of the temple in 70 C.E.). For females, baptism with public witnesses sufficed. The date of the introduction of proselyte baptism is debated. Some scholars think that it was pre-Christian and pre-70 C.E. (McKnight 1991, 84). The silence of Philo and Josephus on this matter, however, has led most scholars to date it to the first century C.E. and to consider it possibly post-Christian. Vermes et al. (1986, 174, no. 89) assert that it was "post-biblical and pre-Mishnaic." McKnight suggests that the origins of Jewish proselyte baptism may have been in the entrance requirements of Jewish Christianity. He says:

The rites in Judaism and Christianity [may] owe their origin to a common Jewish milieu in which water lustrations became increasingly important for converts and that Judaism's rite of baptism may very well have received a decisive impetus from John the Baptist, Jesus, and the earliest Christians. (1991, 85)

In Antioch in Pisidia Paul read Isaiah 49:6 as a command of the Lord for mission to the gentiles when he said, "We turn to the gentiles, for this is what the Lord commanded us to do when he said, 'I have made you a light to the nations, so that my salvation may reach the remotest parts of the earth'" (Acts 13:46-47). What has been demonstrated in this book is that Paul was rooting the Christian mission fully in Old Testament traditions, for "while Israel is the people of God, the people of God is broader than Israel" (Fretheim 1977, 26).

---

3. *Mishna Keritot* 2:1: "a proselyte's atonement is yet incomplete until the blood [of his offering] has been tossed for him [against the base of the Altar]." The translation is from Herbert Danby, *The Mishnah* (Oxford: Clarendon Press, 1933), 564-65.

Bibliography

Achtemeier, Elizabeth. 1976. "Righteousness in the Old Testament." In *Interpreters Dictionary of the Bible,* edited by George Arthur Buttrick et al., 4:80-85. Nashville: Abingdon.

Ackerman, James S. 1981. "Satire and Symbolism in the Song of Jonah." In *Traditions in Transformation: Turning Points in Biblical Faith,* edited by Baruch Halpern and Jon D. Levenson, 213-46. Winona Lake, Ind.: Eisenbrauns.

Alter, Robert. 1985. *The Art of Biblical Poetry.* New York: Basic Books.

Andersen, Francis I., and David Noel Freedman. 1989. *Amos: A New Translation with Introduction and Commentary.* New York, London, Sydney: Doubleday.

Anderson, Bernhard W. 1962. "Exodus Typology in Second Isaiah." In *Israel's Prophetic Heritage: Essays in Honor of James Muilenburg,* edited by B. Anderson and W. Harrelson, 177-95. New York: Harper.

———. 1967. "Creation and Consummation." In *Creation versus Chaos: The Reinterpretation of Mythical Symbolism in the Bible,* 110-43. New York: Association Press.

———. 1977. "A Stylistic Study of the Priestly Creation Story." In *Canon and Authority,* edited by G. W. Coates and B. W. Long, 148-62. Philadelphia: Fortress.

———. 1988. "The Apocalyptic Rendering of the Isaiah Tradition." In *The Social World of Formative Christianity and Judaism: Essays in Tribute to Howard Clark Kee,* edited by Jacob Neusner et al., 17-38. Philadelphia: Fortress.

———. 1992. "A Worldwide Pilgrimage to Jerusalem." *Bible Review* 8:14, 16.

———. 1994. "Biblical Perspectives on the Doctrine of Creation." In *From Creation to New Creation: Old Testament Perspectives,* 19-41. Minneapolis: Fortress.

Andreasen, Niels-Erik. "Festival and Freedom: A Study of an Old Testament Theme." *Interpretation* 28 (1974): 281-97.

Anonymous group from Rennes. 1979. "An Approach to the Book of Jonah: Suggestions and Questions." *Semeia* 15 (1979) 85-96. Structuralist interpretation.

Barré, Michael L. 1991. "Jonah 2, 9 and the Structure of Jonah's Prayer." *Biblica* 72:237-38.

Barstad, Hans M. 1984. *The Religious Polemics of Amos.* Vetus Testamentum Supplement 34. Leiden: E. J. Brill.

Barton, John. 1980. *Amos's Oracles against the Nations.* Cambridge: Cambridge University Press.

Bernhardt, Karl-Heinz. 1975. "Bara'." In *Theological Dictionary of the Old Testament,* vol. 2, edited by G. Johannes Botterweck and Helmer Ringgren. Grand Rapids: Eerdmans.

Beuken, W. A. M. 1972. "*Mishpat*: The First Servant Song and Its Context." *Vetus Testamentum* 22:1-30.

———. 1989. "Servant and Herald of Good Tidings: Isaiah 61 as an Interpretation of Isaiah 40-55." In *The Book of Isaiah/Le Livre d'Isaïe: Les oracles et leurs relectures unité et complexité de l'ouvrage,* edited by J. Vermeylen, 411-42. Leuven: Leuven University Press.

———. 1990. "The Main Theme of Trito-Isaiah, 'The Servants of YHWH.'" *Journal for the Study of the Old Testament* 47:67-87.

———. 1991. "Isaiah Chapters LXV-LXVI: Trito-Isaiah and the Closure of the Book of Isaiah." In *Congress Volume: Leuven 1989,* 204-21. Vetus Testamentum Supplement 43. Leiden/New York/Cologne: E. J. Brill.

Bickerman, Elias. 1967. *Four Strange Books of the Bible.* New York: Schocken Books.

Bird, Phyllis. 1981. "'Male and Female He Created Them': Gen 1:27b in the Context of the Priestly Account of Creation." *Harvard Theological Review* 74:129-59.

Blenkinsopp, Joseph. 1976. "The Structure of P." *Catholic Biblical Quarterly* 38:275-92.

———. 1986. "Yahweh and Other Deities: Conflict and Accommodation in the Religion of Israel." *Interpretation* 40:354-66.

———. 1988. "Second Isaiah: Prophet of Universalism." *Journal for the Study of the Old Testament* 41:83-103.

———. 1997a. "Structure and Meaning in the Sinai-Horeb Narrative (Exodus 19-34)." In *A Biblical Itinerary: In Search of Method, Form and Content; Essays in Honor of George W. Coats,* edited by Eugene Carpenter, 109-24. Journal for the Study of the Old Testament Supplement 240. Sheffield: Sheffield Academic Press.

———. 1997b. "The Servant and the Servants in Isaiah and the Formation of the Book." In *Writing and Reading the Scroll of Isaiah: Studies of an Interpretive Tradition,* edited by Craig Broyles and Craig Evans, 155-75. Vetus Testamentum Supplement 70. Leiden/New York/ Cologne: E. J. Brill.

———. 2002. *Isaiah 40-55: A New Translation with Introduction and Commentary.* New York/London: Doubleday.

———. 2003. *Isaiah 56-66: A New Translation with Introduction and Commentary.* Anchor Bible 19B. New York/London: Doubleday.

Boring, M. Eugene. 1999. *1 Peter.* Nashville: Abingdon Press.

Bosch, David. 1991. *Transforming Mission: Paradigm Shifts in Theology of Mission.* Maryknoll, N.Y.: Orbis Books. Especially "Mission: The Contemporary Crisis," 1-24; and "Mission as *Missio Dei,*" 389-93.

Bratcher, Robert G., and William D. Reyburn. 1991. *A Translator's Handbook on the Book of Psalms.* New York: United Bible Societies.

Brekelmans, Christian. 1981. "Jer 18:1-12 and Its Redaction." In *Le Livre de Jérémie,* edited by P.-M. Bogaert, 348-50. Leuven: University Press.

Brueggemann, Walter. 1965. "Amos iv, 4-13 and Israel's Covenant Worship." *Vetus Testamentum* 15:1-15.

———. 1968. "David and His Theologian." *Catholic Biblical Quarterly* 30:156-81.

———. 1982. *Genesis.* Interpretation. Atlanta: John Knox.

———. 1984. *The Message of the Psalms: A Theological Commentary.* Minneapolis: Augsburg.

———. 1997. "Planned People/Planned Book?" In *Writing and Reading the Scroll of Isaiah: Studies of an Interpretive Tradition,* edited by Craig C. Boyle and Craig A. Evans, 19-37. Vetus Testamentum Supplement 70.1. Leiden: E. J. Brill.

———. 1998. *Isaiah,* vol. 1, *1-39;* vol. 2, *40-66.* Louisville: Westminster John Knox.

———. 2000. "Exodus in the Plural (Amos 9:78)," In *Texts That Linger, Words That Explode: Listening to Prophetic Voices,* 89-103. Minneapolis: Fortress Press.

Burrows, M. 1971. "The Literary Category of the Book of Jonah." In *Translating and Understanding the Old Testament,* edited by H. Frank and W. Reed, 80-107. Nashville: Abingdon.

Carr, Burgess. 1974. "The Moratorium: The Search for Self-Reliance and Authenticity." *All Africa Conference of Churches Bulletin* 7:36-44.

Cassuto, Umberto. 1961. *A Commentary on the Book of Genesis,* vol. 1. Jerusalem: Magnes Press.

———. 1973. "The Prophecies of Jeremiah concerning the Gentiles." In *Biblical and Oriental Studies,* vol. 1, *Bible,* 198-204. Jerusalem: Magnes Press.

Childs, Brevard S. 1958. "Jonah: A Study in Old Testament Hermeneutics." *Scottish Journal of Theology* 11:53-61.

———. 1969. "Psalm 8 in the Context of the Christian Canon." *Interpretation* 23:20-31.

———. 1974. "The Theophany at Sinai, Exod 19: 1-25; 20: 18-21." In *The Book of Exodus,* 340-84. Philadelphia: Westminster.

———. 1978. "The Canonical Shape of the Book of Jonah," In *Biblical and Near Eastern Studies: Essays in Honor of William Sanford Lasor,* edited by G. A. Tuttle, 122-28. Grand Rapids: Eerdmans.

———. 1979. *Introduction to the Old Testament as Scripture.* Philadelphia: Fortress.

———. 2001. *Isaiah.* Louisville: Westminster John Knox.

Clements, Ronald E. 1975. "The Purpose of the Book of Jonah." In Vetus Testamentum Supplement 28:16-28.

———. 1978. *Old Testament Theology: A Fresh Approach.* London: Marshall, Morgan & Scott. Especially "The People of God," 79-103.

———. 1985. "Beyond Tradition History: Deutero-Isaianic Development of First Isaiah's Themes." *Journal for the Study of the Old Testament* 31:95-113.

———. 1996. "A Light to the Nations: A Central Theme of the Book of Isaiah." In *Forming Prophetic Literature: Essays on Isaiah and the Twelve in Honor of John D. W. Watts,* edited by James W. Watts and Paul R. House, 57-69. Sheffield: Sheffield Academic Press.

———. 1997a. "'Arise, Shine, for Your Light Has Come': A Basic Theme of the Isaianic Tradition." In *Writing and Reading the Book of Isaiah: Studies of an Interpretive Tradition,* edited by Craig Broyles and Craig Evans, 441-54. Vetus Testamentum Supplement 70. Leiden/New York/Cologne: E. J. Brill.

———. 1997b. "Zion as Symbol and Political Reality· A Central Isaianic Quest."

In *Studies in the Book of Isaiah: Festschrift Willem A. M. Beuken,* edited by J. van Ruiten and M. Vervenne, 3-17. Leuven: University Press.

Clifford, Richard J. 1972. *The Cosmic Mountain in Canaan and the Old Testament.* Cambridge, Mass.: Harvard University Press.

———. 1985. "The Hebrew Scriptures and the Theology of Creation." *Theological Studies* 46:507-23.

———. 2002. *Psalms 1-72.* Nashville: Abingdon.

Clines, David J. A. 1976. *I, He, We, They: A Literary Approach to Isaiah 53.* Journal for the Study of the Old Testament Supplement 1. Sheffield: University of Sheffield.

Coats, George W. 1981. "The Curse in the Blessing: Gen 12:1-4a in the Structure and Theology of the Yahwist." In *Die Botschaft und die Boten: Festschrift für Hans Walter Wolff zum 70. Geburtstag,* edited by Jörg Jeremias and Lothar Perlitt, 31-41. Neukirchen-Vluyn: Neukirchener Verlag.

Collins, John J. 1985. "A Symbol of Otherness: Circumcision and Salvation in the First Century." In *To See Ourselves as Others See Us: Christians, Jews, "Others" in Late Antiquity,* edited by Jacob Neusner and Ernest S. Frerocjs, 163-86. Scholars Press Studies in Humanities. Chico: Scholars Press.

Cooper, Alan. 1993. "In Praise of Divine Caprice: The Significance of the Book of Jonah." In *Among the Prophets,* edited by Philip R. Davies and David J. A. Clines, 144-63. Journal for the Study of the Old Testament 44. Sheffield: JSOT Press.

Coote, Robert. 1981. *Amos among the Prophets: Composition and Theology.* Philadelphia: Fortress.

Crenshaw, James L. 1968. "Amos and the Theophanic Tradition." *Zeitschrift für die alttestamentliche Wissenschaft* 80:203-15.

———. 1986. "The Expression of MI YODEAʻ in the Hebrew Bible." *Vetus Testamentum* 36:274-88.

Cunliffe-Jones, Hubert. 1973. *A Word for Our Time? Zechariah 9-14, the New Testament and Today.* London: University of London, Athlone Press.

Davies, Graham. 1989. "The Destiny of the Nations in the Book of Isaiah." In *The Book of Isaiah/Le Livre d'Isaïe: Les oracles et leurs relectures, unité et complexité de l'ouvrage,* edited by J. Vermeylen, 93-120. Leuven: Leuven University Press.

Day, John. 1990. "Problems in the Interpretation of the Book of Jonah." In *In Quest of the Past: Studies on Israelite Religion, Literature and Prophetism,* edited by A. S. van der Woude, 32-47. Leiden: E. J. Brill.

Dearman, John Andrew. 1988. *Property Rights in the Eighth-Century Prophets: The Conflict and Its Background.* Atlanta: Scholars Press.

Dialogue and Proclamation: Reflection and Orientations on Interreligious Dialogue and the Proclamation of the Gospel of Jesus Christ. 1991. *Bulletin for the Pontifical Council for Interreligious Dialogue,* vol. 21, no. 2, 210ff. Vatican: Vatican Polyglot Press.

Dozeman, Thomas B. 1989. "Inner-Biblical Interpretation of Yahweh's Gracious and Compassionate Character." *Journal of Biblical Literature* 108:207-23.

———. 1989a. "Spatial Form in Exod 19:1-8a and in the Larger Sinai Narrative." *Semeia* 46:87-101.

———. 1989b. *God on the Mountain: A Study of Redaction, Theology and Canon in Exodus 19-24.* Society of Biblical Literature Monograph Series 37. Atlanta: Scholars Press.

Dumbrell, William J. 2000. "Abraham and the Abrahamic Covenant in Galatians 3:1-14." In *The Gospel to the Nations: Perspectives on Paul's Mission,* edited by Mark Thompson and Peter Bolt, 19-31. Downers Grove: Intervarsity Press.

Eboussi-Boulaga. 1974. "La de-mission." *Spiritus* 56:276-87.

Eichrodt, Walter. 1967. *Theology of the Old Testament,* vol. 2. Philadelphia: Westminster Press.

Eissfeldt, Otto. 1962. "The Promises of Grace to David in Isaiah 55:1-5." In *Israel's Prophetic Heritage: Essays in Honor of James Muilenburg,* edited by B. W. Anderson and W. Harrelson, 196-207. New York: Harper.

Feldman, Louis H. 1993. "The Success of Proselytism by Jews in the Hellenistic and Early Roman Periods." In *Jews and Gentile in the Ancient World: Attitudes and Interactions from Alexander to Justinian,* 289-341. Princeton, N.J.: Princeton University Press.

Fensham, F. Charles. 1962. "Widow, Orphan, and the Poor in Ancient Near Eastern Legal and Wisdom Literature." *Journal of Near Eastern Studies* 21:129-39.

Fishbane, Michael. 1985. *Biblical Interpretation in Ancient Israel.* Oxford: Clarendon Press.

Freedman, D. N., and J. R. Lundblom. 1974. "ḥannan." In *Theological Dictionary of the Old Testament,* edited by G. Johannes Botterweck and Helmer Ringgren, 5:22-36, esp. 24. Grand Rapids: Eerdmans.

Fretheim, Terence. 1977. *The Message of Jonah: A Theological Commentary.* Minneapolis: Augsburg.

———. 1978. "Jonah and Theodicy." *Zeitschrift für die alttestamentliche Wissenschaft* 90:227-37.

———. 1991. *Exodus.* Interpretation. Louisville: John Knox.

———. 1996. " 'Because the Whole World Is Mine': Theme and Narrative in Exodus." *Interpretation* 50:229-39.

Gelston, A. 1992. "Universalism in Second Isaiah." *Journal of Theological Studies* 43:377-98.

Gillingham, Susan E. 1998. "From Theory to Practice: Readings of Psalm 8." In *One Bible, Many Voices: Different Approaches to Biblical Studies,* 232-44. Grand Rapids: Eerdmans.

Glasser, Arthur F., et al. 2003. *Announcing the Kingdom: The Story of God's Mission in the Bible.* Grand Rapids: Baker Academic. Especially "The Whole Bible Is a Missionary Book," 17-28.

Good, Edwin. 1965. "Jonah: The Absurdity of God." In *Irony in the Old Testament,* 39-55. Philadelphia: Westminster Press.

Goodhart, S. 1985. "Prophecy, Sacrifice and Repentance in the Story of Jonah." *Semeia* 33:43-63.

Gowan, Donald. 1994. "Covenant: Exodus 19 and 24." In *Theology in Exodus: Biblical Theology in the Form of a Commentary,* 173-83. Louisville: Westminster John Knox.

Greenberg, Moshe. 1971. "Mankind, Israel and the Nations in the Hebraic Heritage." In *No Man Is Alien. Essays on the Unity of Mankind,* edited by J. Robert Nelson, 15-40. Leiden: E. J. Brill.

————. 1983. *Biblical Prose Prayer: As a Window to the Popular Religion of Ancient Israel*. Berkeley: University of California Press.

Gunkel, Hermann, and Joachim Begrich. 1998. *An Introduction to the Psalms: The Genres of the Religious Lyric of Israel*. Macon, Ga.: Mercer University Press.

Habel, Norman. 1995. "Land as Host Country: Immigrant Ideology." In *The Land Is Mine: Six Biblical Land Ideologies*, 115-33. Minneapolis: Fortress.

Hahn, Ferdinand. 1965. "The Old Testament and Jewish Presuppositions of the Early Christian Mission." In *Mission in the New Testament*, 18-25. Naperville: Allenson.

Halpern, Baruch, and Richard Elliot Friedman. 1980. "Composition and Paronomasia in the Book of Jonah." *Hebrew Annual Review* 4:79-92.

Hamlin, E. J. 1976. "Nations." In *The Interpreter's Dictionary of the Bible*, edited by George Arthur Buttrick et al., 3:515-23.

Hammershaimb, E. 1959. "On the Ethics of the Old Testament Prophets." In 7, *Congress Volume: Oxford 1959*, 75-101. Vetus Testamentum Supplement 7. Leiden: E. J. Brill.

Hanson, Paul D. 1979. *The Dawn of Apocalyptic: The Historical and Sociological Roots of Jewish Apocalyptic Eschatology*. Revised edition. Philadelphia: Fortress Press.

————. 1987. "Israelite Religion in the Early Postexilic Period." In *Ancient Israelite Religion: Essays in Honor of Frank Moore Cross*, edited by P. D. Miller, Jr., Paul D. Hanson and S. D. McBride, 485-508. Philadelphia: Fortress.

————. 1995. *Isaiah 40-66*. Interpretation. Louisville: John Knox Press.

Hartman, David. 1978. "Sinai and Exodus: Two Grounds for Hope in the Jewish Tradition." *Religious Studies* 14:373-87.

Hasel, Gerhard F. 1992. "Sabbath." In *The Anchor Bible Dictionary*, edited by David Noel Freedman et al., 5:845-56. New York: Doubleday.

Hayes, John H. 1968. "The Usage of the Oracles against the Foreign Nations in Ancient Israel." *Journal of Biblical Literature* 87:81-92.

Holbert, John C. 1981. " 'Deliverance Belongs to Yahweh!': Satire in the Book of Jonah." *Journal for the Study of the Old Testament* 21:70-75.

Holladay, W. L. 1989. *Jeremiah* II. Philadelphia: Fortress.

Hollenberg, D. E. 1969. "Nationalism and 'the Nations' in Isaiah XL-LV." *Vetus Testamentum* 19:23-36.

Howie, C. 1959. "Expressly for Our Time: The Theology of Amos." *Interpretation* 13:273-85.

Huffmon, Herbert. 1983. "The Social Role of Amos's Message." In *The Quest for the Kingdom: Studies in Honor of George E. Mendenhall*, edited by Herbert Huffmon et al. Winona Lake, Ind.: Eisenbrauns.

Hyatt, J. P. 1962. "Circumcision." In *The Interpreter's Dictionary of the Bible*, edited by George Arthur Buttrick, 1:629-31. Nashville: Abingdon.

Jeremias, Joachim. 1958. *Jesus' Promise to the Nations*. London: SCM.

Jeremias, Jörg. 1998. *The Book of Amos*. Louisville: Westminster John Knox.

Johnson, T. H. 1953. *Prophecy and the Prophets in Ancient Israel*. 2nd ed. London: Gerald Duckworth.

Kaiser, Otto. 1974. *Isaiah 13-39*. Philadelphia: Fortress.

Kaiser, Walter C. 2000. *Mission in the Old Testament: Israel as a Light to the*

Nations. Grand Rapids: Baker Books. Especially "God's Plan for the Missions in the Old Testament," 15-28.

Kapelrud, A. S. 1961. *Central Ideas in Amos*. Oslo: Universitetsforlaget.

Kaufmann, Yehezkel. 1960. *The Religion of Israel*. Translated by Moshe Greenberg. Chicago: University of Chicago Press.

Kellermann, D. 1974. "Gur." In *Theological Dictionary of the Old Testament*, edited by G. Johannes Botterweck and Helmer Ringgren, 2:439-49. Grand Rapids: Eerdmans.

Khoury, Adel Theodore. 2003. "Abraham—A Blessing for All Nations according to the Jewish, Christian and Islamic Traditions." *Sedos Bulletin* 45:188-95.

Kirk, J. Andrew. 2000. *What Is Mission? Theological Explorations*. Minneapolis: Fortress. Especially "What Is Theology of Mission?" and "God's Mission and the Church's Response," 7-37.

Klein, Ralph W. 2002. *Israel in Exile: A Theological Interpretation*, 97-124. Mifflington: Sigler Press.

Knierim, Rolf. 1981. "Cosmos and History in Israel's Theology." *Horizons in Theology* 3:59-123.

Knight, George A. F. 1959. *A Christian Theology of the Old Testament*. London: SCM.

Köstenberger, Andreas J., and Peter T. O'Brien. 2001. *Salvation to the Ends of the Earth: A Biblical Theology of Mission*. Downers Grove: Intervarsity Press.

Kraus, Hans-Joachim. 1989. *Psalms 60-150*. Minneapolis: Augsburg.

Kuhn, Karl Georg. 1964. "Προσηλυτος." In *Theological Dictionary of the New Testament*, translated and edited by Geoffrey W. Bromiley, 6:727-44. Grand Rapids: Eerdmans.

Lamarche, Paul. 1961. *Zecharie IX-XIV*. Paris: Gabalda.

Landes, George M. 1967. "The Kerygma of the Book of Jonah: The Contextual Interpretation of the Jonah Psalm." *Interpretation* 21:3-31.

Lang, Bernhard. 1985. "The Social Organization of Peasant Poverty in Biblical Israel." In *Anthropological Perspectives to the Old Testament*, 83-99. Philadelphia: Fortress.

Le Déaut, Roger. 1981. "Le thème de la circoncision du Coeur (DT XXX 6; JÉR IV 4) dans les versions anciennes (LXX et Targum) et à Qumran." In *Congress Volume: Vienna 1980*, edited by J. A. Emerton, 178-205. Vetus Testamentum Supplement 32. Leiden: E. J. Brill.

Legrand, Lucien. 1990. *Unity and Plurality: Mission in the Bible*. Maryknoll, N.Y.: Orbis Books. Especially "A Preliminary Question," 1-7.

Levenson, Jon D. 1985. *Sinai and Zion: An Entry into the Jewish Bible*. San Francisco: Harper & Row.

———. 1988. *Creation and the Persistence of Evil: The Jewish Drama of Divine Omnipotence*. San Francisco: Harper & Row.

Licht, Jacob. 1978. *Storytelling in the Bible*. Jerusalem: Magnes Press.

Limburg, James. 1993. *Jonah: A Commentary*. Louisville: Westminster John Knox.

———. 1997. "Swords and Ploughshares: Texts and Contexts." In *Writing and Reading the Book of Isaiah: Studies of an Interpretive Tradition*, edited by Craig Broyles and Craig Evans, 279-93. Vetus Testamentum Supplement 70. Leiden/New York/Cologne: E. J. Brill.

Lindblom, J. 1963. *Prophecy in Ancient Israel*. Oxford: Basil Blackwell.

Lipinski, E. 1974. "צפן." *Theological Dictionary of the Old Testament*, edited by G. Johannes Botterweck and Helmer Ringgren, 12:435-43. Grand Rapids: Eerdmans.

Lohfink, Norbert. 2000. "Covenant and Torah in the Pilgrimage of the Nations." In *The God of Israel and the Nations: Studies in Isaiah and the Psalms*, edited by Norbert Lohfink and Erich Zenger, 33-57. Collegeville, Minn.: Liturgical Press.

Louis, Conrad. 1946. *The Theology of Psalm VIII: A Study of the Traditions of the Text and the Theological Import*. Washington: Catholic University of America.

Magonet, Jonathan. 1983. *Form and Meaning: Studies in Literary Technique in the Book of Jonah*. Sheffield: Almond Press.

Mann, Thomas. 1988. "The Abraham Cycle." In *The Book of the Torah: The Narrative Integrity of the Pentateuch*, 29-50. Atlanta: John Knox.

———. 1991. "'All the Families of the Earth': The Theological Unity of Genesis." *Interpretation* 45:341-54.

Marlowe, W. Creighton. 1998. "Music of Mission: Themes of Cross-Cultural Outreach in the Psalms." *Missiology* 26:445-56.

Martin-Achard, Robert. 1959. *Israël et les Nations: La perspective missionaire de l'Ancien Testament*. Paris: Delachaux & Niestlé.

———. 1984. *Amos and Lamentations: God's People in Crisis*. Grand Rapids: Eerdmans.

Matthey, Jacques. 2001. "Missiology in the World Council of Churches: Update." *International Review of Mission* 90:427-43.

Mauser, Ulrich. 1982. "Isaiah 65:17-25." *Interpretation* 36:181-186.

Mays, James L. 1969. *Amos*. Philadelphia: Westminster.

———. 1983. "Justice: Perspectives from the Prophetic Tradition." *Interpretation* 37:5-17.

———. 1994a. *The Lord Reigns: A Theological Handbook to the Psalms*. Louisville: Westminster John Knox.

———. 1994b. "What Is a Human Being? Reflections on Psalm 8." *Theology Today* 50:511-20.

McConville, J. G. 1993. *Judgment and Promise: An Interpretation of the Book of Jeremiah*. Leicester: Apollos; Winona Lake, Ind.: Eisenbrauns.

McKnight, Scot. 1991. *A Light among the Gentiles: Jewish Missionary Activity in the Second Temple Period*. Minneapolis: Fortress.

Melugin, Roy F. 1997. "Israel and the Nations in Isaiah 40-55." In *Problems in Biblical Theology: Essays in Honor of Rolf Knierim*, edited by Henry Sun et al., 249-64. Grand Rapids: Eerdmans.

Miller, Patrick. 1994. *They Cried to the Lord: The Form and Theology of Biblical Prayer*. Minneapolis: Fortress.

Miscall, Peter D. 1992. "Isaiah: New Heavens, New Earth, New Book." In *Reading between Texts: Intertextuality and the Hebrew Bible*, edited by Danna Nolan Fewell, 41-56. Louisville: Westminster John Knox.

Moore, George F. 1971. "The Conversion of Gentiles." In *Judaism in the First Centuries of the Christian Era*, 1:323-53. New York: Schocken Books.

Moran, William L. 1962. "A Kingdom of Priests." In *The Bible in Current Catholic Thought*, edited by John L. McKenzie, 7-20. New York: Herder & Herder.

Muilenburg, James. 1959. "The Form and Structure of the Covenantal Formulations." *Vetus Testamentum* 9:347-65.

———. 1965. "Abraham and the Nations: Blessing and World History." *Interpretation* 19:387-98.

Neusner, Jacob. 1997. "Exile and Return as the History of Judaism." In *Exile: Old Testament, Jewish, and Christian Conceptions*, edited by James M. Scott, 221-37. Leiden: E. J. Brill.

Newbigin, Lesslie. 1958. *One Body, One Gospel, One World*. London/New York: International Missionary Council.

Nicholson, Ernest E. 1986. *God and His People: Covenant and Theology in the Old Testament*. Oxford: Clarendon Press.

Noble, Paul. 1993. "Israel among the Nations." *Horizons in Biblical Theology* 15:56-82.

Nogalski, James. 1993. *Literary Precursors to the Book of the Twelve*. Beihefte zur Zeitschrift für die alttestamentliche Wissenschaft 217. Berlin/New York: Walter de Gruyter.

North, C. R. 1956. *The Suffering Servant in Deutero-Isaiah: An Historical and Critical Study*. Second edition. Oxford: Oxford University Press.

———. 1964. *Second Isaiah: Introduction, Translation and Commentary to Chapters XL-LV*. Oxford: Clarendon Press.

Noth, Martin. 1962. "The Theophany on Sinai with the Decalogue." In *Exodus: A Commentary*, 151-68. Philadelphia: Westminster Press.

Orlinsky, Harry M. 1967a. "'A Light to the Nations': A Problem in Biblical Theology." In *The Seventy-Fifth Anniversary Volume of the Jewish Quarterly Review*, edited by Abraham Neuman and Solomon Zeitlin, 409-28. Philadelphia.

———. 1967b. "The So-Called 'Servant of the Lord' and 'Suffering Servant' in Second Isaiah." In *Studies on the Second Part of the Book of Isaiah*, 1-133. Vetus Testamentum Supplement 14. Leiden: E. J. Brill.

Oswalt, John N. 1997. "Righteousness in Isaiah: A Study of the Function of Chapters 56-66 in the Present Structure of the Book." In *Writing and Reading the Scroll of Isaiah: Studies of an Interpretive Tradition*, edited by Craig Boyles and Craig Evans, 177-91. Vetus Testamentum Supplement 70. Leiden: E. J. Brill.

———. 1998. *The Book of Isaiah: Chapters 40-66*. Grand Rapids: Eerdmans.

Paul, Shalom M. 1991. *Amos*. Hermeneia. Minneapolis: Fortress.

Pedersen, Johannes. 1926. "The Blessing." In *Israel: Its Life and Culture*, I-II, 182-212. Copenhagen: Povl Branner; London: Oxford University Press.

Polan, Gregory J. 2001. "Zion, the Glory of the Holy One of Israel: A Literary Analysis of Isaiah 60." In *Imagery and Imagination in Biblical Literature: Essays in Honor of Aloysius Fitzgerald*, edited by Lawrence Boadt and Mark S. Smith, 50-71. Catholic Biblical Quarterly Monograph Series 32. Washington: Catholic Biblical Association.

Pontifical Biblical Commission. 2002. *The Jewish People and Their Sacred Scriptures in the Christian Bible*. Vatican City: Libreria Editrice Vaticana.

Pontifical Council for Interreligious Dialogue and the Congregation for the Evangelization of Peoples. 1991. *Dialogue and Proclamation: Reflections on Interreligious Dialogue and the Proclamation of the Gospel of Jesus Christ.* Rome.

Raitt, Thomas M. 1977. *A Theology of Exile: Judgment/Deliverance in Jeremiah and Ezekiel.* Philadelphia: Fortress.

Rendtorff, Rolf. 1968. "The Concept of Revelation in Ancient Israel." In *Revelation as History,* edited by W. Pannenberg. London: Macmillan.

———. 1977. "The 'Yahwist' as Theologian? The Dilemma of Pentateuchal Criticism." *Journal for the Study of the Old Testament* 3:2-10.

———. 1993. "Isaiah 56:1 as a Key to the Formation of the Book of Isaiah." In *Canon and Theology: Overtures to an Old Testament Theology,* 181-89. Minneapolis: Fortress.

Rétif, A., and P. Lamarche. 1966. *The Salvation of the Gentiles and the Prophets.* Baltimore/Dublin: Helicon.

Ringgren, H. 1953. "Einige Bemerkung zum LXXIII Psalm." *Vetus Testamentum* 3:265-72.

Robinson, H. Wheeler. 1946. *Inspiration and Revelation in the Old Testament.* Oxford: Clarendon Press.

Robinson, Theodore H. 1953. *Prophecy and the Prophets in Ancient Israel.* 2nd ed. London: Duckworth.

Rowley, H. H. 1939. *Israel's Mission to the World.* London: Student Christian Movement Press.

———. 1944. *The Missionary Message of the Old Testament.* London: Carey Kingsgate Press.

———. 1950. *From Joseph to Joshua: Biblical Traditions in the Light of Archaeology.* London: Oxford University Press.

———. 1956. *The Faith of Israel.* London: SCM.

Ruether, Rosemary Radford. 1999. "Ecojustice at the Center of the Church's Mission." *Mission Studies* 16:111-21.

Sanders, James. 1984. *Canon and Community: A Guide to Canonical Criticism.* Philadelphia: Fortress.

Sarasson, Richard S. 1988. "The Interpretation of Jeremiah 31:31-34 in Judaism." In *When Jews and Christians Meet,* edited by Jakob J. Petuchowski, 99-123. Albany: State University of New York Press.

Sarna, Nahum. 1993. "Psalm 8." In *Songs of the Heart: An Introduction to the Book of the Psalms,* 50-67. New York: Schocken Books.

Sasson, Jack M. 1990. *Jonah: A New Translation with Introduction, Commentary and Interpretation.* Anchor Bible 24B. New York: Doubleday.

Sauter, Gerhard. 2003. "Jonah 2: A Prayer Out of the Deep." In *A God So Near: Essays on Old Testament Theology in Honor of Patrick D. Miller,* edited by Brent Strawn and Nancy Bowen, 145-52. Winona Lake, Ind.: Eisenbrauns.

Sawyer, John F. A. 1986. " 'Blessed be my People Egypt' (Isaiah 19:25): The Context and Meaning of a Remarkable Passage." In *A Word in Season: Essays in Honor of William McKane,* edited by James D. Martin and Philip R. Davies, 57-71. Journal for the Study of the Old Testament Supplement 42. Sheffield: JSOT Press.

Schramm, Brooks. 2000. "Exodus 19 and Its Christian Appropriation." In *Jews, Christians, and the Theology of the Hebrew Scriptures,* edited by Alice Ogden Bellis and Joel S. Kaminsky, 327-52. SBL Symposium Series 8. Atlanta: Society of Biblical Literature.

Schwartz, Baruch J. 1998. "Torah from Zion: Isaiah's Temple Vision (Isaiah 2:1-4)." In *Sanctity of Time and Space in Tradition and Modernity,* edited by A. Houtman, M. J. H. M. Poorthuis and Baruch J. Schwartz, 11-26. Leiden: E. J. Brill.

Seilhamer, F. H. 1974. "The Role of Covenant in the Mission and Message of Amos." In *A Light unto my Path: Old Testament Studies in Honor of Jacob M. Myers,* edited by H. N. Bream et al., 435-51. Philadelphia: Temple University Press.

Seitz, Christopher S. 1991. *Zion's Final Destiny: The Development of the Book of Isaiah; A Reassessment of Isaiah 36-39.* Minneapolis: Fortress.

Shead, Andrew. 2000. "The New Covenant and Pauline Hermeneutics." In *The Gospel to the Nations: Perspectives on Paul's Mission,* edited by Peter Bolt and Mark Thompson, 33-49. Downers Grove: Intervarsity Press.

Shenk, Calvin E. 1988. "God's Intention for Humankind: The Promise of Community; Bible Study on Gen 12." *Mission Studies* 5:13-20.

Sheppard, Gerald T. 1982. "Canonization: Hearing the Voice of the Same God through Historically Dissimilar Traditions." *Interpretation* 36:21-33.

Simon, Uriel. 1999. *Jonah.* Second revised edition. The JPS Bible Commentary. Philadelphia: Jewish Publication Society. Hebrew original, 1992.

Smith, Mark S. 1997. "Psalm 8:2b-3: New Proposals for Old Problems." *Catholic Biblical Quarterly* 59:637-41.

Smith, Morton. 1984. "Jewish Religious Life in the Persian Period." In *The Cambridge History of Judaism,* vol. 1, *Introduction: The Persian Period,* edited by W. D. Davies and Louis Finkelstein, 219-78. Cambridge: Cambridge University Press.

Snaith, Norman H. 1967. "Isaiah 40-66: A Study of the Teaching of the Second Isaiah and Its Consequences." In *Studies on the Second Part of the Book of Isaiah,* 135-264. Vetus Testamentum Supplement 14. Leiden: E. J. Brill.

Sommer, Benjamin D. 1999. "Revelation at Sinai in the Hebrew Bible and in Jewish Theology." *Journal of Religion* 79:422-51.

Stamoolis, James J. 1986. *Eastern Orthodox Mission Theology Today.* Maryknoll, N.Y.: Orbis Books.

Steck, Odil H. 1991. "Zu jüngsten Untersuchungen von Jes 56, 1-8; 63, 7-66, 24." In *Studien zu Tritojesaja,* edited by Odil H. Steck, 229-68. Beihefte zur Zeitschrift für die alttestamentliche Wissenschaft 203. Berlin: de Gruyter.

Stern, Philip. 1994. "The 'Blind Servant' Imagery of Deutero-Isaiah and Its Implications." *Biblica* 75:224-32.

Stuhlmueller, Carroll. 1959. "The Theology of Creation in Second Isaiah." *Catholic Biblical Quarterly* 21:429-67.

———. 1970. *Creative Redemption in Deutero-Isaiah.* Rome: Pontifical Biblical Institute.

Stuhlmueller, Carroll, and Donald Senior. 1983. *The Biblical Foundations for Mission.* Maryknoll, N.Y.: Orbis Books.

Sweeney, Marvin A. 1996a. "The Book of Isaiah as Prophetic Torah." In *New Visions of Isaiah*, edited by Roy Melugin and Marvin Sweeney, 50-67. Journal for the Study of the Old Testament Supplement 214. Sheffield: Sheffield Academic Press.

———. 1996b. *Isaiah 1-39, with an Introduction to Prophetic Literature.* Grand Rapids: Eerdmans.

———. 1997. "The Reconceptualization of the Davidic Covenant in Isaiah." In *Studies in the Book of Isaiah: Festschrift Willem A. M. Beuken,* edited by J. van Ruiten and M. Vervenne, 41-61. Leuven: University Press.

Trible, Phyllis. 1994. *Rhetorical Criticism: Context, Method, and the Book of Jonah.* Minneapolis: Augsburg Fortress.

Tsevat, M. 1990. "ירושלם." In *Theological Dictionary of the Old Testament,* edited by G. Johannes Botterweck and Helmer Ringgren, 6:347-55. Grand Rapids: Eerdmans.

Unterman, Jeremiah. 1987. *From Repentance to Redemption: Jeremiah's Thought in Transition.* Journal for the Study of the Old Testament Supplement 54. Sheffield: Sheffield Academic Press.

van Winkle, D. W. 1985. "The Relationship of the Nations to Yahweh and to Israel in Isaiah xl-lv." *Vetus Testamentum* 35:446-58.

van Zyl, Danie C. 1992. "Exodus 19:3-6 and the Kerygmatic Perspective of the Pentateuch." *Old Testament Essays* 5:264-71.

Vermes, Geza, and Fergus Millar. 1979. *The History of the Jewish People in the Age of Jesus Christ,* vol. 2. Edinburgh: T&T Clark.

Vermes, Geza, Fergus Millar, and Martin Goodman, eds. 1986. "Gentiles and Judaism: 'God-Fearers' and Proselytes." In Emil Schürer, *The History of the Jewish People in the Age of Jesus Christ (175 B.C.–A.D. 135),* vol. 3, pt. 1, 150-76. Revised edition. Edinburgh: T&T Clark.

Vermeylen, J. 1978. "Les relectures deutéronomistes des livres d'Amos et de Michée." In *Du Prophète Isaïe à l'Apocalyptique,* 2:519-69. Paris: Gabalda.

Vicedom, Georg. 1965. *The Mission of God: An Introduction to a Theology of Mission.* St. Louis: Concordia. Especially "The *Missio Dei*," 1-44.

Vogels, Walter. 1972. "Invitation à revenir à l'alliance et universalisme en Amos IX, 7." *Vetus Testamentum* 22:223-39.

von Rad, Gerhard. 1962. *Old Testament Theology,* vol. 1. San Francisco: Harper.

———. 1965. *Old Testament Theology,* vol. 2. San Francisco: Harper & Row.

———. 1966. "The City on the Hill." In *The Problem of the Hexateuch and Other Essays,* 232-42. New York: McGraw Hill.

———. 1972. *Genesis. A Commentary.* Rev. ed. Philadelphia: Westminster.

von Waldow, H. Eberhard. 1968. "The Message of Deutero-Isaiah." *Interpretation* 22:259-87.

Waard, Jan de. 1977. "The Chiastic Structure of Amos V, 1-17." *Vetus Testamentum* 27:170-77.

Waard, Jan de, and William A. Smalley. 1979. *A Translator's Handbook on the Book of Amos.* New York: United Bible Societies.

Walsh, Jerome T. 1982. "Jonah 2, 3-10: A Rhetorical Critical Study." *Biblica* 63:219-29.

Walton, John H. 1992. "The Object Lesson of Jonah 4:5-7 and the Purpose of the Book of Jonah." *Bulletin for Biblical Research* 2:47-57.

Warsaw, Thayer S. 1974. "The Book of Jonah." In *Literary Interpretations of Biblical Narratives,* edited by Kenneth Gros Louis et al., 191-207. Nashville: Abingdon.

Webb, Barry G. 1990. "Zion in Transformation: A Literary Approach to Isaiah." In *The Bible in Three Dimensions: Essays in Celebration of Forty Years of Biblical Studies in the University of Sheffield,* edited by David Clines, Stephen E. Fowl, and Stanley Porter, 65-84. Journal for the Study of the Old Testament Supplement 87. Sheffield: Sheffield Academic Press.

Weinfeld, Moshe. 1976. "Jeremiah and the Spiritual Metamorphosis of Israel." *Zeitschrift für die alttestamentliche Wissenschaft* 88:17-56.

———. 1981. "Sabbath, Temple and the Enthronement of the Lord: The Problem of the Sitz im Leben of Genesis 1:1-2:3." In *Mélanges bibliques et orientaux en l'honneur de M. Henri Cazelles,* edited by A. Caquot and M. Delcor, 501-12. Neukirchen-Vluyn: Neukirchener Verlag; Kevelaer: Butzon & Berker.

———. 1992. "Justice and Righteousness—משפט וצדקה—the Expression and Its Meaning." In *Justice and Righteousness: Biblical Themes and Their Influence,* edited by H. G. Reventlow and Y. Hoffman, 228-46. Journal for the Study of the Old Testament Supplement 137. Sheffield: Sheffield Academic Press.

Wellhausen, Julius. 1957. *Prolegomena to the History of Israel.* New York: Meridian Books.

Wells, Jo Bailey. 2000. *God's Holy People: A Theme in Biblical Theology.* Journal for the Study of the Old Testament Supplement 305. Sheffield: Sheffield Academic Press. Especially "Blessing to All the Families of the Earth: Abraham as Prototype of Israel," 185-207.

Wells, Roy D., Jr. 1996. "'Isaiah' as an Exponent of Torah: Isaiah 56:1-8." In *New Visions of Isaiah,* edited by Roy Melugin and Marvin Sweeney, 140-55. Journal for the Study of the Old Testament Supplement 214. Sheffield: Sheffield Academic Press.

Westermann, Claus. 1969. *Isaiah 40-66.* Philadelphia: Westminster Press.

———. 1978. *Blessing in the Bible and the Life of the Church.* Philadelphia: Fortress.

———. 1985. *Genesis 12-36: A Commentary.* Minneapolis: Augsburg.

———. 1991. *Prophetic Oracles of Salvation in the Old Testament.* Edinburgh: T&T Clark; Louisville: Westminster John Knox.

———. 1994. *Genesis 1-11.* Minneapolis: Fortress.

Whiston, William, trans. 1987. *The Works of Josephus.* Complete and unabridged. Peabody, Mass.: Hendrickson.

Wilcox, Peter, and David Paton-Williams. 1988. "The Servant Songs in Deutero-Isaiah." *Journal for the Study of the Old Testament* 42:79-102.

Wildberger, Hans. 1957. "Die Völkerwallfahrt zum Zion, Jes II, 1-5." *Vetus Testamentum* 7:62-81.

———. 1991. *Isaiah 1-12: A Commentary.* Minneapolis: Fortress.

Williams, D. L. 1966. "The Theology of Amos." *Review and Expositor* 63:393-403.

Williams, Sam K. 1988. "*Promise* in Galatians: A Rereading of Paul's Reading of Scripture." *Journal of Biblical Literature* 107:709-20.

Willis, John T. 1997. "Isaiah 2:2-5 and the Psalms of Zion." In *Writing and Read-*

ing the Scroll of Isaiah: Studies of an Interpretive Tradition, edited by Craig Broyles and Craig Evans, 295-316. Vetus Testamentum Supplement 70. Leiden/New York/Cologne: E. J. Brill.

Wilson, Gerald H. 1992. "The Shape of the Book of Psalms." *Interpretation* 46:129-42.

Wilson, Iain. 1966. "In that Day: From Text to Sermon on Isaiah 19:23-25." *Interpretation* 21:66-86.

Wolff, Hans Walter. 1966. "The Kerygma of the Yahwist." *Interpretation* 20:131-58.

———. 1977. *Joel and Amos.* Hermeneia. Philadelphia: Fortress.

Wolff, Walter. 1986. *Obadiah and Jonah.* Minneapolis: Augsburg.

Woude, A. S. van der. 1997. "שם." In *Theological Lexicon of the Old Testament,* edited by Ernst Jenni and Claus Westermann, 3:1348-67. Peabody: Hendrickson.

Wright, N. T. 1991. "Curse and Covenant: Galatians 3:10-14." In *The Climax of the Covenant: Christ and the Law in Pauline Theology,* 137-56. Edinburgh: T&T Clark.

Zenger, Erich. 2000. "The God of Israel's Reign over the World (Psalms 90-106)." In *The God of Israel and the Nations: Studies in Isaiah and the Psalms,* by Norbert Lohfink and Erich Zenger, 161-90. Collegeville, Minn.: Liturgical Press.

Index

SCRIPTURE PASSAGES DISCUSSED

The American Society of Missiology Series, published in collaboration with Orbis Books, seeks to publish scholarly work of high merit and wide interest on numerous aspects of missiology—the study of Christian mission in its historical, social, and theological dimensions. Able proposals on new and creative approaches to the practice and understanding of mission will receive close attention from the ASM Series Committee.

Previously Published in
The American Society of Missiology Series

Changing Tides: Latin America and Mission Today, Samuel Escobar

Gospel Bearers, Gender Barriers: Missionary Women in the Twentieth Century, edited by Dana L. Robert

Church: Community for the Kingdom, John Fuellenbach, SVD

Mission in Acts: Ancient Narratives for a Postmodern Context, edited by Robert L. Gallagher and Paul Hertig

A History of Christianity in Asia: Volume I, Beginnings to 1500, Samuel Hugh Moffett

A History of Christianity in Asia: Volume II, 1500 - 1900, Samuel Hugh Moffett

A Reader's Guide to Transforming Mission, Stan Nussbaum

The Evangelization of Slaves and Catholic Origins in Eastern Africa, Paul Vincent Kollman, CSC